Angel Whispers

by *Russell Forsyth*

WITH MANY BLESSINGS.

Russell

Introduction

Everyone has an innate ability to make connections to spirit, a higher power, God, loved ones, and everything else that exists beyond the physical plane. Energy found beyond the veil is part of a Divine Matrix connecting all of us. In truth, we are always connected to a source of energy that is one with the fabric of our essence. In a commitment to accessing that part of me, I began creating *Angel Whispers* that took the form of a weekly newsletter.

In the process of devoting energy to making a connection with the light beings known as angels, I discovered my ability to listen to spirit. By repeatedly engaging in this activity, I honed the gift inherent to all species on the planet.....intuition. Intuitive connections helped me to discover that the issues, words and topics that were finding resonation in me were also touching other people at the same time. This led to countless affirming communications from my readers, while providing the inspiration to go deeper into the whispers from the spirit world.

The freedom that my readers gave me to explore the outer regions of human psyche supported the permission I gave myself to take this experience to the fullest. Little did I know that the weekly commitment would last for four years and evolve into a body of work that is a unique collection of short stories, each with the added twist of a message from the angels. It could be similar to a journal, except that the discoveries are not all about me. They are about life on Planet Earth, raising questions that mankind faces every day.

Rewards such as those offered by the *Angel Whispers* have brought me personal joy, peace, and a greater connection to people than I have ever felt. I hope that you find the same vibrations in this collection, and part of my intention is that you can use the book like Oracle Cards. Simply close your eyes, ask a question or set an intention, then let the pages of the book fall open to the one that wants to speak to you. For digital book readers, close your eyes and scroll until you feel it want to stop. Open your eyes and read the page on your reader.

In hopes that you find your connection with spirit, peace on Earth, and the discoveries that allow you to live to the fullest, I offer this book with many blessings, Russell

Beckie Forsyth

Table of Contents

Glenna Forsyth

Russell Forsyth

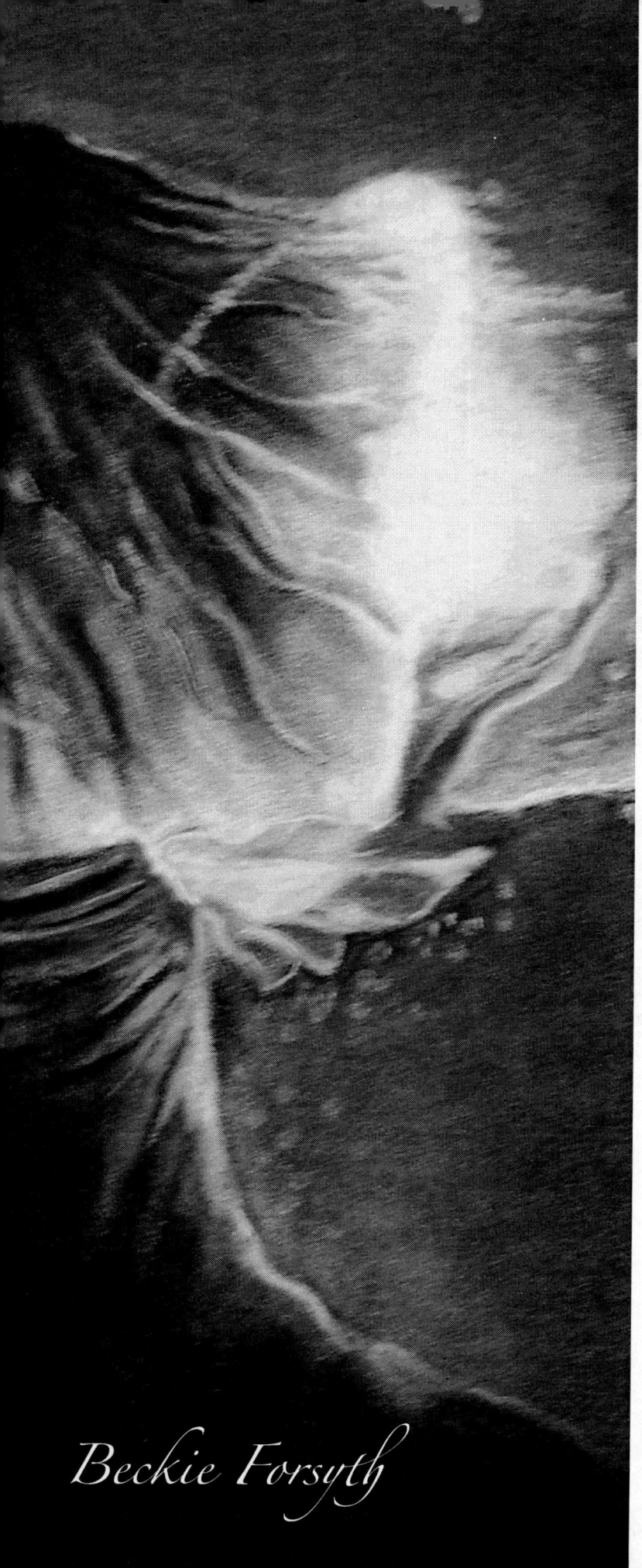

Beckie Forsyth

Glenna Forsyth

Glenna Forsyth

Angel Whispers 2007-2011

Abundance   *Sunday July 22, 2007*

    Abundance is to money what spirituality is to religion..........they go hand in hand. So when I say abundance, most relate it strictly to money. When in fact 'plentifully supplied' is the true meaning of abundance. It is our society's attachment to money that blurs this meaning and is difficult to separate the two, because there is little separation in our real world of today.

    The work that I am doing has its own struggle in the areas of finance and money. There are so many people that have told me that it's not right to accept money in exchange for healing or energy work. On the other side, are the folks that insist that an even exchange of energy is a vital element of ones healing.

    In a leap of faith and a test to satisfy my skeptical mind, I erased on my website page all the rates that I had so carefully put together. Cancel, Alt Delete as Dr. Virtue would say. I put in their place, love offerings. I have since received more money for every session that I had done prior to erasing the rates page.

    So now I am consciously attaching abundance to every areas of my life to try to balance the significance between finances and my plentiful environment. This has brought about within me a gratitude for the abundance that surrounds me. I have adopted a new way of thinking about money as it relates to my life. I try to see it as a flow of energy like everything else in the universe. But I started this new way of thinking about abundance only after this whisper:

    I am the Source and Divine Presence. When you worry or think of lack, you take away my powers to flow as Source. When you lose these emotions tied to lack, you become one with your surroundings and nature.

    Would a forest squirrel worry about a lack of nuts? Well in the same way it would be nuts for you to worry about lack. That is you saying to yourself, "I am not worthy to receive the abundance that surrounds me". If you place that on yourself, you will manifest just that.

    You have given of yourself and now it's time to receive. You have learned the value of your own self worth and love for yourself. Loving yourself enough to act responsibly is Divine. Begin to accept the responsibility of abundance and you will notice that even the word has 'dance' in it. This is the dance of life, learning to give and receive responsibly.

    I am the Source of all abundance; unfailing, omnipresent and real. Abundance can come from the stars in the form of knowledge about the mysteries of the universe. Sacred geometry, Atlantian healing, words of thought and artistic expression, vibrational technology, relationship to spirit and infinite possibilities through Source are there for you to experience the abundance.

    There is abundance around you like the air and the angels that surround you. Tap into the flow and rejoice in the Divine Source. Sing like angels and the angles will join. Love like children without conditions and joy will fill the moment. Love the moment and a moment filled with love will follow. Follow love in the moment and it will lead you to Source.

Alisha writes, *"I was wondering if you would be willing to do a whisper on abuse by people and abuse to yourself. I would love to see what the angels would say about it."* Thanks, Alisha, for the whisper suggestion, and what a deep subject!

The angels often whisper in my ear that my client has suffered abuse, which is often framed as spiritual, mental, verbal, sexual or physical. Some might argue that, according to such a broad scope, who hasn't taken on some energy of abuse in their lives? *Abuse can be defined as the systematic pattern of behaviors in a relationship that are used to gain and/or maintain power and control over another.*

Alisha also wants to know what the angles say about the act of abusing ourselves. We can abuse ourselves in many ways, such as over-indulging in food or drugs, defeating thoughts and language, or behaviors that generally serve to lower one's self-esteem. What causes that type of response, and how does a person free themselves from an energy that supports abuse?

Let's hear from angels on the subject of abuse:

Mankind has followed a pattern of domination through intimidation, and it will take a collective effort to overcome abusive behaviors of individuals, groups and states. With a deep-seated belief that says suffering is the pathway to salvation, humans have developed behaviors that mirror the need for such salvation. This energy can be directed at the self with a sub-conscious motivation to create change.

The key is found in the response to abusive situations. Will you find the deepest lessons of love penetrating your being in order to form a response that allows you to take the best care of yourself? Within truth, the light of love transcends the energy of fear and allows for a transmutation to occur. An instantaneous understanding forms within an energy contained by boundaries of belief and triggered by the loss of free will in a moment of abuse. When the free will is taken and personal authority is compromised, your vulnerability holds lessons of love that serve everyone you come in contact with.

Becoming a partner in an expression of abuse, creates a form of release with faceted energy in that moment. Within the expression of abuse and subsequent energetic release, there is an opportunity to follow an enlightened path that holds a deep understanding with a need to learn forgiveness of the self. Forgiveness does not condone any actions; it simply is a commitment toward your willingness to release toxins from your heart and a way to present yourself in the manner that aligns with your higher voice.

What a meaningful word with an energy that soothes the soul. In our deepest moments of healing and reflection, acceptance speaks living, breathing and intentional words to the heart. Grief, love, life-purpose, relationships and our very existence hinge on our personal abilities to accept.

When I engage in the energy of acceptance, my thinking can often mislead or derail me. A recent project that was holding my excitement fell through, and in order to hide my disappointment I simply stated, "Oh well, I don't care." The newly improved, remodeled, spiritually enlightened Russell (tee hee) drew red flags of danger at the mere utterance that I did not care. That was a non-truth for me because I did care! In that moment I realized a pattern of coping used throughout my life that was disconnected from my heart.

Acceptance means the act of accepting; a receiving what is offered, with approbation, satisfaction, or acquiescence; esp., favorable reception; approval; as, the acceptance of a gift, office, doctrine, etc. "Being happy doesn't mean that everything is perfect. It means that you've decided to look beyond the imperfections." This quote from an unknown source speaks to the relationship between happiness and acceptance.

It is difficult to accept certain aspects of life like the characteristics and beliefs of others, the loss of something or someone in our lives, destiny and the uncertainty or mystery of life. It is time to accept a whisper on the wings of an angel:

Acceptance energy is in the vibrations of love: love for yourself and others, love of God and Divine Source, love of life and the sanctity of life. If you are struggling to accept certain truths about your existence, first make sure it is the truth that is hard to accept rather than an illusion built to support another passion.

If within the walls of your own discernment you find a truth that is hard to accept, then you are facing a lesson of some sort. This lesson could be around having faith in a Higher Power that everything is in Divine order, including your life. Your lack of acceptance illuminates purpose in your journey around awareness and understanding.

Being unhappy with who you are demonstrates the need for clarity, while being unhappy with the journey of others demonstrates lower energies at work. The ego will offer judgments as a way to lead you through illusions to test your faith, but you can reach a time when you overcome those issues within the light of truth. At that point, you set new intentions with awareness that the lessons are complete in order to break the patterns set in place by the teachings.

Don't make this difficult; it is as simple as tuning in a dial on the radio. Once the message is being received without static, you have arrived at the point of alignment with the vibrations of the core truth. Enjoy the beat of your own heart and listen to the sound that makes your soul dance. Learn acceptance to gather others around the circle of unconditional love.

People often turn to alternatives as part of their process of due diligence. But others appear to be acting solely out of desperation. I will openly admit (with grins) that I have reached that final-straw point myself at times, and it feels more like giving up than anything else.

What brought up this whisper concept was a moment of pondering the energies around healing. Some people are skeptical about an alternative to medicine until they face a healing crisis. At some point, an opening occurs which might be created in a moment of desperation.

I have to say that in my opinion any form of surrender can lead to faith, so maybe desperation and faith can be closely linked. But if you've reached a point of saturation that leaves you desperate, then maybe it's time to clear some energy and boost your faith before moving forward with decisions. Let's engage in faith for a whisper on acts of desperation:

The human journey will ultimately bring you many tests of faith. Abandonment of hope leads to desperation and could anchor you in the subconscious energy you have created over a lifetime with your belief system. Sudden faith without basis could create an illusion around an outcome, eventually leading to disappointment, confusion and frustration.

If you are feeling desperate around a situation, that could be a sign that it is time to boost your faith in some way. Researching information, reading stories of those who overcome great challenges, connecting with a spiritual community, spending time in nature, and reflecting on the blessings in your life are just a few ways to boost faith.

Desperation is also a sign that the mental body needs to be purged of all the clutter that has built up to cause a lack of clarity or feed an obsession. It is easy to create illusions during moments of desperation, so this is the time when faith is most needed.

Your higher self knows the answers to all questions in your life as it centers energy in the heart area that connects to the Cosmic Heart of the Universe and to the great void of silence. It is here that you will find the answers to your questions that no other source can give you as they are illuminated by truth. This is the stream of love that lifts you from the mired energy of human drama and struggles.

Start by believing in yourself in order to create upward movement with faith, and you will find peace, love, joy, acceptance and a healthy distance from desperation!

I have been writing on some heavy subjects and thought it was time to lighten it up. There is no better subject to do that with than angels. Besides I couldn't wait to get this whisper to shed even more light on the subject.

Angels: 1. One of the immortal beings attendant to God. 2. A kind and loveable person.

Well, which one is it?, I pondered as I read the dictionary account? *How can it be both?* I have certainly encountered Earth Angels. In Christian beliefs, angels are referred to as 'ministering spirits' where thousands often gathered for key biblical events with more than three hundred mentions in the Bible

It has been somewhat surprising the way angels transcend all religious boundaries as they are easily accepted by many as part of their own spiritual belief system. Even Native Americans have a belief in these loving beings. Another aspect of angels that really appealed to me is that their messages are always based in love.

Angels cannot talk to us in the way that humans talk to each other, so we are dependent on the utilization of the 'Clair' senses to receive their messages of love. Clairvoyance (clear vision), Clairaudience (clear hearing), Clairsentience (clear feeling) and Claircognizance (clear knowing) are the methods by which we can connect with these loving beings.

I think that our individual beliefs are mostly based on personal experience, so for someone to truly know angels they often need to experience their own sign, encounter or event regarding angels. Working with angels has given me a more personal connection to God and Source, which was somewhat unexpected and certainly a bonus.

I could expand on this subject for several pages, but I think it's time for a whisper:

Angels are heaven's mediators. They often negotiate with the soul to arrive at a loving conclusion to the events of mankind. When you ask for their help, the negotiation begins. This can be in the form of a 'soul contract' or life purpose. There is often a deeper meaning attached to the actions of man.

If you take the time to look beneath the surface, you will find the loving basis for the action. Whether you are here to discover the light through a journey into the darkness, or simply a 'kid in a candy store' that has arrived as an evolver, everything starts with the clarity of negotiating with the angels.

There is a knowing that you bring into this life that is often lost in your childhood. If you listen to your inner voice, there is a connection with the divine that can be guided by angels. The sole purpose of the angels is to be there for you whenever you call, and to assist in opening a gateway to Godliness found in all spirits.

Angels are the divine and timeless essence of your spirituality. Therefore, angels can bring a balance and harmony to body, mind, and spirit. Walk with the angels to experience true love and an opening into the loving light itself.

This subject arose with incredible fashion during a crystal release session this week. My client released load after load of anger into my healing space. I felt the energy pass through me like a wave. He left with an unusually large smile on his face which made me laugh as he rode away on his Vespa.

I went straight into my office where I received an unpleasant email from a family member. I really got angry over it and fired off a response. It stunned me the way my uncharacteristic rant manifested and took form so quickly. When Beckie came home, I was like a kid with his mother, saying, "I got mad." I told her about my session and she immediately asked if I cleared the healing space and myself. Oops!

How many times have your thoughts wandered to an event in your history that gave you that feeling of anger? You know the kind that makes your chest or stomach burn like fire. This feeling is the result of 'etheric cords of attachment.' These unhealthy cords can be anger, manipulation, guilt, fears, jealousy, pity and a host of others. It's these negative attachments that affect the major energy centers and become unhealthy.

I personally spent a year and half of my life doing what I refer to as my forgiveness work. Part of that work was to relive the painful experiences that I didn't process or experience in the way that was most healthy for me. Basically, I was 'cutting cords' by feeling the event one last time before releasing the energy. To stay clear, I have to complete the experience in the 'now' and be unwilling to carry it forward.

My client called the next day to tell me his face was hurting from the foreign activity known as smiling. I have cleared the healing space and cut my cords of attachment as I continue down the healing path with the help of my angel whisper:

Anger is the result of confusion, misunderstanding and the ego's defense of actions. To truly understand and see the light in all humans, you must remove the layers of expectations and false hopes.

To conquer your anger, you must see the world in the truest light. From those eyes you will see the world with acceptance, tolerance and the patience that comes with compassion. The anger you hold will reveal some of the truth about who you are.

When love replaces anger, there is a joy that breathes of hope and the healing energy. In all beings exists the potential for loss of control through anger. That is the time to extend your capacity to love into the face of anger.

Apply all your freedoms to the pursuit of life without anger and you will truly know the meaning of unconditional love without borders and boundaries. In loving light you bathe the angry heart while cleansing the soul. Anger does not exist in the landscape of the divine.

This is the dawning of the Age of Aquarius, or so the song goes. That Age of Aquarius refers to an astrological term and *an **astrological age** is a time period believed by some to parallel major changes in the Earth's inhabitants' development, particularly relating to culture, society and politics. There are twelve astrological ages corresponding to the twelve zodiacal signs in astrology. At the completion of one cycle of twelve astrological ages, the cycle repeats itself. Astrological ages occur because of a phenomenon known as the precession of the equinoxes. One complete period of this precession is called a Great Year or Platonic Year of about 25,920 years.*

Many experts believe that the Age of Aquarius has arrived recently or will arrive in the near future. On the other hand, some believe that the Age of Aquarius arrived up to five centuries ago, or will not start until six centuries from now. The Age of Pisces that we are leaving is symbolized by the two heads of a fish facing each other, which also represents Christianity. Jesus is often referred to as the avatar of the Age of Pisces.

The Age of Aquarius is thought of as the age of care and a time for mankind to advance to the next level of understanding. So perhaps we stand in a moment of time where history will mark great changes in our development. With the age of caring comes a new kind of sharing that involves releasing our old paradigms and shifting into a new consciousness.

According to the calendars of many ancient civilizations, including the Mayans, we are at the end of an Earth cycle that started almost 26,000 years ago, and that may mean the Age of Aquarius is about to repeat. December 21, 2012 is the date of the winter solstice and a day marked by ancient mathematicians and astrologers as the transition into the Age of Aquarius. I will look toward the stars and ask for a whisper:

With every New Age comes an energetic shifting of vibrations. This can be felt by everyone and can bring unity to thoughts, prayers and a connection to a Higher Consciousness. With the movement of the stars and Universal alignment of Cosmic Energy, mankind can leap into the future with cohesive momentum.

As you resonate with the wisdom that comes with sharing, you can strip away layers of repressed evolution with a single heartbeat of the Earth. Ancient civilizations were tapped into the Divine Source of earth energies and therefore saw the future of their own species as represented by the stars. The Power of the Earth is completely present.

In the depths of your Soul lives the essence of energy that is connecting every cell in your body to the Universal rhythms. The only thing that can distance you from this Cosmic Cord of love is living in the Lower Self. Open your heart to the spirituality of the Age of Aquarius and breathe in the light of life that shines at the deepest level of the human experience. Your soul has journeyed a great distance to find love in the Age of Aquarius and now is the time to find freedom through evolution and planetary alignment.

I guess it is human nature to want things that can be rare or illusive, such as an apology (lol). My personal experience has taught me to expect a battle with the ego when mustering any conversation that begins with those curious words, "I'm sorry," An expression of sorrow can come in many forms, I am sure of that. Even this newsletter could be just that (tee hee).

In a recent discussion, a neighbor was describing an argument with his ten-year-old son. The basis of the disagreement was over the father's contention that once an event had passed, it could never be changed. At the child's insistence that it could, the father challenged him by asking, "Just tells me one thing that can alter the effects of a past event." His son quickly replied with large, innocent eyes, "An apology." Wow, are these kids sharp!

When you put it in that perspective, it sounds so simple and effective. This also raises questions in my mind as to how an apology is received. I am sure most of you have experienced an apology that felt empty and, in that moment of facing acceptance ... well, you soon begin to see how complicated this subject can be. Let's see if we can get an angel whisper on the action of an apology:

The resolution found in a moment of expressed regret or sorrow has, within the energy, several layers of emotional movement. The one that expresses the apology has the opportunity to release toxic emotions, such as guilt, anger and so on, which could be stored at deep levels in the human body's energy field. The person receiving has a chance to speak words of forgiveness and understanding to replace an ego's defensive stance.

If an apology is rejected by an implied or energetic response, the individual is left with finding other ways to release the energy, without the active participation of others. In most situations where feelings have been hurt, this is necessary internal work, regardless. The emotional response from within the human body, when released in the energy of love, can be felt at the core of existence, across the world and beyond.

The balance of giving and receiving can be found in the discernment of apologies. Simply ask yourself who is to be served in a moment of expressed regrets, and the answer will enlighten you with answers to such questions. After all, this energy is anchored in love, love for yourself and others that can manifest to deeper levels from your action steps.

Within love, there is truth and the occasional mistake that can lead you to an apology. In that instant of awareness, you grow inside a space held for the lessons of love you came to experience, all the while leading others by your example. Now that's love!

The Biblical definition might go something like this: ***Archangels*** *are superior or higher-ranking angels. The only angel ever clearly named as being of the order in the Bible is Michael. Archangel Michael is also known as Saint Michael, has a name with the Hebrew translation meaning "he who is like God" and is often depicted as the angel commander, guardian of the Orthodox faith, advocate for Israel and a fighter against negative energy.*

The archangels Michael, Raphael (he who heals) and Gabriel (he who communicates) are venerated in the Roman Catholic Church with a feast day on September 29. This recent discovery of the feast day gave me that tingly feeling since that is also my birthday. An angel reader born on the archangels feast day, you can't make this stuff up!

I often tell people that the archangels can be all places at once, so you are never disturbing them with anything to little or too large. I invite you to call upon these beings of light and feel the power of their connection to everything that is spiritual for help with your intentions and dreams. I will now call on the Archangels for a whisper of reflection:

If you collected the souls that have walked the Earth and chose the most wise and loving sampling of these spirits, you would be setting those individuals aside and apart from the rest. These spirits would then feel called into service for being honored in this way. This is the same as the Archangels. We are a collection of the most evolved in our group of light-filled servants to the Divine.

As your leaders have taken on roles in the society that best fit their gifts, so have the Archangels. This gives us the ability to call in 'specialists' for every situation. For this reason prayers and requests take discernment on many levels and many layers. Weaving your story into the environment of your heart and landscape of your soul is exacting when it comes to fitting your life purpose.

If you think your prayers are going unanswered, know that they are always heard. Look deep into every situation to know whether there is an answer or whether you have overlooked the message generated from your prayers. The best form of communication with the Archangels is the intentional transmission of thought to Divine Source using angelic energy as a conduit. This becomes a form of surrender, gratitude, faith, passion and love for the body, mind, spirit and all forms of life.

Love is the wellspring from where mankind finds meaning, purpose peace and energy. The Angels and Archangels can connect you to this flow like a wave connects you with the ocean. In the exploration of life, the playful and joyful spirit of a child shines through and touches the angels in the same way that they touch you. Breathe in the air that surrounds the angelic realm and breathe out all that does not serve.

"He who is like God" is the meaning most associated with the name of this Supreme Being in the angelic realm. Hierarchy, religious structure and spiritual framework surface for many at the mention of this name, while I have found an energy that has old-world charm, the ability to lighten things up and something mysterious that feels like a spiritual partner within my personal connection with Archangel Michael.

During a session one day, Archangel Michael delivered a simple but powerful message to my Jewish client. "*You know me as Saint Michael*" was the endearing communication that stirred my curiosity. After the session, I searched for the meaning using the Google gods (tee hee) and discovered that Saint Michael was considered to be the advocate and protector of the children of Israel! In that moment, I also discovered that my birthday is the same day that Saint Michael's feast day is celebrated.

This is a typical example of what can happen when you follow your instincts and some direction from a pure, loving source. I will now ask Archangel Michael to deliver a message on any subject today as we form a whisper from an angel:

Spirituality can be found in every moment and every aspect of life if you are willing to look. The form that this takes is simply that which mankind chooses. Within each individual is thirst for knowledge that serves to answer the questions of life. If you look to the Lower Self energies, like guilt, shame, anger, greed, jealousy and such, you will be drawn away from the Higher Self. But if you choose to look to the higher regions of thought, purpose, love and responsibility, you will find faith and a Higher Power.

You are the only one that can make choices based on what is best for you with direction that will lead you to the love, happiness and joy offered by the life experience. Your willingness to engage in certain activities could represent a level of expressed needs that could bring balance and harmony to your life. Conscious decisions around repeating and addictive behaviors or cravings can create action steps that initiate changes with energy that brings you into total alignment with your core existence.

Move through life with purpose as you integrate teachings from the past with acceptance around the lessons that you hold as truths. Show caution when diving into the future to avoid building illusions. Display reckless abandon in the present moment as you allow passion to fuel the heart, love to light the way, integrity to be your mantra and overwhelming waves of unrepressed emotion that propel you across the oceans of time. As you fill your soul with the breath of Divine Life on Earth, fill your heart with a love for life that teaches everyone you touch the truest meaning of love.

Merriam-Webster defines **ascension** in Christian terms as *a celebration of the Ascension of Christ into heaven; observed on the 40th day after Easter.* Many words have multiple meanings, and for ascension, this is also true. *To rise or create an upward movement such as the ascension of a hot-air balloon* is another meaning. In astronomy, *the rising of a star above the horizon*, thus we have ascending planets in our charts.

In his book *Conscious Living,* Sol Luckman writes: "Many ancient traditions worldwide maintain that humans not only inherently possess the potential for fully incarnating light at the physiological level, but that some have already achieved it, and millions more will do so in the very era in which we live." The historical literature suggests that there are "unusual physical, as well as psychological, consequences in humans to the attainment of the exalted state of mind known as enlightenment," writes biochemist Colm Kelleher. "These reported changes include, but are not limited to, sudden reversal of aging, emergence of a light body and observed bodily ascension." While many of these descriptions associate the light body with death, Kelleher makes it clear that a number of reports indicate that "transformation of the body can happen independently of death." Let's ascend together on a transformational whisper:

There are many levels of human development, and mankind is currently reaching for new heights in the spiritual realm. Ascension is not limited to this realm as there are many ways to achieve a raised consciousness. Near-death experiences, incredible physical feats and walking in the light of truth can all produce this effect.

The Ascended Masters have achieved this high level of consciousness and are now teaching larger numbers of people. The New Age brings an energetic shift to the human experience as many people tap into the fount of intuitive wisdom with trust, belief and hope leading the heart. This 'shift' allows for the release from past hurts, ego judgments and limiting factors as a way to find freedom in the experience of the deepest levels of love.

Ascension in simple terms means to rise above in conscious and intentional living. The significance at this time is that the focus of one person creates the ripple effect. Instead of a wave that comes crashing with energy, there is a subtle effect from a flow of connection with spirit and oneness. One human tribe comes together in a cosmic experience full of unity and comfort found in the arms of spirit.

Mystery and miracles are partners in the process of ascension, and all you have to do to discover these feelings is to breathe your way into a willing and open heart that speaks to the greater love that is available to you. From there it is a lot like a hot-air balloon ride: fun, exciting and peaceful vibrations, complete with an elevated perspective and breathtaking view of the world!

I have been reading some old texts and have been quite entertained by my observations and insights with this material. It seems that what some people are describing as "New Age" is anything but new. The wording might easily reflect the times, but the messages are the same.

One word that I saw frequently was **aspirant**, which, according to the website Mudrashram.com, means *a seeker after spiritual knowledge. The aspirant typically reads spiritual books, attends seminars and lectures on meditation and spirituality, visits spiritual teachers, and learns techniques to meditate and pray. The great task of this aspect of spiritual development is to learn to unite with the Soul and to travel consciously through the inner vehicles and within the Planes of the Great Continuum of Consciousness.*

Many people are searching for answers to the deepest questions of life, and that search leads them to look at the truth regarding their lives. Some have asked me why that is so hard, and they claim that the self-help books leave the degree of difficulty out of the equation (tee hee). Nonetheless, the Lightworkers and spiritual warriors of the world are united in a thirst for knowledge like never before. Let's search together by requesting a whisper from an angel on information regarding an aspirant.

The human race has reached a point in evolution that says it is time to leave the old paradigms and structures that have long impeded personal and spiritual growth. Great change is coming, and the aspirants are preparing the world in ways that may not be apparent. A collective consciousness is linking people to this energy of change and to each other in a Oneness that transcends all barriers.

Aspirants are the students and the teachers who will usher mankind into the Age of Aquarius. Like a child graduating from school, the human species will rise to accept the responsibility that comes with knowledge. Individuals will come together with similar actions and deeds that are beyond the teachings of the past. The final frontiers of discovery will not be in outer space or the depths of the ocean, but instead, it will be in the outer reaches of the soul where great peace will be found.

What drives the aspirant to these discoveries is the inspiration and motivation that can only come from a Source so powerful that the limitless potential has never been viewed by humans. Like great detectives unraveling a mystery, the aspirants will move forward with intuitive senses that connect the heart of a person to the heartbeat of a Cosmos. So put on your happy face and get ready for the ride of your life!

As I was working with a client this last week, she was being guided toward a more assertive approach to a situation. She responded by saying, "I guess anything but the assertive truth is a form of manipulation." That comment sent me into deep reflection and a somber accounting of some recent situations (grinning) that held the energy of passive aggression.

In yoga teachings, you should not speak if your words would be hurtful to another. Reading a person's response to your unspoken words becomes subjective, and makes it easy to become a total people-pleaser to the extent that your truth is never fully spoken or heard.

Assertiveness could be defined as *a form of behavior characterized by a confident declaration or affirmation of a statement, without need of proof; this affirms the person's rights or point of view without either aggressively threatening the rights of another or submissively permitting another to ignore or deny one's rights or point of view.*

That sounds simple and effective, two things the angels often encourage in most communication efforts! Now I will assert myself with a loving, yet firm (tee hee), request for a whisper from an angel on the subject of assertiveness:

You can use language that is assertive and loving at the same time, but that style of communication takes practice, awareness, integrity and a willingness to spread truth. Your aura shines a little brighter and broader when you stand in the light of truth with the courage to speak from the heart. When attached to ego, assertiveness becomes confrontational, and words are lost from one's ear.

Like an athlete depends on instinct to make split-second decisions regarding a course and direction, your Higher-self knows how to make choices regarding the subtle energies around the truth. Knowing when to speak your truth is as important as delivering the actual message. You intuitively know when people are open to receiving and when they aren't, which demands your discernment.

The truth isn't always what you want to hear, but change and alignment begin as soon as the energy leaves your body and lands on another's body, mind and heart. Humans adapt very easily, so you must show others how to lend support for you and your beliefs. People won't know if they are crossing your boundaries unless those lines are clearly established, respected and occasionally pushed upon.

Assertiveness takes a certain amount of passion, which can be fueled by emotions ranging from hate and anger to faith and love. By making a stand, you state an unwillingness to betray your emotions. But under certain conditions, assertiveness combined with benevolence creates a union of the hearts. Inside this union is an energy of thought that connects with Source, and even though some might disagree, most will find ways to enter the light of truth.

Everyone has dealt with an attitude or belief that seems so negative and unreasonable that understanding seems difficult. There is nothing more frustrating than trying to work through a problem, only to come up against a person with a negative attitude. People often close the door on a solution due to a belief or thought that a certain outcome is inevitable, and that energy seems to intensify when your own belief is that all things are possible. Bo Bennett was quoted as saying, "Having a positive mental attitude is asking how something can be done rather than saying it can't be done."

My experience tells me that it isn't often a person changes their mind by simply facing a positive demeanor. Is that my attitude? (lol) Many people have great attitudes, and it has been my experience that a positive outlook creates a more comfortable space in which to solve problems.

*The word **Attitude** means a complex mental state involving beliefs, feelings, values and dispositions toward acting in certain ways.* William James once said, "Whenever you're in conflict with someone, there is one factor that can make the difference between damaging your relationship and deepening it. That factor is attitude."

So how do we deal with life in a positive way when facing obstacles and people with bad attitudes? Let's ask the angels for a whisper on attitude that helps me and you with ours:

You have been receiving messages around this subject with studies on words like optimism, highest potential and now attitude. The essential ingredient to leading a happy and purpose-filled life comes from the way that you view and approach your existence. In order to find the higher vibrations of joy, love, passion and wellness, you must put effort toward clearing away disharmonious thoughts and beliefs associated with the feelings around your guilt, anger, fear and shame.

Everything will return to your view on life and your faith with a higher power. If you support beliefs that you are a victim in life by using negative thoughts and ego judgments, your positive attitude will suffer. Holding beliefs that support everything is in Divine order and that certain events in life, no matter how harsh, generate deep and meaningful lessons, allow a positive view of the world to form a bond with your core frequency.

Your attitude is your choice and is guiltless by nature, which allows each individual to shift their perspective. In other words, it is your free will that determines the emotional outcome before you ever face it. The Universal Laws of Attraction ensure that you will attract that which dominates the focus of your thinking. Choose your thoughts carefully and when facing an opportunity to resolve an issue in your life, seek the resonance with the higher vibrations that help you know truth, hope and resolution.

In faith you will find the most positive attitude, while in darkness you will find the lessons that challenge you to make choices regarding the happiness you seek. When you find that thread of true happiness, do not let your attitude close the door.

I'm using the word today to imply 'spiritual awakening,' as most people don't go around referring to their 'awakening' as the first thing they experienced that morning. Most definitions of awakening are brief in their description of a morning routine or a religious epiphany of some sort.

A Course in Miracles put spiritual awakening in the context of: In religious experience, or a sacred experience where an individual comes in contact with transcendental reality. Religious experiences are by their very nature preternatural (surpassing the ordinary or normal); that is, out of the ordinary or beyond the natural order of things. They may be difficult to distinguish observationally from psychopathological states such as psychoses or other forms of altered awareness.

That sounds really serious (tee hee)! Some would argue that the most profound spiritual awakening occurs in the depths of our pain and suffering. Could that be true in the sense that the weakened spirit of an individual surrenders to a greater power, which becomes the awakening? Well, I am starting to ask those questions which usually mark a segue to a connection from an angel who whispers on the subject of spiritual awakening:

It is a lot like waking up in the morning as you go from one reality to another, and that transition calls for a response. Awakening to the new dawn can be literal or figurative, and as you grow and learn, there comes the moment when you rise to the occasion that you may not have known you were preparing for. Those opportunities to rise often appear at times of great challenge and distress, but how else could you be drawn into events that hold profound meaning?

A person's transition from a period of higher vibration has only one direction to go, and the beauty of polar opposites is that within a moment of darkness, light can lift humans from their suffering. The subtle preparations for that moment of spiritual awakening provide the platform needed to feed a constant energy that is building for a date with destiny.

The awakening is defining a return to what you already know through a medium that you do not. The Godself creates a pathway for the illuminated truth to surface at the moment an opening or willingness transcends the thought, beliefs, actions and projections. By offering a glimpse through the lens of Divine love, you make the choices that determine key aspects of your path to ascension that further define your free will, integrity, faith and capacity to love.

The Universe does a pirouette to enlighten, entertain, nurture and evoke your spiritual awakening, as food for the soul enters the stream of the Christ Consciousness.

In the metaphysical or conceptual sense, **balance** is used to mean *a point between two opposite forces that is desirable over purely one state or the other, such as a balance between the metaphysical law and chaos—law by itself being overly-controlling, chaos being overly unmanageable, and balance being the point that minimizes the negatives of both.*

I would change that definition to read at the end: " … balance being the point that maximizes the positives of both." The other way sounds like we have to constantly settle for less in order to achieve balance in the metaphysical sense.

Some common Divine prescriptions given today to help swing the scales into balance would be to: have more fun; make room in your schedule for some self-time; lower the bar on your goals so you can feel more success in your life; nurture yourself in some way; forgive yourself; go a few weeks without casting a judgment on yourself. These are ways to bring balance to a situation or aspect of life.

Some experts say that in order to balance key social issues such as discrimination and oppression, the scales must first counter-balance before coming to rest in true equality. This may be true when it come to the body, mind and spirit as well. This raises the question to me: Do we have to flirt with the edge of the extreme before we can find true balance with a deep issue? It is now time for me to do just that as I flirt with a whisper:

Certain Universal Laws are in place to ensure a harmony of balance. Mankind is testing the limits of these boundaries when it comes to the Earth. That is why you have ever-increasing awareness as a race of beings that you must care for your planet.

This is the global example of the human experience. The loss of balance triggers the awareness in all areas of existence as described in the phrase 'the balance of life.' Without darkness, there is no light. Without the negative ground, there is no positive charge. Without the void, there is no space for energy to exist.

Balance is the co-existence of these things with the true values of partnership. Your balance in life comes from embracing the undeniable truths of your existence as partners. Love is not felt at the same level of depth without the experience of loss. The greatest triumphs of mankind have sprung from tragedy. This may not be desirable, but it can be accepted as you surrender and release your attachments to an outcome.

Spiritual balance is achieved with the acknowledgment that a higher power exists. The higher the level of acknowledgment becomes, the more you create a movement away from the self that brings you into a real and true perspective of life. The act of moving beyond this life creates the purest balance in your reality and challenges you to accept the magic and the mystery that surround your own personal belief system.

I feel so blessed to be able to share time with so many that I consider to be hovering somewhere around the creative genius level. That in itself is inspirational! Today as I tapped into the energy of inspiration, I set an intention to feel the flow of creative juices move through my body in waves of inspiration.

Within minutes I was walking out the door before stopping to pull an angel card. Doreen Virtue's message from the angels came through with 'Giving and Receiving' which quickly took the form of breath. The Daily Guidance card read, "When you only exhale (give) or inhale (receive), you become out of balance with the universe."

In that moment, I stood there and focused on each breath. With every inhale I was receiving and with every exhale I was giving. I immediately felt a tingling sensation all over my body. As some of you may know from Yoga practice, your exhale is longer than your inhale, so that added gift at the end seemed even more divine when my energy reached a balanced Nirvana (Sanskrit word meaning 'to cease blowing', tee hee).

As I practiced this for a moment, I felt absorbed in gratitude in the realization that I just tapped into the creative energy of inspiration. That entire thought was expressed in such a soulful way, there was no doubt that through breath, love, intention and gratitude, I had connected with energy from a Divine Source. I should now engage my breath in hopes of connecting with angels for words of love and a whisper on balancing breath:

The breath of life is that which brings balance, even when the body ceases to breathe. The balance that occurs in that instant is beyond measure or comprehension. The soul continues to breathe in the Universal flow of loving energy. Some place themselves in the middle of this energetic strand of connecting light, while others surf around the edges.

Even at the Soul level you will find beautiful differences between spirits as a way to mimic nature with every nuance. The Universal rhythm and evolutionary cycles require this aspect in the make-up of the core ingredients that work in harmony to create life.

The balance achieved through breath and intentional living reflects the simplistic nature of energy. Therefore the innocence of a child can be serving in the sense that things don't have to be complicated. The way that humans grow and change into their later years illustrates a return to innocence. For this reason and more, you should be careful of what you 'breathe' in and pay attention to how you breathe it out.

When you sleep, your breath flows in long and steady rhythmic patterns. You fully balance your energy with peace and harmony as you open to the many functions of the body, mind and spirit that occur during rest. The dream stage is mostly a psychological manifestation of expressions through balancing breath that act as a gateway to connection with the Higher Self and Spirit. In your waking hours, inspire others through the innocence and simplicity of balance with breath.

Beckie and I have taken on the completion of several projects in 2011. These goals pertain a lot to our personal space and the structures that are meaningful in our lives. The underlying theme with these projects was to beautify our world and the world of others. In some cases, some of these projects began as far back as 2003.

A few summers ago, we shared some time in New Mexico with friends, and each of us took turns creating an activity for the entire group to participate in. I was surprised by my friend Craig's project choice, which was for all of us to beautify a specific area of the property where the Casa Angeles sits. This area was the septic tank (tee hee), and we had a lot of fun stacking rocks and building mock structures out of the pine needles and branches in order to adorn a neglected area.

This was a project that I never would have conceived of (grinning)! The result was transformative to the property, the friendship and apparently to the deer that frequented the property, and who now seemed more interested in what was going on in that area. What was going on was beautification! That experience was a teaching around the way we react when beauty comes into our everyday world through our own efforts.

Speaking of beauty, let's see what the angels have to whisper on the powerful effects of focusing on bringing beauty into our world.

Part of the loving energy that fills the spirit world comes from an elevated view of the beauty that exists everywhere. When you create something that adds beauty, you transmute the energies of fear, sadness, worry and all the lower energies in an artful manner. Beauty creates a space for spirit to communicate in ways that are intangible and, therefore, difficult to comprehend solely through a mental process.

Beauty is language that the heart and soul understand, because it connects you to the world of the Divine. Beyond the veil, there is a world filled with beauty, without limits or constraints, where the lowest vibration is love and highest is a unified vibration of energy. When you beautify your world, the God or Goddess within awakens to the sweetness of life as it connects you to a Divine matrix of light and sound, or the essence of all creation.

If you can imagine yourself as a free energy being drawn upward and pulled into a stream of light without effort, this is what awaits you. Practicing this upward movement while in the body is a great exercise! So why not create the experience as a way of easing suffering for yourself and others? Beauty not only fills the eyes of the beholder, it expands the energy of the heart and soul.

Spend time beautifying your world at every level, and you will be drawn into a comfortable space that looks like home and feels like home. Your effort will bring forward the gentle nurturing energy known as self-love.

One of the beauties of life is that we get to choose a significant part of our existence, thanks, in part, to our free will. A recent study shows that people who are considered 'negative' live an average of 7 fewer years that those who have a positive outlook on life. Behind that half-empty glass is usually a person who is basically unhappy with life and is choosing to focus on the negative aspects.

Choosing to be happy can be directly tied to your belief system, and so faith and your view of life can be extremely important to the body, mind and spirit. What we believe is a choice based on several factors, such as the way we were raised, our environment, experiences and the mental patterns we formed based on these aspects. *A person's individual **belief system** can refer to life stance, world view, religion, philosophy and ideology.*

I think we need to be careful with the way we treat our thoughts in respect to the things mentioned above, and be cautious with our minds, which can be just as fragile as life itself. Everything we ingest can have consequences, especially the thoughts we choose to entertain. Let's entertain some thought around a whisper from an angel on belief system:

Your spirituality is part of an ever-changing landscape that revolves around your belief system. Placing limitations on your beliefs can be a way for you feel safe and secure as you experience contrasts in order to create a slow, methodic rise to the surface of unconditional love. Being stuck without movement within those limitations can ultimately lead to unhappiness and negativity.

There are simple ways for you to break free and expand your feelings around spiritual teachings if you are willing to explore options. The human body is a complex, yet creative organism, designed to reach new heights in an evolving state, and free will is in place to help you with that ascension. An open mind can influence a heart opening and an open heart can influence the belief system.

In one single instant, the wall in place around your belief system can be torn down through experiences that form new paradigms. The unlimited potential that exists within you is best seen through the eyes of love, joy and understanding, which are somewhat dependent on your happiness. Every aspect of life can be viewed through the lens of different perspectives, and it is up to each individual to define the path of their happiness.

Your day-to-day choices in the minutia of life are like pieces of a puzzle that, when fully assembled, create a dazzling picture. Sometime this "big picture" cannot be seen in each individual piece, but you can know it's there with a vision and with foresight anchored in the highest levels of faith. Choose each piece of the puzzle out of laughter, joy and happiness in order to unveil the glorious life you were born to live

As I was working toward a very calculated outcome, things went south in a hurry one morning. The shift that occurred was really no one's fault, but the blame game began. Since I was ultimately responsible as the one in charge of the whole operation, I quickly blamed myself. It occurred to me that taking responsibility was called for, but the negativity I felt around the blame was not.

I went into deeper thoughts around the energy of blame, realizing that in today's world some people are not always accepting of responsibility. That tendency could lead toward a stronger emotional response, such as blame. By definition, ***blame*** *means to find fault or to place or hold responsibility.* Hubert Humphrey once stated, *"We believe that to err is human. To blame it on someone else is politics."* Boy, does that ring true!

Maybe it is way too easy to find fault in human behavior. The real trick is to find the truth that allows love and compassion to eliminate finding fault by replacing that energy with equal measures to finding answers and solutions (tee hee). I will seek to hold responsibility with the interpretation of a vibration or a whisper from an angel on blame:

Energy that appears to be on the opposing side of any argument almost always elicits some sort of response. These emotions, considered to be polar opposites of your considerations, attract a type of balance to any situation. The education of a soul requires specific needs to be honored and fulfilled in order to bring that balance or some resolution to an apparent resistance.

If everyone on the planet aligned with their Divine Life purpose and released the struggle around responsibility, blame would become a thing of the past and be replaced by an acceptance or understanding. But until that day comes, blame will continue to awaken the senses of the Warrior Spirit within.

Discernment around responsibility is important for self-discipline, accountability and personal growth. The way that focus on responsibility is presented to an individual can undo the effects when bitter condemnation and judgments offer conflict above all else. When challenged in this manner, the ego will stand and fight with energy that can lack purity in reason and thought.

It takes conscious awareness and focused intention to rise to an elevated perspective that directs energy toward truth and light. Refuse to be led down the path of confusion by those who would choose to distract you with the lower energies of guilt, blame and manipulation. Instead, be the one who uses assertive, yet loving, guidance that gives direction toward a grounded and simple solution.

Allow your actions to be the gentle reminder of who you are, why you came here and what you life-path holds as truth for you. That should be more than enough to hold your attention and keep you occupied!

The whisper on 'Aspirants' had me thinking about all the searchers whom I come in contact with. I have noticed a common thread in the angel messages that many are receiving. The future appears to be unscripted to a large extent, which can seem unsettling for some.

For me, the past several months have been so full of every kind of emotion that any thoughts of the past or future have felt somewhat eclipsed. The upside is that I have been able to stay more in the moment. The downside is an uncertain future, but that is not unusual. Maybe the concept of a blank canvas goes against a type of social programming that says a Higher Power has it all mapped out?

If I let go of that programming, the idea of a blank canvas can feel exciting, challenging, expansive and mysterious. There is an aspect to the co-creation process that begs us to answer the questions around what makes us happy, what path leads to the most joy and what serves the highest good. Let's give the blank canvas to the angels and see what impressions can be communicated from a whisper:

Never before have so many been offered such a profound and unique opportunity. Like a painter stepping up to blank canvas with all the paints, colors, the inspiration and an idea, you have many choices to make around the creation that will mirror your personal expressions around life-purpose, family, relationships, and commitments.

Of course, you can always insist on a path that leads to more suffering, but you can also choose to go in an entirely different direction. The collective consciousness that you carry is now offering a type of freedom, freedom from the past and from the future. The bonds of time are lifting, and you are free to experience the sensation of humans in flight!

The blank canvas gives you a rare glimpse into the mirror in order to see the alchemist within. By combining the precious elements that you hold as truths, you get to create magic in the enchanting forest of your dreams. Every person is being gifted with a blank canvas at some level of their existence, and each of you bears witness to the energy that sweeps the planet.

In order to bring balance to a world that appears chaotic, organize your thoughts so that you may see life through the eyes of love. See the good and the inspirational without allowing the focus to be directed toward what is not good. Your energy is transformational and is currently creating the collective consciousness to be held by the future generations.

Birds   *Sunday April 18, 2010*

It has been my experience that birds have an important place on our planet and with mankind. The cardinal seems to have a special relationship with our deceased loved ones, often delivering a comforting energy to those in grief. Also, I have found a common thread in most spiritual teachings that speaks to signs from Angels being delivered by winged creatures.

In a recent workshop, a man spoke of a magic moment with a bird that came to his window. The bird, who claimed to be a General (tee hee), transferred what I believe was important information regarding the birds' place in the spiritual realm. The bird claimed to have purpose around healing this man and another person living in the complex. What followed was an energetic shift attached to strong feelings.

In addition, the bird indicated that the reason they flock together and create such visual beauty in flight was for the conscious shifting of energy for the humans and the Earth. This reminded me of a moment when I was looking out over the river that flows through Austin at sunset and witnessed a flock of birds spiraling high into the air, followed by diving toward the water with incredible continuity and harmony. The cumulative effort formed an outline similar to the shape of a single candle flame.

That moment moved me to the depths of my soul with feelings of the beauty that surrounds us in nature while connecting me with the Highest Power of the Universe. Let's call upon the birds' winged partners that we call Angels for a whisper on birds.

If you study ancient text and Native American philosophy, every animal has a specific meaning and are referred to as totems. These teachings came from Spirit and those meanings were transferred energetically. The Renaissance painters saw Angels as highly illuminated balls of light that, when transferred to canvas, became a winged human form. Once again, this was an energetic transfer.

Birds have the ability to bridge the physical and the spirit world with incredible compassion as they are free from limiting beliefs and have eyesight that is aligned with both worlds. Did you think they were simply nervous creatures? Look deeply into the eyes of a bird and listen to their vocalization in order to receive their divinely orchestrated apocalypse.

The paths of the bird and of mankind are closely aligned, with the birds being slightly ahead of man in the evolution process, in the sense they have lifted off the ground in ascension known as flight. Birds have not always flown and there is still evidence of that. In this context, you learn a lot about life on Earth as a casual observer of nature and, in particular, birds. Freedom of flight is something you will experience in your soul journey, for some day you will soar with the eagles, dance with the clouds and sing your own individually defining song of the heart.

Note: When I was receiving the whisper, I clearly heard the word apocalypse, *which had a negative connotation to me. When I finished, I looked up that word and to my surprise found the definition to be "Lifting the veil"!*

I love getting requests for an angel whisper from my loyal readers, especially when it is my mother (tee hee). In the news lately, we have seen an increase in the stories and the harsh effects of bullying. Recently, we have seen where a victim of bullying took extreme measures when they took their own life. This raises an awareness of something that is becoming unacceptable to our society and can solicit a strong response of compassion, caring and the need for change.

The dictionary describes **bullying** as a form of abuse that is comprised of repeated acts over time involving a real or perceived imbalance of power, which may be social power and/or physical power. The victim of bullying is sometimes referred to as a target.

Besides individual attacks, there exists a form of group bullying, like the Westboro Baptist Church whose members hide behind the First Amendment to spread hate at the private funerals of our fallen heroes. This type of bullying brings pain and suffering to entire families! In addition, some countries bully other countries as a way to control or hold power over a large group of people in order to achieve some type of gain or authoritative control.

Now I am getting mad (lol), so I know it is time to set aside any preconceived notions and ask for a loving whisper from an angel to better understand the essence of bullying:

There are those who need to express an abuse of power and exertion-of-control energies on another human being or group. This need usually springs from low self-esteem and internal judgments that are tethered to lower energies. By allowing the energy you define as bullying, one becomes a partner in the energy of being a victim. Once the soul has agreed to allow the abuse to occur, power is given over and this fuels the personal authority of the abuser. The result can serve to bring a type of energetic balance for the abuser, but when this occurs, both souls are wounded.

What this tells you is that by taking action to defend yourself from suffering the abuse of a bully, you can save deep emotional scars from both parties. There is always a way to bring those with rational minds into any situation as a way of neutralizing the abuse, bringing awareness to a problem, and offering psychological support.

It can take a Warrior spirit to shoulder the abuse from a bully so that same passionate soul can stand up for themselves and avoid the wounding effects for all parties. Fear is real, but so is faith. Don't build an illusion around an outcome that holds you in fear, as that will anchor you within that energy until the experience completes the attraction that was created.

Bless the hearts for all involved with bullying. As you stand in truth for the mistreated and become the advocate for change, you will be holding a space for justice from a Higher Power to prevail within the situation.

If you are one of my friends on Facebook (if not, send me a friend request), then you may have seen the stories about my neighbor's cat whom we call Stubbie. Stubbie appeared at our doorstep one day during the time that my father was making his transition and insisted on coming in the house and getting in my lap.

We have never fed or watered Stubbie. Her motivation was a social one, with unusual habits that include the ability to open our screen door and walk right in. The folklore around the Stubbin Manx is that when the rains became heavy, Noah became impatient with the cat and closed the door to the Ark on their tail. This breed has no tail or nerve endings to indicate it ever had a tail, and apparently Stubbie does not like it when you go to close a door either (tee hee).

Some think the breed evolved from a bobcat, and Stubbie's 16 pounds of female furry flesh and large clawed feet are an intimidating reminder of the forces found in the wild. Her breed is known as the 'dog cat' and for good reason: Stubbie will follow you around, lie at your feet, growl at strangers and even bark a little (lol) as she truly lives up to the breed's reputation.

After a friend made the comment that Stubbie was a Zen Master with her all-knowing eyes and attitude, I started writing "The Continuing Adventures of Stubbie" on my Facebook, and now she gets more friends and attention than I do! She showed up and comforted me at an important time in my life, so I wrote a song for her called "One Conscious Stream," as a testament to her loving presence. Let's get a whisper from an angel on cat energy:

Cats have earned their place in the domestic animal kingdom because of their unique abilities and uncanny senses. They teach lessons around independence, self-sufficiency, sensuality and detached love, while simultaneously showing you how to land on your feet in a crisis.

Cats have an inner sense and completely trust their instincts in a sometimes extreme fashion in order to display nature living life to the fullest. Rarely do you see a cat with a broken spirit because they know how to deal with adversity, often choosing the people or environment they prefer to be around.

As you hold and pet a cat, you can feel the essence of a lion and the warmth and playfulness of a kitten at the same time. Fiercely independent, there is a determination and dedication to survival that comes with strength in bringing focus to the task at hand and combines that with the embodiment of the energy known as free will.

Cats can tune into energy and give you information if you are willing to receive. Watch a cat around someone's passing and you will know the meaning of these words. The steady purr of a cat is one language that everyone understands as a transmission of pure love!

As you bring this year to a close, remember the celebration for life that is an integral part of your successful journey. Even if you have lost a loved one recently, or this is an anniversary of your loss, celebrate the life that is eternal by giving gratitude for the opportunity to know, love and be connected to this special person in your life. Give them the gift of your acknowledgment and acceptance, for that kind of love is yours to share.

You have an ability to balance your energy and align every dimension of your being with the truth that flows through you. Complicated energy systems hold resistance until they become simplified through a gracious reception of the truth. Balanced energy supports your divine mission to find the happiness and abundance that is God's gift.

As the awareness of the human species increases in 2012, problems will not disappear. Yet the knowing achieved through heightened sensitivity will connect you to the Oneness that supports all of life. Even within the most subtle experience, such as feeling a gentle breeze, detecting an odor that holds memories, watching a child's eyes light up when they open your gift, or enjoying a simple moment of silence, a beautiful opportunity presents itself.

When you accept a gift of love, the rewards are met at a soul level as your experiences reflect the love you bestow upon yourself and others. Self-love is the language that whispers to the Universe a message that you are ready to surround yourself with loving friends, families and situations that mirror your commitment to love.

Within your heart, there is a willingness to let go of the things that hold you back from experiencing peace, joy and happiness. Your soul chose this incarnation, but nobody told your body what to expect from the physical experience of life and death. The pain you may have encountered with the learning lessons of life contains blessings that will help you achieve success in all areas of life. You have learned how to protect your heart to know that unconditional love opens your heart to life itself, and the only thing that will hold you back is fear. It takes courage to open the heart, and your strength comes from knowing that your fear is something you can overcome.

When you take time to celebrate, exchange gifts and express love, you create beauty and wellness in yourself and others. Celebration brings joy and peace as it eases suffering. One moment of shared love can create a lifetime of balance, with a focused intention to live life consciously, with purpose and reasons to celebrate.

Thanks to Shenal for the request to do a whisper on chaos that might explain how to find peace in a state of disorder. According to the web dictionary, chaos is *a state of extreme confusion and disorder. But it can also hold meaning around the formless and disordered state of matter, before the creation of the cosmos.* Then perhaps we evolved out of some kind of chaos?

In Greek mythology, Chaos refers to *the most ancient of gods; the personification of the infinity of space preceding creation of the universe.* So chaos is cosmic (tee hee)! When it comes to physics, chaos is a *dynamical system that is extremely sensitive to its initial conditions.* By that definition, it appears that humans embody chaos.

The definitions of chaos surprised me in many ways, but the possibility that a structure of creation can emerge from a system that seems chaotic sounds intriguing. We know that peace comes from within, but how do we bridge the emotional gap between centered calmness and the frenetic, stomach-churning chaos that can come with challenging relationships, events, earth energies and situations?

Let's calm the chaos for a moment, so that we may listen to the whispers of angels:

There are global energies that merge to create storms, but below the surface are unseen forces that are only sensed from beyond the body. Unlike the atmospheric pressures that are forecast, giving time to prepare for a coming storm, these global energies travel undetected by even the most sensitive people. These unseen energies are chaotic in nature.

In other words, the vibrations that are interpreted as chaotic are always present in some form and you get to choose how to align yourself with an evolving creation. Anchoring yourself in faith is one way to feel at ease with a cosmic structure of emerging growth. Preparedness for all aspects of life comes from prayer, meditation, intentional living and, of course, the energy of love.

One single stream of love can provide a bubble of peace that surrounds and nurtures the soul through any experience. Finding the energetic stream of love that awakens peace in a time of chaos brings awareness that aligns your vibrations with the highest potential. You become a co-creator, heightening a state of love in a chaotic moment, which in turn brings peace and joy to the forefront with a focus on the blessings that exist within each minute.

Fragmented energy that comes from chaos circles and returns in the form of enlightenment to create acceptance and understanding when energy is transmuted by love.

Clarity is something we all need. In today's fast-paced environment it is easy to get lost in the mental clutter that often accompanies such a lifestyle. When I think of clarity, I also think of truth. When the truth is hard to look at or accept, I find that some clarity is lost.

Clarity is the property of being clear or transparent. Clarity can refer to one's ability to clearly visualize an object or concept, as in thought, understanding, and the "mind's eye," as well as the traditional notion of visual perception with the eyes. Clarity may also refer more broadly to 'perspicacity' (intelligence manifested by being astute), the Zen concept of 'no mind,' or other terms denoting general clear and unperplexed cognition.

I see several clients that are searching for this conscious state to become prominent in their lives. I find that some days are better than others when it comes to being clear about who you are. I find it interesting that some of the time others are more clear than I am with their observations regarding who I am and what I stand for.

I personally love those times when things seem so clear and present. I also think there is a connection between clarity in the present and our relationship to the future. We don't know our future, but clarity in the present moment can bring some peace to the questions of the future. If you can look back at your past with the same clarity, your mistakes can become accepted and released, to bring clarity into the present.

The clarity I feel when I am engaged in a whisper seems to be even more profound, and this must speak to the value of clarity when directing energy to Source. It is clearly time for a whisper on the word *clarity*:

Clarity is connected to the Divine and therefore easily reached when you make this commitment your intention. The prominent people in the history of mankind had clarity with their purpose that surpassed the judgment of others.

In the absence of clear thinking, there is an energy that is missing as it relates to clarity. The journey for some is built around the search for this blissful yet powerful station in life. That path leads to the newborn child and beyond into the vastness of Nature.

Love, truth, harmony, balance, faith and several key goals are found through this one state of being. When your mind, body and spirit have found clarity, everything else falls into place. Everyone and everything is connected in ways that are entwined beyond imagination or science. This is true of your emotions as well.

The clarity of the spirit is achieved through the opening of the heart combined with acceptance of the mind. With the truth comes light, and with light comes the illumination of crystal clarity. With clarity, there is acceptance followed by Divine love.

Sol Luckman writes, *"The ancient Greeks were well aware of [torsion]energy, calling it "aether" and understanding that it is directly responsible for universal manifestation. In the 1950s Russian scientist Nikolai Kozyrev conclusively proved the existence of this life-giving subspace energy, demonstrating that, like time, it flows in a sacred geometric spiral resembling the involutions of a conch shell. In the face of overwhelming evidence of its existence, Western scientists are returning to the notion of aether, using such phrases as "zero point energy" and "vacuum potential" ... This breakthrough research in the temporal physics of subspace establishes that torsion energy permeates the entire multidimensional galaxy and not only is responsive to, but may actually be, consciousness creatively experiencing itself in time."*

I love it when science offers their take on energy and explains things from that perspective, as most definitions of co-creation that I found refer to business models. As co-creators, the angels need to hear, see and feel the vibrations that you establish through dreams, wishes and desires that can ultimately place you in the flow, or, as some say and science seems to agree, the vortex.

Let's discover a model of life we can resonate with as we co-create from the etheric plane, a whisper from an angel:

You are constantly evolving as humans, and co-creation is part of the answer to the deep mysteries of life. You must participate in the process of co-creation as an equal partner with spirit and the Universal energies that flow in and around you. We may help you create an illusion that leads you to an unexpected situation, but you must have faith that you will ultimately arrive at your desired outcome.

If your life isn't going the way you would prefer and you are feeling resentment, lack of faith, anger or frustration, you may be experiencing a contrast between empowerment and the victim mentality as it relates to you personally. This contrast can be teaching you lessons that enable you to know your place in the world.

We angels are here to assist in co-creating the highest vibrations of your Divine life purpose. The life you were born to live can offer resistance to accepting the cards that you have been dealt, yet facing responsibility for your life offers freedom in the form of movement within truth and love energy. The limiting factors that you face can be viewed as lessons co-created by you and your beliefs, as a way to resolve issues.

In the spiraling vortex of energy, there is a geometric language spoken by spirit that voices your deepest alignments. By connecting with this energy, your abilities to manifest are heightened, your love deepened, your purpose feels fulfilled and your light is spread throughout the galaxy. Validate your existence within your being by co-creating the joy, the love and the innocence founded by your soul as it chose to co-create the seed that now blooms in the unfolding experience of life in physical form.

Casa Angeles is the name that Beckie and I lovingly gave our second home in the mountains of New Mexico. Located at the southernmost tip of the Rockies, we can leave the Texas heat in the morning and be in the tall cool pines of the Lincoln National Forest by the afternoon. After a nap and a short trip into town to get some of the local flavor, we settle in to the comfort offered by our cabin home-away-from-home.

A typical day at the Casa might include the choice of several day trips to mystical places. You can experience everything from great hikes, expansive views, shops and galleries, fine food and drink, and of course, those marvelous hot springs that New Mexico is famous for. Or you can sit by the waters of Cedar Creek in the front yard of the Casa and read a book, watch the birds or even come face to face with a deer, elk or wild turkey. Last night we pumped up the air mattress on the upper deck and, with a heated blanket beneath the comforter keeping us toasty, we watched the most amazing nighttime heavenly display.

When I read the journal kept for those who visit the Casa, I realized the rewards of creating such a comfortable environment and then sharing that creation with others. The word 'comfort' appeared in almost every written expression, and with that comfort came prayers for Beckie's and my well-being, along with gratitude and goodwill toward others. That sounds like my whisper; let's see what the angels say.

In the middle of the most chaotic environment, comfort can be found and created. Part of the human journey includes some form of suffering, but the purpose is around learning and therefore the focus should be too. Within the space of comfort, life's learning is integrated and accepted without the need to know the details or even achieve total understanding. Simply stated, there is love in comfort.

Comfort brings a gentle nurturing and a softened edge to relationships, environments, health, social status and most aspects of defining one's self. If you are unwilling to give yourself comfort, that could signal the need for healing in the area of receiving. Being out of balance with an overt desire for comfort could indicate the need for healing in your space of giving.

Casa Angeles carries the intentions of bringing shelter, peace and comfort to all who grace the door. An intention that carries purpose, love, faith and high vibrational energy, when combined with effort created from the higher perspective, yields unimaginable rewards. It is in the nature of every human being to create comfort beyond the limits of perceived conditions.

The dreamscape of the human imagination is forged on the landscape of the spiritually grounded who are operating with some energy of hospitality and service. Define your comfort to greater enhance the steps you take to create the opportunities for healing the body, mind and spirit, yours and those around you.

One of the beauties of engaging in "Angel Whispers" can be found not in the insights and perspectives, but in the occasional glimpse of prophecy. Last January, Archangel Michael told us that we might find ourselves outside our comfort zones as we examined the relationship that love plays in the foundation of our lives. Looking back, this could have been grossly understated, Michael (tee hee)!

Like many of you, I found myself swimming in and out of my comfort zone over the last year. As a witness to the spiritual growth of the wonderful people that I am in contact with, I am better able to see the many visions of the future set forth by others coming true in the form of a mass rising of consciousness. My thoughts in this area have raised questions regarding my ability to grow within the warmth and complacency of my comfort zone.

Most of you know my classic segues into a whisper, and this brought a new epiphany for me today. In some ways, working on a channeled message from the angels took me out of my comfort zone and now, after two years of doing these Whispers, I find myself in a comfort zone as I write. This shows me a lot about love, spirituality and the benefits of stepping outside our comfort zone. Angels, please tell me more:

It is easy to find a place where complacency and comfort provide a safe harbor for your thoughts and emotions. Staying in this space for extended periods can remove you from the experiences that life offers, just as removal from the process of change can create stagnation of the energy around your soul; much like physical clutter slows the energy in your house and environment.

Some people have challenges in expressing who they are, and this can be their reaction to life in a society that can offer harsh judgments. If you believe that communicating who you are and how you feel is exposing yourself or your vulnerabilities, you have just defined an area of your comfort zone. In some ways, this is a form of repression that anchors you in a space to possibly form a barrier around your heart.

Expanding your comfort zone with a willingness to experience the different avenues presented in your soul journey can be rewarding beyond most analytical comprehension. The highest levels of the quality of life are often found by stepping beyond those limitations that you place on yourself.

View the world as your personal playground and let go of what others think in order to allow new experiences to flow to you. You can spot when your ego is creating your personal comfort zone when you feel the energy of control. By releasing limitations and raising your consciousness, you are joining forces with many in the stream of unconditional love, and creating an example unmatched in the history of mankind. There is a rightful inheritance here on Earth for you, and by accepting that everything is in Divine order you have just illuminated the path that will lead you to abundance through playful joy and boundless love.

After last week's whisper on indecision, I made a choice on this week's word and now it is time for a commitment (tee hee). Commitment is defined as the act of committing, or putting in charge, keeping, or trust; consignment; esp., the act of committing to prison. As you know I like quotes and this one by Margaret Mead is no exception: "Never doubt that a small group of thoughtful, committed citizens can change the world. Indeed, it is the only thing that ever has."

Commitment usually relies on focus, personal sacrifice and some aspect of taking charge in order to accomplish some task. Feeling guided into a commitment can make it easier for me to fully extend myself in any situation. This week I followed that guidance to find a high level of commitment in a process that seemed to take me off the path. At times it seemed irrational to spend my energy in a direction that, on the surface, appeared to remove me from my mission. Ultimately, though, the result was a feeling of being divinely blessed for having stood firm with my commitment.

There have been times when I had to back off a commitment and found it difficult to overturn my mindset, even though it was the smart thing to do. Some unusual sense of honor overcomes me during times like that and I am working through that (lol). I committed to writing these 'Angel Whispers' and, in some way, so did the angelic guides. Let's look for a nugget of information on the energy found in the word *commitment*:

The Universe will expand with every personal sacrifice that you make and to some, this can bring in fear of the unknown. It takes courage, patience and perseverance to accomplish goals in life, but the rewards of fulfilling commitments bring eternal satisfaction to the soul. This energy of success in the area of commitment rewards and supports self-love in a way that feels nurturing.

Before making your commitment, it is always wise to discern who or what is being served by your actions and to answer the question "Is there purpose?". Perception and ideas of what it means to make a commitment can lead to indecision, passive or negative behavior patterns, and missed opportunities. It is important to have clear focus on the commitments that are in alignment with your core truth, which will place you in the flow or vortex of energy that represents your highest vibrations.

When you follow guidance into a commitment, you have shown faith in a Higher Power. By assessing your personal commitment to life, you can set priorities that will ensure the highest quality found in the journey. Then by committing to those priorities, you will lessen the stress, anxiety and resistance that may stand between you and your joyful success. The commitment to love always fills the heart with warmth and leaves you feeling complete.

Many people are searching for fulfillment in life with a desire to find love in the areas of relationship, career, environment and community. When the economy is going strong, the tendency is to focus on the bank account and retirement through wealth-building. When the economy is weak, the focus shifts to matters of the heart and building community.

*In sociology, the concept of **community** has caused infinite debate, and sociologists are yet to reach agreement on a definition of the term. There were ninety-four discrete definitions of the term by the mid-1950s. Traditionally a "**community**" has been defined as a group of interacting people living in a common location. The word is often used to refer to a group that is organized around common values and social cohesion within a shared geographical location.*

Social cohesion and common values brought a few people together unexpectedly this morning while I was on my bike ride. I found a toddler wandering the streets of my neighborhood with a small dog at her side. Another motorist stopped when they saw the situation, and together we coaxed a reluctant and protective dog to show us his tag, from which we found an address that was down the street. It felt good to return the beautiful child to a very relieved mother who had just discovered the missing child and a door opened by the dog. Helping return that child helped me tap into community energy!

Paul Newman once said, *"I respect generosity in people, and I respect it in companies too. I don't look at it as philanthropy; I see it as an investment in the community."* It seems like we need community now more than ever in order to find family, support, comfort and the company of the caring individuals with whom we share our lives. Let's get a whisper from the community of angels:

Gathering and connecting with others is an important aspect of the human journey that brings teachings through shared experiences. Lessons of life can be observed and empathized with if you are willing to see through the eyes of another, which can offer growth opportunities by your helping others and forming relationships in a state of conscious living.

Capitalism has a brief history on the planet and has helped form illusions about the path of mankind. In truth, man has survived for centuries by building social economies through communities. The framework of communities has been altered by those that work to control the masses for the purpose of greed and power. Each purpose-filled life has the ability to bring change and create communities within new structures of thoughts and ideas. Many are pioneering new ways to leave old paradigms, and this is creating energy that is building community.

If you are feeling isolated or separated from your community, you might find it helpful to volunteer some time and effort to a worthy cause that is dear to your heart. Helping others in a community atmosphere can give you relief from your problems, help you feel supported by others and pay forward energy that the Universe will return many times over. Your community is this world and this Universe, which makes planet Earth your communal playground.

Good communication is something we all need, especially during a Mercury Retrograde! It could arguably be the most important aspect of our relationships and maybe even our lives whether it is work or pleasure.

Some years back, Beckie and I were on an airplane and the flight assistant noticed how we were holding hands, smiling and generally just being happy. She finally asked us how long we had been married and at the time, was about twenty years. When we told her, she said "I have to ask, what is your secret?" Beckie and I both gave our answer simultaneously like we are known to do. "Communication" I said while Beckie said "good sex". "Communication about good sex" I quickly followed.

The truth is we have always communicated to each other on all levels to the point that we have questioned ourselves about the possibility of running out of things to say. We are in our thirty first year and we still find things to talk about. We have had our share of challenges just like everyone else, but when you communicate in all areas, you are bound to speak from the heart on occasion (LOL). So for this important whisper, I went straight to the master and asked for some insight on this word...........communication.

It is always surprising to see how humans limit themselves in this important area of the earthbound experience. You have been given several tools to use to express yourself. From the face to face voice, to the phone, to the printed word in email and letters, communication can be very simple. But the voice sometimes has trouble conveying a message because of the way it is spoken or heard.

The voice of anger, fear or anything that elevates the true sound often goes unheard while the voice filled with love is always heard. The voice of your life partner hears all aspects of the spoken word and is delivered in a range of emotion because of the isolation that follows your busy lives. Sometimes the only person that you have to bounce things off of is that one close person. That's why it is important to have friends and counselors to confide in and talk to for a different perspective. This practice is as ancient as mankind and as simple as talking within your tribe.

You should learn to communicate in all the ways that were given to you to truly understand this gift. You can communicate with telepathy, ESP, music or even a single thought. A motion or gesture can speak volumes while an act of kindness can be wordlessly deliver a divine message.

When you look into the eyes of an animal, you can easily get a message. Oh he's hungry or wants to go outside. This can be applied to the people you want to communicate with. The left eye is the window into the soul and I invite you to look deeper into the eyes of your friends, neighbors and companions to see what message they communicate.

Prayer is a form of communication and emanates from the brain with information from the heart. This is a collaboration of body, mind and spirit for the single purpose of communicating a thought or desire to a higher power. So if you really want to communicate, step outside the proverbial box and see what happens! Your communication is only limited by you. Good communication can be as rewarding and fulfilling as good sex!

Complacency

This word keeps coming up in my time with others and appears to be, at times, a negative influence. We all have times that feel good with everything in some sort of order, and a period of complacency can feel like receiving the fruits of our effort. I can also look at complacency as time to integrate lessons of life, like a pause in our breathing.

Complacency *by definition means a feeling of quiet pleasure or security, often while unaware of some potential danger, defect, or the like; self-satisfaction or smug satisfaction with an existing situation, condition, etc.* I like this quote from Thomas Huxley where he states, "The rung of a ladder was never meant to rest upon, but only to hold a man's foot long enough to enable him to put the other somewhat higher."

All the definitions that I found for complacency speak of the danger that is possibly hidden within a person's complacency, which I found interesting because the angels sometimes relay this sense of danger. When I think of the potential dangers, I tend to think about our senses resting during times of complacency. I will now ask for a whisper from an angel without the energy of complacency to better understand this meaning:

Times of complacency can bring positive reflection on past, present and future activity, therefore positive energy can result. This can come in short bursts to positively affect your life as you integrate new ideas, life changes, spiritual growth and acceptance through taking pause.

Within those positive features, you reach a point where you have attained maximum potential. To carry complacency beyond that moment can be detrimental to your intentions, purpose and goals. When you decide to put off decisions and action steps due to your complacency, you have decided to stop conscious movement forward. A decision of putting off action with a 'wait and see' attitude is a choice or actionionable energy within itself and can be attached to ego.

People who are experiencing success rarely stop that momentum for any reason, so resting in the energy of complacency can be a sign of fear or resistance. You might think of complacency as energetic clutter that allows feeling and emotions to "stack up" like clients in a waiting room, eager to get your attention.

A momentary pause to feel the vibrations of your true direction is guide focus. Holding on to what you have is the energy of control. True acceptance of all aspects of life is love for God and Spirit. Love is the light to entice you to move beyond complacency, and you will leave old thought patterns, paradigms and repetitive behaviors.

What a juicy word to contemplate with so many twists and turns that can lead you right down the path of enlightenment. There are so many levels of consciousness of the body, mind and spirit, and many of us are trying to reach those higher planes in order to better understand our place in the world today.

Consciousness is a state that defies definition, but which may involve thoughts, sensations, perceptions, moods, emotions, dreams, and an awareness of self, although not necessarily all of these. Julian Jaynes has emphasized that "Consciousness is not the same as cognition and should be sharply distinguished from it. The most common error is to confuse consciousness with perception."

Ned Block divides consciousness into **phenomenal consciousness**, which is subjective experience itself (being something), and **access consciousness**, which refers to the availability of information to processing systems in the brain (being conscious of something).

And then there is the deep mystery of the energy that surrounds the sub-conscious mind and those things such as behavior and perception that appear outside of our consciousness. I find it interesting to think that the Higher Self can operate from the extremes of conscious behaviors to the outer edges of sublime realities. I will try to maneuver through a balance of these extremes while I wait for angels to whisper:

Consciousness is directly connected to the 'Clair' senses and when you are using Claircognizance, you are tapping into the knowledge and energy that surround your consciousness, even though they are distinctly different. Do not let ego or lack of trust block you from this Source.

There is a direct relationship between the consciousness of an individual and the levels of ascension that have been reached. The exalted emotions flow from the Higher Self with ease when connected to the thoughts of Higher Consciousness.

It is important to carefully discern in this area of your personal energy. The vibrations of truth will resonate with your consciousness and the denial of truth will not. Consciousness is part of the basis of your reality, so be careful with your mind. Be nurturing to your heart by believing in your ability to see the big picture. Allow the details of daily existence to flow through your essence with energy from your consciousness and simply trust in your intuition.

Your consciousness stays with you throughout your soul journey as you ascend to the next level. Your evolution as a human rests in your being, like a sleeping giant that is stirred by the passion of your consciousness. To awaken the giant, dive into the well of consciousness, passion, love, desire and truth.

How ironic is it that I am contemplating contemplation, which indicates there is a noun and a verb that stem from this word. I am currently at the southernmost tip of the Rocky Mountains, pondering the meaning of contemplation (lol). I have been accused of over-analyzing words, actions, situations, over-contemplating, you name it.

Blaming an aspect of your own personality for anything sounds like a victim mentality, but I am a Libra! Therefore, I am destined to see all sides, contemplate and then decide what my position is, before choosing what form my actions will take. You should hear Beckie and me contemplate where to go for a meal (tee hee).

I would say that contemplation is part of the process of discernment, yet not committed to an outcome. I am wondering if the physical world is the only place to experience this mental exercise and if so, should we value that aspect even more? With time as a constraint, we often rush through our contemplation lest we be called indecisive.

How much of a part does ego play with this process and how much is inner guidance or divine guidance? As I contemplate contemplation I am raising more questions than answers. I think I just proved all of the above. I need a whisper from an angel to help me contemplate the divine language of life:

Contemplation is the intellectual stimulus that allows for the formation or awareness of your vibrations. From thought to contemplation, followed by decision and ultimate action, the process used by human spirit to raise awareness, follow dreams, and to witness miracles starts with contemplation.

Think of contemplation as a way to take a moment to pause and reflect on information collected, the feelings experienced and the alignment with your essence. True growth and spiritual development evolve from contemplation, as a profound and moving understanding becomes an epiphany.

An artist contemplates the expansion of visual discoveries through the mind's eye, and then transfers that image of color and light onto canvas. The more clarity found in the process of contemplation, the more creative and truly representative are the results. This type of transmission is present in all aspects of life.

Contemplation, for these reasons and many more, can bring peace to the heart and soul through acceptance, stillness and a willingness to explore beyond the surface in order to see the truth in all situations. Contemplate without ego judgments to reach the highest vibrations of resonance with the Higher Self.

Contentment (Santosha)

In yoga, Santosha *translates to contentment, and we are encouraged to cultivate such an attitude. Diligent practice and active acceptance will remind you to simply be happy for what you have after a series of heart openings.* So in theory, the heart could be closed on some level if you are discontent or unhappy with certain areas of life.

Discontentment seems to be going around in some of my circles these days, and I am curious whether this is the gauntlet that leads to an open heart. Many are extremely discontent with their discontentment (tee hee)! I do believe we can have almost anything we want to manifest in life. So, what's the problem (grins)?

Let's join together in a heart opening that allows the reception of a whisper from an angel on contentment:

It is possible to reach a certain level of contentment with the creation of heart openings. A closed heart does not allow happiness into your energy, and so the vibrations might be escaping you in some level. You would be guided to go beyond the symptoms of discontentment in order to reach the cause.

Maybe you are seeking validation from the outside world, and those external energies are not fully supporting your contentment. The relationship that you have with yourself and God, or the Highest Power, IS the most important relationship. Whatever it takes to shift away from the symptoms and get to the cause is essential for you.

It is a part of your Holy mission to be happy and content with your life, which requires validation from within. That stream of love available to you cannot enter to offer resolution without your free will agreeing to a willingness to open the heart. Heart closings are relatively easy to produce in the constant contrasts that are offered. So it does take determination, willingness and a process that facilitates your intentions around achieving peace and happiness.

Most have experienced deep levels of pain at some point in their life, which places you at risk of closing the heart to avoid future pain. But wellness can be created within a healthy boundary. Closing the heart brings discontent and establishes patterns of behavior anchored in the lower energies, which then repeats until your awareness gets back to the root of the issue.

You can start by taking small steps with upward movement toward happiness, but remember, your happiness will never be dependent on anyone but yourself. So allow your actions to reflect Santosha by acknowledging the many blessings on Earth that bring happiness. Then you have created a foundation of peace on which you can stand with an open heart.

On October 31st, celebrations were happening around the world in anticipation of our greeting baby number 7 billion's arrival into the world! Those celebrations were somewhat tempered by the awareness that the planet is struggling to support the human species. What a contrast!

The Koch brothers (American oil tycoons) funded a study designed to gather opposing information that would discount the theories on global warming, in an effort to weaken the EPA and clear the way for fewer regulations and more profits for the oil industry. The study has backfired, in that it supports what some scientists have been saying for years: The planet is warming at an alarming rate.

Contrast can be defined in many ways, which makes it a fun word to study. One simple definition might be: ***Contrast** is the difference that makes an object distinguishable from other objects. The state of being strikingly different from something else, typically something in juxtaposition.*

I believe that life offers a contrast in order for us to understand opposing views. Within each 'whisper', there is often a contrast offered that drives the point home. Let's see what can be gleaned from an angelic whisper on the subject of contrast:

A contrast offers the opportunity to fully know someone or something. Human nature is to focus on the defect, the mistake, or what energy is opposing. Part of the shift that is occurring right now is helping people break free of that pattern in order to spotlight what is right in the world today, such as the beauty, joy, love and any energy that moves in an uninterrupted flow.

Unlike a child that makes demands upon their desires, your future demands will come in the form of requests generated at the soul level. Contrasts will bring clarity, commitment and truth through a process of removing the things that are cluttering your energy. Personal responsibility and spirit-driven integrity will provide the foundation that will support the greatest change the planet has ever witnessed!

The age of technology will bring transparency and truth to those who seek it, and contrast to those who don't. There will be few opportunities to hide from the mirror that reflects truth and light into the life you were born to live. Resistance is becoming more of a conscious choice, which signals the erosion of old paradigms and the emergence of a new order of life on Earth.

This shift will not be without challenges, for it will be the collection of individuals standing up in a light of peace-filled integrity that will bring the greatest change and the greatest chance to bring forward the evolving energy of love.

It seems like we have less and less control over our lives these days. With the recent financial collapse, even those who were responsible with their money are now facing effects that are outside of any personal control.

Control *is used in a variety of contexts to express "mastery" or "proficiency." E.g., "Music students attending a master class are expected to have full control of basic skills such as rhythm and pitch." More generally it implies an ability to purposefully direct (including suppression of) change.*

That's an interesting definition since I was not relating control to mastery, but of course they are related. I am having my own epiphany as I am writing! That's a good sign to my wonderful readers. The direction of or suppression of change is good food for thought, too. It feels like when people act controlling, they are really resisting change, and maybe I should address that in a whisper of judgment (tee hee).

I struggle with control in the areas of finding balance. In other words, part of that balance is knowing when and how I should exert control, along with discernment of whether that serves me or anyone else. In the past when I have given up control, others have viewed that as a lack of interest or passion. Maybe it's because I have uncontrollable passion (LOL). I will passionately and without control sit quietly to listen for the frequency that is the whispers of angels:

There is an order in the Universe that connects you to Divine energy at its highest vibration. Everything works in optimal order when reaching complete balance of the systematic order. This is found at the essence of energy and all living matter. When you master multiple areas of your life, you have harnessed the energy of control.

The Angels want you to know that control is a very important energy in the world around you. The more you try to control things that are outside of your responsibilities, the less room there is for angels to help you. It is only when you surrender and release control that the Spirit, God and the Angels can help bring balance to the natural order of the Universe with grace and love.

The gift of free will allows for every living being to make choices in the creation of life and lifestyles. Imposing control over another is like playing a game of tug-of-war. Once you have the rope it is hard to let go without falling. If you turned loose of all your ropes, who around you would be left standing? Those are the ones that love, honor and respect you for who you are.

Unconditional love is the highest form of loving energy, and to master this you must learn love from a detached heart. The types of control that serve are those detached from the heart and connected to the soul where purpose is found. Without attachment to an outcome, the energy of control transmutes to love, passion and cords of light.

Allow the breath of God to fill your sails and carry you across the water with Spirit, while you keep one hand on the rudder.

This word was suggested by Jenny, my copy editor and partner in the *Angel Whispers*. We have fun bouncing these back and forth. At first, I couldn't quite wrap my head around what she was talking about. That didn't last long.

One of my intentions for the New Year was to get back to my writing. So I decided to get organized with my computer, clear some things out and get started! I was cleaning my 'draft' folder and instead of Delete, I accidentally hit Send on an email entitled 'A Mother's Prayer,' which many of you may have received. I was then unable to send a follow-up 'oops report' due to a strange glitch in my server.

The result was a flurry of unexpected emails from a variety of people, some of whom I had not communicated with in some time. A few days after that email went out, I received one from an old dear friend. She expressed a desire for an angel reading. As soon as I received her email, I fired one back saying that I had a brief window of time right then.

She came over shortly and I directed her to park in my driveway behind my vehicle at the end of the driveway (something I never do). After an incredibly beautiful crystal bed session, she talked about her experience. I soon found that I had to leave to go to my doctor's appointment and told her we would have to finish the session by phone.

The angel guides apparently were not down with that. As she tried to leave, her vehicle would not start. There had been no sign of any trouble prior to this. I had no jumper cables and was forced to call my doctor and change my appointment to an hour later.

It all seemed like Divine timing and orchestration that started with a perceived mistake. The end result is here I am writing about it, which brings me back to my original intent for last Friday. I was taken off my path with a cross-purpose that became an integral part of my intention. Let's see if we can find out more on this word with a whisper:

You are asking about inner guidance, spiritual communication and the willingness to be open at critical times. This is a good example of the flow of life. Had you fought the stream of consciousness, your outcome would have been quite different.

When you awaken to your life purpose, the cross-purpose will repeatedly appear. It can be a test of your faith, intuition, resolve, clarity and even love. Will you stop and see which path is illuminated more than the other?

When walking in nature, the trail can split and you must make a choice. If you notice closely, you don't think much about it. You feel it and off you go! You will also notice that the path eventually leads to the same place, the higher self.

This also speaks to the mysteries of life and how you deal with that aspect of your being. Fall in love with the journey, and the path becomes glorious and without resistance. You can do this with the knowing that Divine Source will be with you on every pathway.

Crystals are fascinating in their uniqueness, and I didn't always appreciate these gems like I do today. The vibration that is given off by a crystal is an exact match with that of the human body, 456 kHz, which is also the same rate of vibration of water. This measurement tells science that crystals are moving atoms forming an animate object.

Defined as *a homogenous solid formed by a repeating, three-dimensional pattern of atoms, ions, or molecules and having fixed distances between constituent parts*, crystals might be hard to understand as multi-dimensional beings like me (tee hee).

Crystals are also transducers of information and are the key ingredient to most communication devices. This gives the crystal an ability to transmit information from thought-form vibrations directly into the human body at a molecular level. Healing intentions are communicated with the healing energy of these natural wonders.

If you have ever listened to a radio and dialed in a frequency to hear your favorite station, you have just used liquid crystals to help find your way. I am sure there is a wealth of untouched information that has generated my interest in this week's word from an angel that I call the angel whisper:

Crystals are the timekeepers of the Universe as they store the events that are mapped by the stars. These beings occupy the realm of the elemental kingdom, so the view of history is from nature's perspective. This perspective programs the crystal to assist the immediate area with information and vibrations that bring truth and unity to the inner and outer workings of the planet.

From the Middle Earth, crystals surface with a vibration that connects with mankind as a traveler in time and space. From the Ages come knowledge that is lost to all except those who occupy the domain of raw elements. The crystal is the anthropologist from another world, digging into the knowledge of history, telling the story of man, speaking in a language felt by the stars and faraway galaxies, holding a space for truth and spiritual light to move within a dimension known as time.

With time comes healing and with awareness comes enlightenment. This knowledge stored in crystals provides a platform for healing the body, mind and spirit. That healing power programs the environment with the information needed to facilitate change through natural and loving energies. Crystals will not participate in furthering an effort that stands in the complete absence of love, sending a clear message of integrity to the Universe.

Clear quartz crystal silicon is the material that is generally used to manufacture a crystal singing bowl. This material is one of the few on earth known to vibrate at the same rate as the human body. This natural affinity with the body, combined with the fact that crystals can transfer information, come together in unique fashion.

It is believed that the sound of the crystal bowls carries the note for each chakra (or energy center) along with the ability to transfer light into the human body through the wavelength of sound. When this occurs, the body can release blocks through vibrations that open pathways for energy and light to travel at optimum levels.

*At the present time the Hopi American Indian prophecy is being fulfilled with the "Coming of the Rainbow People," through the keepers of the **crystal bowls**. This ancient wisdom has emerged to heal and uplift the consciousness of the universe through a **crystal sound**. Edgar Cayce predicted, "Crystal Sounds will be used for healing before the end of this century," while Nostradamus foretold the healing of cancer through pure tone by 1998.*

Many ancient cultures recognized music, sound and tones as having healing powers, so for centuries, sacred ceremonies have included the use of drums, chanting and various methods to produce tones for the specific purpose of bringing balance to the inner self. Let's listen for a sound made by a whisper on crystal singing bowls:

The thread that connects life can be found in the frequencies and pathways of sound. The ancient civilizations had great knowledge with respect to sound, and this knowledge is returning as part of the awakening spirit of change. If you want to hear the sounds of life, you must create the environment that best suits that intention.

To hear as your ancestors did, crystal singing bowls can play a big role in the modern world. The restoration of sound harmony in the body creates the strongest physical connection with spirit through energy movement and a doubtless knowing.

If you could hear the sound of the Sun, you would shine so bright in the child essence. If you could hear the sound of the moon, your passionate energy of love would travel like a beam of light connecting the Father Sky to your soul in an instant of profound awareness. If you could hear the sound of the Mother Earth, it would sound like the breath of God conducting the symphony with your heartbeat.

Vibrate in rhythm with your being to find your true sound essence as you allow the crystal singing bowls to surround you in connective energy with the sacred tones of your life. Find peace and balance with the sound of anger evaporating in the vibration of love, the resonance of heartache replaced by the movement of joy, and by filling the void of disappointment and loss with the voices of the heavenly choir. Choose to live in the vibration where sound meets your heart and time is eternal.

It seemed a little odd when the angels whispered an exercise that would be good for me while on sabbatical at the foot of the sacred White Mountains. *"Walk as if you were holding a cup of energy so that you don't spill a drop"* was the mental body exercise given to me as I made my way up the stairs leading to the upper deck with my full cup of coffee.

That afternoon, as Beckie and I played disc golf at Grindstone Canyon, I traversed the mountain landscape with grace and with ease. Using the image of holding a cup of energy, I moved in a way that seemed to connect with the Earth. With each climb, I used less and less energy with the method created by the simple exercise.

A simple whisper transformed me for that day as I felt connected in ways I had never experienced. In the moments when I forgot the exercise and walked normally, I often stumbled or moved in a way that now felt clumsy, out of step and without regard to the environment. This ultimately reminded me why I share the angel whisper with my whisperees (as one reader puts it). In gratitude, I ask for a whisper on the cup of energy.

The whisper on the cup of energy came at a time of focus when you could easily listen and understand. By acting on the guidance, you were available to one of the lessons that nature provides to those who are willing to get in touch with energy. The connection you felt was the one that exists between the subtle layers of sensory perceptions and hidden realms of the Earth, which is energy triangulated by God or the Highest Power.

By being open, aware, receptive, and willing to take small action steps, the guidance manifested into an experience that you might not have ever been in touch with by other means. This truly demonstrates the purpose and position that angels and archangels have in the lives of people. It is a partnership in a co-creation process that feeds and nurtures endless possibilities with illumination on the times.

Energy travels with focused movement and will do so throughout your lifetime. You get to choose where your focus and your energy are directed. When you find methods that quiet the mind-chatter and allow the senses to touch life, you are purging the mental body of cluttered energy. Your focused intentions allow you to take responsibility for the things that you control, like your happiness and well-being. The result is freedom to feel the vibrations of love, peace and joy.

Over the past few months, I have had a closer relationship with this subject than I would have chosen. I know there are many profound lessons for me in my recent discoveries as I have felt a shift in my own consciousness. The truth is that the sooner we gain a healthy perspective on this aspect of our being, the sooner we can evolve into our true purpose on Earth.

The loss of a loved one can be the most profound, personal, and private experience that we will ever face. No matter how intellectual or spiritual we are, no matter what each of our beliefs supports, no matter how strong we think we are, the death of a family member, friend or acquaintance can alter our lives forever. In this moment of reflection, I will ask the angels for a whisper:

Death is not the opposite of life any more than completing college is the opposite of learning. The euphoric discharge of energy of crossing over creates the opening for the essence to leave the physical world. This represents the end of a cycle of life and marks the beginning of ascension into the light of love and the open arms of the Divine.

Part of the mystery of the physical world is the overlapping of planes. Most people are fearful to mix these realms and therefore they stay separated by belief systems. In reality, your deceased loved ones are more present and available than ever before. There is a freedom of the soul that allows for a merging of consciousness within the physical plane. The only way to access this is through understanding, removal of fears, prayers, intention and, above all else, love.

The social structure builds boundaries that create the paradigms in which you live. If you have no vision of the possibilities that exist for you, the paradigm remains. You could compare this to the phenomenon of apparitions of deceased loved ones people have reported. These experiences help expand the mind of the few so that others may learn. Many claim that there is no God because they have never witnessed anything that makes it real for them. In truth, they have closed their minds and hearts to the possibilities. Death challenges your belief system to build faith on what you cannot see.

If you have ever witnessed the wonders that surround your life on the physical plane, there is little to deny you the Divine experience. This Divine moment cannot be placed in a box, yet even today's science points toward the Divine Matrix that connects all living matter. This connection is whatever you want it to be! Universal laws are in place for this reason alone. The conscious decisions regarding life and death are yours. Eternity is now and if you are focused on the inevitability of death, think of the inevitability of life!

You have heard the saying 'Live every day like it is your last,' and it usually refers to death. This tells you something very important about the process of death and the common views that are shared. If you could allow the basic premise of this statement to alter your psyche without the threat of death, your heart would grow wings, your breath would move mountains and your purpose would inspire everyone you meet.

Dedication is defined in some circles as the act of setting apart or consecrating to a divine Being, or to a sacred use, often with religious solemnities; solemn appropriation or the act of binding yourself (intellectually or emotionally) to a course of action.

In the exploration of certain commitments of mine and looking at the different levels, I started to examine my dedication under the microscope. A careful discernment of my dedication to the people and things involved can be affirming in regards to how I feel about my action steps. Personally, I might have a tendency to have such a narrow focus on my dedications that it would be easy to miss something coming up behind me (tee hee).

And then there are priorities. When does the commitment to one thing take precedence over another? It can be amusing at times to see where others dedicate their energy, like those who might listen for a whisper from an angel (tee hee). It must be time to dedicate some energy to a divine perspective on the meaning of dedication:

Unlike commitments, dedications are usually evoked from the heart with a range and depth of feelings and emotions. Your dedications connect to the emotional body in a way that distributes your passionate feelings to every energetic cell in the body. Any thing that takes you out of balance can disrupt those energies and bring questions to your dedications in life. The example would be an event that compromises your faith with a response that shifts your desire to worship.

There is also a connection between your dedications, your belief system and your spiritual purpose. Feeling free to release loving energy in the direction of your heart's desires gives your dedicated activities purpose, which rewards your efforts in meaningful ways. Dedicating yourself to unconditional love and letting go of anything that doesn't resonate as truth will direct your focus to the important features that surround your existence. You are then fully awakened to the life you were born to live, which speaks to the importance that dedication plays in your spiritual life.

For the greatest vibrational response, you can ask yourself one question: "Does my dedication to those efforts bring me closer to my divine life purpose?" Asking the question connects you with a higher power and opens you to receiving an answer. No matter how you receive, your willingness to ask the question will eventually lead you to the direction and guidance that you seek.

In your dedication, the God self intones to the Universe.

PS. I had to look it up after the angels whispered the word "intones" in that last sentence. I think they meant "speaks in musical or prolonged notes"(lol).

Human nature can provide the most entertaining and exciting theater of all. Just when you think that normality is going to prevail, some crazy human does something completely unexpected and out of the box. But even the most enlightened person can fall back into an old paradigm or behavior pattern. That is what I am referring to as the default position (tee hee)!

As in the theater, every actor and prop has a 'mark', a physical location where they must be at any given time. From an investment standpoint, defaulting on a futures contract occurs when one party does not fulfill the obligations set forth by the agreement. From this definition, there could be emotions around not fulfilling some part of our soul contract, or our personal futures, that dims the light within, causing us to shrink into apathy or a type of default.

In any case, I for one do not want to default on my obligations or contracts, especially those at a soul level. I must hold a space that allows me to see the truth, act on my responsibilities, pay my debt and create movement with dialog from a space of love. Now I need an angel to whisper soothing energy that will help empower me away from my default position:

Remember the whisper that communicated 'the path of least resistance often leads to nowhere'? Your journey is filled with opportunities to escape your responsibilities and then use your rational minds to find ways to validate your choices. The default position may provide a comfort zone that is quite possibly void of vital components of your reality. Therefore, it is an important exercise to take inventory of your life from time to time in order to qualify your position in the light of truth and give you a platform that supports your true position.

How will you single-handedly save the world if your house is not in order? It's not that you have to wait for the perfect moment to make your intentions clear, but to serve, your foundation must be solid and one that starts and ends with your integrity. You can distract yourself from the fully illuminated path by giving to an imbalance as a way to resolve and support all your actions. But the world will not change as a whole unless the individual spiritual principles are clearly defined and upheld.

If you want to serve the world and rise from your default position, you must pay the personal debts that are holding your energy static. In your upward movement of energy that is facilitated by the freedom felt at the soul level when you awaken to the responsibilities of life, you lift others into a collective consciousness defined by your actions and willingness to operate from the truth.

If it sounds simple, that's because it is. The inner child knows nothing but the illuminated truth that connects every living being on Earth.

Thanks, Alisha, for the request to engage in a whisper on a phenomenon that emerges from the human psyche. I am sure that almost everyone has had some history with that feeling known as déjà vu. The Princeton site called wordnetweb describes paramnesia as a disorder of memory in which dreams or fantasies are confused with reality. Déjà vu, sometimes referred to as paramnesia, is defined as the experience of thinking that a new situation has occurred before.

No matter how déjà vu is described by others, it does feel more like an experience than a disorder to me. My disorder (grins) hits like a wave that seems to transcend time as life goes into slow motion. A type of energy shift occurs and I tend to stop, to pause for a moment, with what some might describe as psychic shock.

However you define it, a moment of déjà vu seems profound and meaningful. I tend to receive those moments with warmth and openness, like I am connecting with an old friend. That old friend is probably 'Deep-Down Russell' (many tee hees). I am starting to crack myself up, so it must be a sign to turn it playfully over to the angels for a whisper on déjà vu.

The moments of a déjà vu experience are a type of vibration in constant movement around your body and the energy field that surrounds your physical being. These vibrations hold information, knowledge and wisdom within a luminous structure. When you align yourself with these vibrations, it is as if you are tuning in to a radio frequency.

Those vibrations could be described as 'tubes of light', each one holding a distinct pattern filled with information contained in the light of truth. Discernment is the key to interpreting the information that is being passed in a moment of connected energy. Akashic records are encoded in these energetic strands of light, making it possible for those in the physical plane of existence to have a sensory experience. This could include an experience of standing in the footprint of the past, present and future.

The déjà vu experience allows a person to tap into the Source energy that connects the Universe with the Cosmic Heart of the soul. The natural bridge that spans between the physical and spiritual worlds is created when the soul travels across the astral plane to incarnate into physical form, like a spelunker carrying a rope down into that mysterious cave. The 'umbilical cord' provides spiritual sustenance as it carries forth the vibrations from the heavens.

The birth process evolves from a mystery into a magical reality, full of endless possibilities and creations. Déjà vu is a simple reminder of the mystery that connects the soul with the energy of love through an all-knowing, self-loving, mystical, magical experience.

The Cosmic energy that surrounds us for the next few months as we close out 2010 is asking everyone to answer the question: "Do we deserve _____?" Whatever you are working to manifest goes in the blank. The intention is that in order to move forward in the direction of my dreams, I must answer this question to see where the resistance may be hiding.

Deserve is defined as *worthy of being treated in a particular way.* As I try to define myself, it is hard to know the depths of my perspective on deservedness. Surely, my self-esteem helps to support my deservedness or lack thereof.

As the stars align through this holiday season, I am working on alignment within myself. In order to create the life that deserves my full attention, any underlying energy that could block my manifestations has got to go (lol)! Without thoughts of worthiness, I will listen for the wind to carry a whisper from an angel on deservedness.

The life experience offers many opportunities for growth at all levels. You are a multi-dimensional being that has several energetic bodies which form layer after layer, like a fine furniture finish with depth, color and a unique vibration. You are constantly tuning each layer, like dialing in your favorite radio to see what's playing, in order to tune your body into the frequency that holds a balanced resonance.

Within these layers, there are areas that hold interference which slow down the movement of energies. Inside the area of the senses that deals with energies around deservedness, you will usually find guilt and other repressed emotions. Your willingness to release anything that doesn't serve you is part of the path that resolves issues to deservedness, as you may be carrying weight that does not belong to you.

In the quest for an awakened life, you are guided to release judgments about yourself and others to a Higher Power, removing any framework that holds you to a limiting belief. Be willing to view the world from an elevated perspective which will invite love to stream through your heart and soul as you detach from lower energies.

Issues of entitlement may cloud the answer you seek around deservedness, so these questions are best answered in front of the mirror that reflects the energy of forgiveness and enlightenment.

"You will always, almost always, most of you, choose negative emotion over no emotion because emotion indicates desire. It's exciting!" That is a quote from the Abraham-Hicks' daily word and I am including it as a follow-up to last week's whisper on 'Negative Thinking.' This represents a different way of looking at things to me. Maybe all that negativity is a cover-up for our true desires.

In *Passions of the Soul*, Descartes writes of the passion of desire as an agitation of the soul that projects desire for what it represents as agreeable, into the future. Desire is also the preservation of objects already present, as well as the desire that certain effects not appear, that what affects one adversely be curtailed and prevented in the future. Moral and temporal values attach to desire in that objects which enhance one's future are considered more desirable than those that do not, and it introduces the possibility, or even necessity, of postponing desire in anticipation of some future event.

In Aristotle's *De Anima*, he acknowledges that desire cannot account for all purposive movement toward a goal. He brackets the problem by positing that perhaps reason, in conjunction with desire and by way of the imagination, makes it possible for one to apprehend an object of desire, to see it as desirable. In this way reason and desire work together to determine what is a 'good' object of desire.

This resonates with desire in the chariots of Plato's *Phaedrus*, in which the soul is guided by two horses, a dark horse of passion and a white horse of reason. This does not suggest the dark horse be done away with, since its passions make possible a movement toward the objects of desire. But he qualifies desire and places it in a relation to reason so that the object of desire can be discerned correctly, so that we may have the right desire. I now have a desire for a whisper:

The struggles of mankind are marked with desires. In the evolution of the human being, you have reached a point where the future is determined in the mind with feelings from the center or the heart.

You can easily have desires that lend themselves to a negative outcome and that illuminates the need to rationalize with moral judgments. Your desires can also resonate as the best path to your future needs, regardless of how you label them.

Desire is energy just like passion, free will, anger, love and a host of others that can override a single goal. When you put into perspective your heart's true desires, you are shining a light on your soul journey that can enable you to reach for your dreams.

If you translate your desires as being the same as your needs, you can easily lose clarity about your life in general. When you address your specific needs without ego judgments, you have just selflessly made the world a better place filled with desires.

Have you ever wondered why gifted psychics and intuitive people may struggle when it comes to gaining information around their personal lives? It seems like a gifted intuitive could easily tune in and receive the winning lottery numbers or anything that would support their idea of abundance.

A strong feeling of wanting to have something or wishing for something to happen could describe the word 'desires' as a noun. My experience tells me that intuition is a type of interpretation that lives within a vibration. The vibration can easily be affected by desires, whether they are mild or obsessive. So when I am tuning in to the needs of another, I am doing my best to remain totally neutral.

Staying detached from outcomes, desires, and ego-based thinking is a lot easier to accomplish when in service to others. The challenges for me to read myself have been a learning with lots of opportunity for growth and understanding. And then there are times when I receive beautiful guidance, only to choose another path. Is that when desires override every other voice inside my being? It's time to neutralize my thoughts in order to receive a whisper from an angel on desires:

The vibrations of desires run deep as they weave the fabric that connects the conscious mind to the sub-conscious mind. Each thread influenced by the color, shape and sound of the one that opposes and supports, divides and unites, holds together and stands alone. The expression of passion creates the tapestry of energy that is laced with desire, love, ego, surrender and free will.

It's natural for you to hold desires, but like other elements of life, the need to balance the energy of desire will expose itself to you. The angels want to hear your desires and wishes, as well as your dreams and visions. Yet if those are anchored in the lower energies, the response from your prayers could evoke a challenge to experience lessons that bring personal growth.

Expansion of energy while walking in human form is best accomplished when desires are met with the peace that comes from a life with some focus on faith. Out of faith the best relationships are formed, especially the one with yourself. Remaining open to all aspects of life allows light to enter and illuminate the unending truth from which you find alignment.

If you can temper your desires with the proper perspective and attitudes, balance and peace will come to assist the manifestation process. Anchor your desires in the sea of love that surrounds every living creature. Your choice to incarnate was truly based in a desire to merge with the Divine love, and that energy was so strong that you agreed to the path with the most resistance and the greatest reward. Congratulations on your journey so far!

Is there a roadmap to our lives that each one must follow? The answer to the burning questions around destiny may never be fully explained, but some insight might be helpful (grinning). According to the Wikipedia, **destiny** *refers to a predetermined course of events. It may be conceived as a predetermined future, whether in general or of an individual. It is a concept based on the belief that there is a fixed natural order to the cosmos. .*

Is the natural order to the cosmos fixed? I like the part at the end of the movie when Forrest Gump stood beneath the ancient tree where his beloved Jenny lay at rest and tried to answer the question of destiny when he said, "Jenny, I don't know if Momma was right or if, if it's Lieutenant Dan. I don't know if we each have a destiny, or if we're all just floating around accidental-like on a breeze, but I, I think maybe it's both. Maybe both is happening at the same time."

I love that simple explanation! I believe that we each have a destiny, and our free will, or the free will of another, is the 'wild card' in the game of life. One person plays that wild card and the direction of the entire game changes. Let's see what destiny will hold in the form of an angel who whispers:

A person's destiny is a creation that takes form over lifetimes, years or in a split-second, and carries a potential to shift and change in order to meet energy demands. In those instances, a part of you is choosing a path, or direction, anchored in a focused analyzation, an emotional plea, a sub-conscious desire or a moment of spontaneous reaction.

The chosen path, or destiny, emerges from a partnership forged between the inner-self and the Universal Divine matrix that is the structure which moves the energy of love. The higher-self co-creates a projection into the future that facilitates the upward movement of energy. Even when that energy spirals downward, the destined moment can be created to bring balance between positive growth and the need for learning.

A natural state of being can include withdrawal from a destined path, or acceleration into the far reaches of potential directions, as free will becomes the largest component of controlling energies within the human body. The more you place effort toward illuminating the truth and infusing love into all situations, the more peace comes to the destiny creation process.

Change is inevitable in the movie of your life, so be ready to ad-lib part of the script. That will allow you the freedom to position yourself and receive the greatest rewards that come from facing each chapter in the highest vibration. Destined moments spring forward from the foundation of your faith, your wisdom, your connection to Source, and your thirst for the mysteries of life on planet Earth.

Just think what kind of world it would be if everyone took responsibility for their actions! All my guidance around spiritual growth points toward the need to take care of our dharma (responsibilities) in order to experience the highest level of enlightenment.

The term **dharma** *is an Indian spiritual term that means one's righteous duty, or any virtuous path. The word* dharma *translates as that which upholds or supports, and is generally translated into English as 'law'. According to the various Indian beliefs, beings that live in accordance with dharma proceed more quickly toward Nirvana or personal liberation. The antonym of dharma is* adharma, *meaning unnatural or immoral.*

I think it is interesting that while some take on more than their share of responsibility, others avoid it like the plague and can even take this avoidance to extreme levels. I sometime witness those on a spiritual path giving over all powers to the concepts of angels and God, which is fine unless that includes giving over their dharma. Some movies that teach Quantum Physics leave out pieces of information that can lead you into a practice of "just think it and it will be so." To me this teaching lacks information and therefore integrity, which can lead some down the wrong path. Let's see what the angels say about holding our responsibilities and the deeper meaning of dharma:

You might think of dharma as a sensibility instead of a responsibility. Personal freedoms and spiritual liberation emerge from a strong focus on the truth and the responsibility found within such truth. There is a partnership that exists between the spiritual body and the physical body. In order to find a healthy balance between the two, it is essential for all energies to participate in steps leading to your desired outcome.

Your mind, body and spirit often experience comfort and self-love in the effort to uphold your dharma, while disharmony can result in the denial of one's true responsibility. The Universe provides a platform that will support you in all aspects of dharma, yet the true recognition of dharma can be without conscious form. Therefore, it is your intention that connects inner knowing with your action steps in relationship to your dharma.

Asking about dharma raises questions around the complex meanings given to this word over the centuries. It is often left up to an individual's belief system to make an assessment of responsibility in response to even the smallest decisions. This means that dharma shifts and conforms to knowledge and awareness. When one builds faith, one builds dharma in the same way that nature builds life.

Everyone must walk on a path that views the world through a lens that brings focus on dharma, so make no mistake about it. This is an elevated view that aligns with the Christ Consciousness, where there is no illusion of right or wrong. From this perspective, truth brings illumination to the Big Picture as your energy dances around the bright light of passion, like flames moving in harmony around a heart-shaped fire.

As you think about direction, have you ever felt like you were standing at a precipice? You don't want to go backwards since you have already been there, and moving forward is full of fears around the unknown. Finding direction in life can be challenging, especially given all the decisions and perceptions that we face.

Unlike our ancestors experienced, today's world offers more choices in every aspect of life, offering an invocation to simply decide what we want to do with our life. ***Direction** can mean the act of directing, of aiming, regulating, guiding or ordering. Guidance, management, superintendence, and administration such as the direction of public affairs or of a bank* brings full circle the literal translation of direction and the influence of leadership.

Aviator and author Antoine de Saint-Exupéry once said, "Life has taught us that love does not consist in gazing at each other, but in looking outward together in the same direction." Like a river that flows with constant energy, the direction of our energy can move in a similar fashion as we maneuver the path in search of the elusive choices of minimum resistance.

Sometimes we need help with direction, and it is in those times we can turn to our "Scouts" or "Guides" to get a bearing on just where the heck we are (tee hee)! That guidance can come from within, or we can look to external sources for signs like you would find on any freeway. Let's see if we can get a glimpse of the signpost ahead written on a whisper from an angel:

Like everything else in life, you are making the choices. Choosing a direction and then feeling like a victim within those choices can be an indication that more than one area of your life needs some focus or direction. A series of misguided action steps illuminates the need for a quiet mind to see certain truths regarding your existence.

Circumstances and events can form an illusion around your direction that could make you feel as if there is only one answer, or no clear response to your situation. This can be a way of leading you to a great teaching or karmic resolution, as well as a sign that you are complete in that area and ready to move forward.

Duality teaches you acceptance and understanding so you do not have to repeat patterns as you become anchored in your faith. Without faith, your passion is compromised along with your clarity of consciousness which can, in turn, open the door to ego judgments and self-defeating behaviors.

You might consider interviewing yourself with questions like What direction takes me closer to my Divine life purpose?, What does my heart desire?, and What purpose in life vibrates with my core existence? or any question that might unveil one of your deepest answers to life. There you will find the direction that you seek.

The holiday season offers many opportunities to feel disappointed. Between the stress, time off work and a busy social schedule full of gatherings, it is relatively easy to build illusions.

Disappointment *can be defined as the emotion felt when a strongly held expectation is not met or the idea that you have been defeated or disappointingly unsuccessful.* Henry Ward Beecher gave us some insight with this quote: *"One's best success comes after their greatest disappointment."*

The psychological effect of feeling disappointment can hold devastating results that sometimes carry a passionate response leading to an internal search for answers. When things don't quite work out the way we planned, questions around faith, spiritual empowerment and even the meaning of life can be brought into full focus. This can ultimately lead to experiencing spiritual growth.

It is easy to say that by lowering expectations we can avoid disappointment. Yet how is that accomplished without the loss of hope? If the focus is on the highest potential, there could be disappointments and let-downs that bring harsh criticism from within. The perspective found in disappointment ultimately affects the outlook on success, decision-making and life itself. Don't disappoint me now, angels (tee hee); please give me a whisper on this meaningful word:

People and situations will always offer the opportunity for disappointment, which is a natural and normal response. These vibrations can remove you from your core alignment in an instant, so this is one emotion that you should really give attention. Within the energy of disappointment you will find a treasure chest of understanding and a road map to spiritual empowerment.

Disappointment requires and almost demands that you take a look at the situation from a higher perspective. Without some level of understanding, the challenges of accepting disappointment spread into the minutia or the details of life. These challenges can result in removing you from your heart by giving importance to thoughts that are missing substance in truth. Being out of balance or alignment is a symptom of resting too long in the energy of disappointment. Ego judgments can take over during prolonged periods of unresolved disappointment, and this represents a downward spiral into the lower vibrations.

Faith builds hope and creates understanding around the way the world works. Your total acceptance or surrender is better served outside the feelings of any measuring of success whatsoever. Acceptance and understanding around the sweet and bittersweet is the duality that reflects the truth of your existence. By raising your consciousness, you will limit the effects of disappointment, which will help you create action steps that will fulfill and enhance the realities of life on Earth.

In one moment of disappointment, you can discover the truest light needed to illuminate your pathway to a purpose-driven life.

When I first started doing these *Angel Whispers*, I had some resistance to the commitment. With some angelic guidance reaching the 'nagging' level, I decided that one full year would be the length of this focus on words and their meanings. I am well past that first year, thanks to the unexpected rewards of the undertaking.

The benefits have been wide-ranging, from the interesting perspectives of my readers, to my own spiritual uplifting. My commitment of time and expense every week has paid big dividends in areas that were well outside of my own discernment.

Discernment is a term used in Christian tradition to describe the process of discerning God's will for one's life. In large part, it describes the interior search for an answer to the question of one's vocation. Disturbances of the imagination and errors of sensibility thwart the operations of the intellect and will by deterring the one from the true and the other from the good. The Creator willed that there should be communication between angels and men, and as the angels are of two kinds, good and bad, the latter try to win us over to their rebellion and the former endeavor to make us their companions in obedience.

Part of my weekly discernment is in the search for the meaning that resonates with me the most. The above definition came from the Wikipedia, and I must admit that I never met an angel I didn't like or that I would remotely consider bad (lol). I will also admit that things do exist outside my realm of experiences.

According to Miriam-Webster, this word was born in 1586 with a meaning that expresses the *"quality of being able to grasp and comprehend what is obscure."* That's my cue to dive into the pool of obscure communication for a whisper on discernment:

Discernment is engaging in the energy of discovery and often leads to illumination of the truth. It can also lead to the creation of illusions. If you are finding resistance in the body or heart area, it is time for some discernment. Resistance is often a signal that there is something the soul needs to balance energy. Failure to discern the resistance is a delay response and can signal that you are not willing or able to go there.

Your life path is always an area of discernment, unless you are feeling love and divine flow present throughout your day. The landscape is constantly changing and that is the reason why some of you awaken to a discontent that was not in the awareness the previous day. Meditation, counseling and acts of reflection during these moments will help you with discernment.

If you want to engage in discernment, the first action would involve the opening of the heart, mind and soul. This allows a deepening of spirit to enhance the moment of perception that will bring truth into discernment. Impulsive behaviors can limit the experience by eliminating time for discernment. This bypass can be beneficial for greater understanding, such as learning patience and tuning in to the vibrations of guidance and intuition.

If you want to learn, take a moment to discern.

A friend and I were talking about this word recently and its true meaning to each of us. *Discipline*: 1. Training intended to elicit a specified pattern of behavior or character; 2. A condition of order based on obedience to authority; 3. Punishment meant to correct or train. This meaning doesn't seem to fit my definition, as it reads like we all need a personal drill sergeant. My friend's take on the word was that he thought it meant learning from your mistakes and taking action to prevent making that same mistake again.

Discipline is derived from the word *disciple*, meaning one who follows a particular teaching with the commitment to become perfect in it and to bring others a sense of its truth. This is about a body of knowledge which takes some time, effort and skill to master. The word's origin brings a quality of mastery of self or a refusal of self-indulgence in the pursuit of something that is not easy to attain.

Over the weekend, I attended a homecoming football game to watch my nephew play. His team had one player who repeatedly committed unsportsmanlike fouls against his opponents, resulting in several penalties. I don't have the tally but I am sure that he single-handedly bore the responsibility for more than one hundred yards in penalties, and some were at critical times in the game, which ended in a 6-6 tie.

This is a case where one person's lack of discipline affected the entire group of players, coaches and parents. Was he not learning from his mistakes, or did he just refuse to take action to correct them? There was no question about the lack of discipline in this case. I will now use my own discipline for a whisper:

Discipline is a characteristic that can define who you are as person. Going to the next level in life is directly linked to your discipline. To build discipline, you must build on your faith.

The greatest spiritual leaders in your society have displayed great discipline. From this you must realize that discipline can be serving mankind as a whole and the individual, while a lack of discipline can be destructive to the group and the self.

In order to achieve the best results using discipline, it is important to focus on a desired outcome. This can be the motivating factor that drives discipline. If you struggle in this area, spiritual intervention is the prescription. The rewards for your efforts in this area can be confidence, commitment, fellowship and love for who you are.

When you teach discipline through example, you breathe inspiration into the heart of the human experience. The development as a race and society is built on the foundation of discipline and therefore speaks to the evolution of a people and a planet.

I already love the energy and duality around this word! I had another word in mind but eventually decided it was a distraction (tee hee). The *inability to attract* might be my first pass at a definition. In a world full of distractions, it is becoming a rare experience to find lasting and meaningful eye contact with another human.

Distraction can mean: *1. the act of distracting; 2. the state of being distracted; 3. mental distress or derangement; 4. that which distracts, divides the attention, or prevents concentration; 5. that which amuses, entertains, or diverts; 6. division or disorder caused by dissension, tumult. Distraction* is also a British game show where the contestants answer questions while being distracted in bizarre, painful and humiliating ways (lol).

So distractions can painfully cause mental distress, divide our attention or be very entertaining and bizarre. It sounds like one of the key features in the human experience! I have come to believe with my thinking around this word that distractions can be both serving and a waste of time. To me, it comes down to discernment around the distraction as a way to ensure the proper response.

During times of extreme grief, I think it would help the soul to engage in a distraction like laughter or entertainment. But I also think sometimes we are distracted in order to find our resolve or measure the depth of our passion. Let's distract an angel for a moment of Divine clarity around distractions:

The duality of life is clearly displayed in this energy that gives meaning to what one might consider a distraction. Procrastination tendencies, indecisiveness, measuring life around perfectionism, illusions and blocks can all be enhanced by distractions. Seeing the truth, protection from harm, raised awareness and conscious connections can result from a single distraction. So you can quickly form ideas around serving aspects of distractions.

If you are experiencing difficulty in focus and clarity due to what you consider to be distractions, this could be your message that speaks to the balance in your life and situation. Is a distraction taking you away from your Divine Life Purpose? Are you being led down the path of ego due to distractions? Are you forming illusions that distance you from truth? Sometimes you have to wander in the darkness to find your light, and for that reason life offers many distractions as opportunities to raise awareness through knowledge gained in the life experience.

Distractions are a way of 'checking in' with your truth, trust, presence, compassion, consciousness and love in order to affirm what you already know or give you epiphanies and enlightenment. Action steps beyond that will determine the level of learning needed for you to stand in your own light and find presence in the moment. As you limit distractions in a way that allows you to focus on the deepest meaning of your life, you are standing in the pillar of light that does not cast a shadow.

According to a book written by Gregg Braden, a series of groundbreaking experiments revealed dramatic evidence of a web of energy that connects everything in our lives and our world—*the Divine Matrix*. From the healing of our bodies, to the success of our careers, relationships, and the peace between nations, this new evidence demonstrates that we each hold the power to speak directly to the force that links all of creation. What would it mean to discover that the power to **create joy, to heal suffering, and bring peace** to nations lives inside of you?

Some call this field the nature's mind or the mind of God. Western science is just now embracing the fact that there is a divine field of energy that bathes us constantly. The ancient healers tapped into this field thousands of years ago with knowledge of its power. Within this field, we have an ability to communicate healing to our bodies and produce what many would claim is a miracle.

A description of this energetic grid and instructions on its use were edited out of the Bible. They were within the forty-five books that were removed from that text in the fourth century. Prior to that, this technology was part of our culture. The rediscovery of the Dead Sea Scrolls flushed out this information and history.

From the beginning of time, the information on the Divine Matrix has been used by indigenous and ancient cultures. Without the information, the practices of these cultures seemed ancient or outdated. Scholars and scientists are now discovering that this information was lost and incomplete as a part of our history.

With the introduction of this field at the time of the 'Big Bang,' this energy grid expanded into our universe as a substrate or framework that provides a container within which our Universe exists. It is a bridge between our inner and outer world. Maybe I can bridge the two worlds with the Divine Matrix to produce a whisper from an angel:

The Divine Matrix is felt by many on a level that translates a feeling of Oneness. The energetic grid connects all of life to form points of light at the intersection of life and Spirit. The positive and negative relationship within all of living matter keeps an even movement and flow to this energetic field. The complete acceptance of each individual from the perspective that everyone is unique is essential to understanding how the matrix works.

If you think of the matrix in a form similar to the human body, you would find God or Source Energy at the heart. Like the flow of blood that passes through the heart in the human body, that same Universal energy flows within the Divine Matrix to give each person a connection to the Highest Power.

When you are released from the body, you are drawn to enter the stream that is one with all living things. This is how you will fully connect to the divine, travel to your heaven transmitting love to your family, witness other planes of existence and create your soul journey beyond your lifetime in the physical.

Healing with love is always fully present in the Divine Matrix. You can choose to be one with nature or you can resist the flow of life to experience the outer edges of the human drama. Your choices make up your karmic destiny while your faith builds the aura around your pathway to ascension. The true journey of the soul is at the core of existence with illumination by a rainbow of light called the Divine Matrix.

Doldrums

Thanks for the request to study the word *doldrums*, which is an unusual and rarely spoken word these days. *Doldrums* has been associated with sailors over the years, but may sneak into our landlocked holidays and the shifting sands of our time on Earth.

__Doldrums__, according to Merriam-Webster, means a spell of listlessness or despondency or state or period of inactivity, stagnations or slump. Doldrums is also a part of the ocean near the equator abounding in calms, squalls, and light shifting winds. The exact etymology of "doldrums" is not certain, though it is believed to be related to the Old English "dol," meaning "foolish" — a history it shares with our adjective "dull."

Everyone gets the __doldrums__ — a feeling of low spirits and lack of energy — every once in a while. The doldrums experienced by sailors, however, are usually of a different variety. In the mid-19th century, the word once reserved for a feeling of despondency came to be applied to certain tropical regions of the ocean marked by the absence of strong winds. Sailing vessels, reliant on wind propulsion, struggled to make headway in these regions, leading to long, arduous journeys.

Maybe the term is not as distant from the sailor's experience, in that, as we experience our journey, there can be a loss of momentum or passion to keep us sailing on our way. Let's get some wind in our sails with a whisper from an angel:

Spirit moves incredibly fast and is substantially slowed down inside the vessel known as the human body. When the body experiences a slow-down or pause, the result can be the doldrums, just as sailors experienced from a deep connection with the ocean. Sometimes you may feel like you lack direction or desire, and this can feel uneasy, as if you're stuck in time and space with no fuel to get things going.

The human body responds to the stars in the same way that the tides of the ocean are responding. The alignment of the planets brings forth an energy that is felt on deep levels and in a variety of ways within the human journey. For example, a Mercury Retrograde is akin to an adult time-out. This is a period of reflection where you go inside to answer questions around how you handled and presented yourself to others. These questions are usually connected with your personal integrity, and the purpose is to illuminate the needed changes and spiritual growth in your life.

The depth of a moment of doldrums can be very serving and can signal that you are integrating sometimes harsh lessons around grief, loss and trauma that can reach back into your entire life. The mirror of reflection ultimately provides insight into spiritual growth, so move through these periods with patience, understanding and nurturing energy as you integrate your experiences with the same resolve and high vibrations normally present in your life. The wind will return to fill your sails as you continue on your journey toward the horizon. Hold the never-ending faith, curiosity and innocence that were naturally yours as a child as you maneuver through the doldrums.

It doesn't take long when you are living in Austin to realize how much we love our dogs. I recently did my first canine crystal treatment on an eleven year old named Jake. When Jake greeted me at the door, I heard a little voice say "I am set in my ways" as Jake curled up on his bed in the living room.

Jake had the unfortunate experience of lightning hitting the house while his Mommy and Daddy were away. The storm managed to take out three TV's, the mechanical system and other electronic devices. Since that day, Jake begins to worry and pace the floor ahead of any storm, and as you know we have had more that our share this summer in Austin.

As it turns out, it was an experience of confinement as a puppy that was the source of his fears. The storm was bad, but the lightning strike while he was alone was the culprit. He was so comfortable and set in his ways that he fell asleep and snored loudly during most of the treatment with an occasional glance at Mom.

While I was on the other side of town with Jake, a good friend was finding out that cancer was overtaking his companion of 11 years. He told me that Laszlo gave him one look that said it all about his fight with cancer. Please help me, I am done. Now my friend has gone through a lot in the past few years, yet putting down his beloved dog was one of the hardest things he has had to do.

I was recently sent an article about Oprah's golden retriever that died suddenly when a rubber ball became lodged in the throat. You could tell in the writing how difficult the loss was her. Oprah referred to him as her 'Earth Angel', as she described hearing his playful bark by the pond where he passed. Like my friend, watching the life leaving his eyes was extremely difficult.

This was a communication of love from the eyes of a dog to his owners' receptive heart. Most of you have experienced some sort of animal communication at some time in your life. I remember the first time that I was asked, during an angel reading, for a message regarding dogs. This was my dog whisper and if you spell it backwards is God whisper (LOL).

Dogs are unique to the animal kingdom in several ways. They are totally loyal to humans and therefore will follow their master forever. They can hear and see things on the other side of the veil.

Dogs are accustomed to the sight of angels and are very comfortable in the angelic realm. So when you ask if there are 'dog angels', I will show you a visual of a dog with wings. This is your answer.

Dogs are here to serve mankind and fully accept the responsibility. This is why there are so many 'working dogs' in different jobs around the globe. This is also how you can tell when the animal's purpose is being fulfilled, by the smile on their happy faces.

One reason it is hard to let go of your canine companions is their unconditional love that they freely give. What makes them so unique is their unequalled love, compassion, loyalty and trust that is their gift to mankind.

Dreams are the images, thoughts and feelings experienced while sleeping, particularly strongly associated with rapid eye movement. I have had a fascination with this subject for years and as a result have attended dream circles, journaled my own dreams and often refer to a dream dictionary. My wonder around these mysterious and random occurrences might be linked to the nature of my own experiences.

Long periods of time cam lapse between my dream cycles as I can go months without one nighttime morsel. But then I can go into an intense dream merry-go-round for days on end. I have vivid dreams rich with story, plot and action that allow me to awaken, leave the room, return and fall back to sleep only to pick up right where I left off. This can happen throughout an entire night and several waking moments in between.

Isn't it fun when other people tell you about their dreams? Some abstract and often impossible happenings within their psyche can describe the life-changing phenomenon of the effect a dream can have in a way that makes them unforgettable. Let's see what the angels can dream up on this subject:

One way that we help guide you is through the co-creation of an illusion. This process helps give you a vision of your path while illuminating your desires and intentions. The end result is often more rewarding than the vision that you originally created. This partially explains the role of Divine Energy and dreams.

In the dream stage, the human mind, body and spirit are sometimes open to other dimensions and realms. This can provide an opportunity for communication through all of the senses. When you have awakened from a dream with the scent of the flowers that you were holding, this is your Clairaudience.

The Mind's Eye becomes a witness to your dreams in order to help you with visions, projections, and manifestations while serving as an integral part in shifting paradigms. Dreams have several practical applications, from emotional release to physical healing, all while serving the entire human body in some form.

Dreams are like movies to the soul playing the soundtrack of the heart to create a distraction for the mind with an occasional message with meaning. To enjoy your dreams, clear and shield yourself regularly, release fears and cords of attachments and drift to sleep in gratitude.

The journey of the soul and the evolution of mankind are connected to dreams and waking visions. Follow the trail of Divine Energy and you will arrive in a space filled with dreams, faith, love and eternal joy.

This word comes up frequently in my work and seems to appear on many different levels. In scientific terms, every cell structure is formed with polar opposites, and the movement generated between these parts provides the basis of all energy in the Universe.

When you apply that principle to the combination of cells that form the human body, it becomes apparent that we receive cumulative energy in this form. This could explain why an imbalance at some level depletes our energy. In theory, opposites that are equal to each other make up our Universe and present a dichotomy to every aspect of life. Without darkness, there can be no light and vice versa.

Duality*: a situation or nature that has two states or parts that are complementary or opposed to each other.* Complementary is the word I was looking for to describe how opposites attract in a serving manner. Eckhart Tolle says, "When you live in surrender, something comes through you into the world of duality that is not of this world," while Sri Guru Granth Sahib is quoted as saying, "Burn the pen, and burn the ink; burn the paper as well. Burn the writer who writes in the love of **duality**."

Oooops, why do I suddenly feel cursed (lol)? It's not that I love duality as much as I am trying to understand how it applies to my life. Let me stretch the limits of duality with a whisper from an angel:

Words often form limitations in the mind of those who speak them without understanding the true meaning. The tone of judgment within the language can block reception as truth meets opinion. Duality helps illuminate the truth when all sides are displayed without ego or manipulation.

If you are willing to reach for understanding and knowledge, opposing forces can unlock information stored at the deep levels within the body, mind and spirit. Engaging in the process of acceptance of duality creates opportunities for spiritual growth through human experiences, while simultaneously exposing core truths and beliefs.

Bringing balance to extreme conditions enlightens the soul or essence through energetic transfers of information. This allows for discernment in all areas of life with an opportunity to shift repeating patterns and addictive behaviors, which opens the door to manifesting dreams and desires.

As you breathe in and then breathe out, you experience the duality of giving and receiving in the most natural cycle of awareness. Breathing in unison with another individual connects the Cosmic Hearts. Breathing with a group through song, meditation or chants sends balanced love across the Universe as light intersects with dark. Understanding propels the energy of love and acceptance that whispers in your ears and tells you that everything is in Divine order.

Have you been feeling a little wonky lately (tee hee)? I am not sure what wonky means, so maybe the correct term is off-center. We have just entered a Mercury Retrograde, one of four this year instead of the normal three, and that always brings in a bag of tricks from the Universe. A Mercury Retrograde evokes questions like "How have I presented myself?", "How do others view me?", "Why am I here?" and so on. This period also brings challenges around communication with ourselves and others.

In addition, the Earth is going through some major vibrational shifting, such as earthquakes, intense storms, tidal waves and volcanic eruptions. The earthquake in Chile created a shift on the axis that resulted in the loss of one second of time. That doesn't sound like much, but the event is rather significant to the humans who dwell in time. This shifting is connected to the path of mankind, as it is facilitating great change in human consciousness that is reflected by current major world events.

As we move into the new Age of Aquarius, mankind will climb another rung of the evolutionary ladder on the path to human ascension. We could individually hold up a protest sign that says "No More Change" (tee hee), or we can try to gain understanding in order to move through these energetic shifts with as much grace and ease as possible. I hope the angels can help me with a better understanding around the effects of the Earth and the Stars:

You are being presented with a lot of information regarding Universal oneness and the Divine energy that connects all of life. The Earth and the Stars are a big part of that Divine Matrix which places everyone in a single stream of energy that some refer to as the Christ Consciousness.

In a state of ascension, there is a presence that enables some to put form around the concepts of God. The Earth and Stars energies combine to create lessons and teachings that ultimately bring you to a centering around love. While some resist this invocation, every soul surrenders to this stream eventually.

In order to raise your consciousness, there are times when some sort of illusion or 'trick' is necessary for you to receive the information that will facilitate change. Everyone has the free will to choose the time and place where this will occur, even if the soul journey involves a surrender that is beyond the physical existence.

The Earth and the Stars can give you valuable insights around your life purpose through a vibrational response that comes in the form of an invitation. You decide whether to join the party and do the dance of life, or to stay on the couch to ponder further the method in which you will eventually express your true self. Either way, all paths lead to the same outcome; in other words, there is no wrong choice. What may look like the path of least resistance may include the harsh lessons that will illuminate surrendering with grace and ease. The Earth and the Stars are the Mother and Father teaching their children lessons of life while offering Divine Love.

On last week's whisper of *Quantum Entanglement*, Terry writes: "Better yet, exactly what is the ego and who is it accountable to? Is there a hierarchy like the angelic and other realms? What is missing? What is it that is needed to be known?"

Ego is defined as the self, especially as distinct from the world and other selves. In psychoanalysis, the division of the psyche that is conscious most immediately controls thought and behavior, and is most in touch with external reality. Ego can mean an exaggerated sense of self-importance or conceit.

Controlled behaviors based in the ego are not always viewed as preferred, yet people may be inspired to achieve greatness under that control. Did my ego just try to defend my bad behaviors (tee hee)? It can get confusing to pursue a balanced ego, but Terry's question was directed toward the bigger picture and what happens to the ego when we cross over.

That question creates an opening big enough for bands of angels to fly through (grins)! Let's see what can be done with the ego to accommodate a whisper from the angels limited to what we need to know:

When the energy of purpose intersects with the energy of need, the ego interprets the response as one energy evoked with some element that relates to survival. The survival mode, activated by ego, requires a certain amount of faith to support the action steps required to draw the desired experience. The purpose that dictates the response and action steps usually solicits an emotion created to find resolution on some level.

Resolutions can range from issues of surface emotions to deep-seated healing or transformation, with various subtle energies appearing throughout the incarnated journey. The physical experience can be supported by a balanced ego that gives a conscious choice, some clear markers for direction. But the ego can also block energy and serve as resistance to finding a completion to your current incarnation.

Should resistance prevent a completion to your physical experience, the ego energy connects with free will in yet another dimension that offers resolution in regards to your purpose. Upon completion of your specific purpose, moving into the light offers a stunning metamorphosis. A beautiful shedding of the energies that existed solely for the physical incarnation experience occurs to allow energy to fall away gracefully in the transformation to a neutral state of pure love.

Ego, like many components of a fulfilling life, is exactly what you make of it. If you pour light into energy, it becomes an asset. Darkness serves to support lower energies and offers the greatest resistance to finding resolution. Ego energy is part of the mystery that keeps life unpredictable and interesting, because without it, everyone could easily settle into their eternal bliss.

To start the thought process on this word study, the first thing that comes up is defining the ego. That's interesting because I spend a lot of time in session talking about the ego and ego judgments, and now words of definition escape me. Is it related to a thought process, a social paradigm, a primal essence of who we are, or all three?

Id, ego and super-ego are the three parts of the "psychic apparatus" defined in Freud's so-called structural model of the psyche; they are the three theoretical constructs in terms of whose activity and interaction mental life is described. According to this model, the uncoordinated instinctual trends are the "id;" the organized, realistic part of the psyche is the "ego;" and the critical and moralizing function the "super-ego."

Psychic apparatus sounds good, but why would we need the critical and moralizing feature (tee hee)? Even as I ask the question in print, I feel like there is a connection between our ego, the soul and our spirituality. The ego judgments we face within ourselves may provide the challenges that define us as human beings and give us inspiration to overcome. Maybe that means that the ego judgments of others are the deepest expression of who they are and really have nothing to do with us.

I try to teach a method of rejecting the ego judgments through awareness and practicing a routine. The desired effect would be the natural and almost unconscious rejection of the critical and demoralizing emotions triggered by the ego. I have to believe that evolution hinges on mankind's ability to transcend the super-ego at some level. I must set the ego aside to have any chance of hearing a whisper from the angels on ego judgments:

The ego is the most natural way to ensure the survival of man on the planet. To be enlightened is to be on a path that includes seeing truth illuminated. The Higher Self ascends in the light of truth with a distancing from the psyche and the ego judgment.

Ego judgments may appear to be generated from the darkest of human emotions, yet the fuel for the ego is passion. Anger sends out vibrations of passion in linear waves with direction, intent and purpose, while the passion of love is omni-directional. Abusive ego judgments are the release of pain that the body has stored without means of movement. Often, adrenalin is released in certain situations as a stimulant or trigger for the release of such energy.

When you detach from the ego judgments, you are simply surrendering to Spirit the willingness to carry those burdens. You are then free to expand your mind and accept the faith, trust and a belief in yourself that transcends the energies of the Lower Self.

Be careful with your thoughts by using nurturing kindness, profound courage, and integrity of truth in a way that helps you feel faith beyond finding fault, compassion free from blame, love without boundaries and support beyond measure. Live in the footsteps of your vision for who you are. Teach only love!

I want the angels to tell me why people spend their time and energy stealing information from others. Even large companies should have some sort of conscience when it comes to invading a person's privacy. When my email was compromised, hundreds of links to a Canadian pharmacy, with great deals on Viagra (ha ha), went to all my family, friends, bankers, in-laws, acquaintances and clients.

It was interesting to see the response from people, especially those whom I had not heard from in quite some time. That aspect was a blessing hidden between the emotions of feeling like a victim. Many people trusted me enough to click on the suspicious link, and I am saddened that my younger friends may have done the same.

There was humor too! Some thought that my link was sent as part of my intuitive work and the gentle nudging was a gift, like I had tuned into something! I suddenly found myself privy to information regarding the sex life of people that I never dreamed would be sharing such things with little ole me. What trust!

Learning became an important feature of the event as I studied what happened and what action steps could be taken. Changing my password took an act of Congress (tee hee). Removing contacts from online sources took a technical genius. Dealing with it all took patience. And now I seek further understanding from the voice of spirit:

There is much to be learned in your world today, in areas from technology to spirituality, and beyond anything you have imagined so far. The landscape is changing at a pace that often encourages people to act without regard to consequences. The result is shifting energies that are raising the awareness of every being on the planet.

Adaptation to change is best absorbed with a presence and awareness that give information around the effect each individual creates in the world. The focus on the self is a streaming energy with movement that, when held in a space of integrity, ripples out into the world with positive effects. Through making conscious choices with pure and clear motivation, unity is expressed in the form of energy that becomes a catalyst of change for nations.

Your choices are to pay attention to the details that directly affect the quality of life, or to gloss over the subtle energies of your life as if nothing ever happened. The completion to an aspect of the soul journey is available to you, and there will be many distractions on the path. Facing life by dealing directly with issues that degrade the quality of your life will carry many rewards.

Some of those rewards will take the form of lessons; others will take the form of love. If the experience creates a downward spiral of energy, you learn how to present yourself by placing your best foot forward. If your experience, no matter how devastating, takes you into an upward spiral of energy, you have just been shown the fruits of your labor.

As a medium, I have some rather unique experiences that have changed the way I view life and life after death. Just when I find a little comfort in thinking I have seen it all, something happens that puts me back in my humble beginnings (lol).

Upon arriving home from a week in Mexico, I was shocked to find some rather unusual emails in my current inbox. There were nine emails grouped together that really opened my eyes and heart. Five were from the publisher of my first book, Mariposa, followed by two from the artist who created the book cover, followed by two more from the publisher. The shock was that my artist friend had passed almost a year ago to the day.

The email from her was a loving message that was making reference to a file from the book publisher. It was late and I was tired from the travel day, so I simply went to bed in amazement and wonder. The next day, the nine emails had vanished without a trace and couldn't be found, even in the history folder where I store all book-related emails.

I decided to contact my publisher and was even more shocked when the reply came back from her husband that she had passed more than two years prior. I have had experiences with unusual emails from deceased loved ones in the past, but this experience takes the cake! Let's see if an angel who whispers can shed some light on the case of the emails from deceased loved ones:

When the body ceases to function, the energy from within experiences a freedom that births the next phase of the soul journey. In a state of pure energy, movement becomes a learning process, much like a baby learning to crawl. This process has, in simple terms, been forgotten during the incarnation and travel across the etheric plane.

During the initial transition, there is a greater focus on communication with those who are left behind, which provides a pathway to resolution. Since computers operate on energy, there is an opportunity to engage in a process that facilitates communication. The effort to make such things happen is greater than you might imagine and a testament to a person's free will.

This holiday season, take the time to send love to your departed loved ones. Your grief can be released in the acknowledgment of their energy and the love from your heart. You may not have them in the physical, but you will always carry them in your spiritual body. Your open heart will invite your loved-ones to communicate a message in the energy of pure love.

You can breathe the air, yet you cannot see it. You can feel the wind, even though you cannot touch it. You can know your loved ones, even when you can't hold them. You can hear angels when there is no audible voice. You can believe in God when there is no proof of existence. And the beauty of creation is that you get to choose.

This is a word that is near and dear to my heart, especially since my job is to evoke inspirational messages for the purpose of empowerment. But is empowerment real or simply an overused term without much significance? As I searched for meanings, I discovered that the term "empowerment" can be a complex and multi-dimensional concept.

Some of the qualities of **empowerment**, according to the National Empowerment Center, might include *having decision-making power, having access to information and resources, having a range of options from which to make choices, assertiveness, feeling that the individual can make a difference (being hopeful), learning to think critically, learning to redefine who we are (speaking in our own voice), learning to redefine what we can do, learning to redefine our relationships to institutionalized power, learning about and expressing anger, feeling part of a group, understanding that people have rights, effecting change in one's life and one's community, changing others' perceptions of one's competency and capacity to act, coming out of the closet, growth and change that is never-ending and self-initiated, increasing one's positive self-image, and overcoming stigma.* All that inside one word (tee hee)?

In addition, I discovered that empowerment has institutional applications that rarely involve personal decisions and choices. John F. Kennedy's quote *"And so, my fellow Americans: Ask not what your country can do for you. Ask what you can do for your country"* was designed to lift up the whole country, by empowering each individual. Let's see if there is a common thread between empowerment and a whisper from an angel:

Empowerment is the energy that occurs in defining moments of conscious shifting. Whether it is during a healing crisis or a profound moment of inspiration, empowerment occurs when your awareness creates change that brings you more in alignment with your Divine life-purpose.

Within the core of your existence, there is a truth that aligns with your vibrations like a radio that tunes into that perfect frequency in order to transmit information. Enlightenment, illumination of the truth, vibrations of your most loving essence and connection with the Highest Power occur in the energy of empowerment in a stream of Divine Love.

It is wise to discern the feeling of empowerment in the human body to allow for an unobstructed flow of energy. Divine energy is always empowering as it connects your soul to the meaning of life and the reason for your incarnation. When a person or situation takes your power away by using ego judgments, control or negative energy, the empowering response comes in the form of boundaries.

Personal empowerment could be supported by surrounding yourself with like-minded people, finding the joy in life and building faith through conscious living. Stand in the light that emits the sound of your heart and then touch others with that beautiful song to feel the energy of empowerment.

I heard this term used in a description of Casey Anthony, also known as 'Tot Mom'. She was found not guilty by a Florida jury for the death of her 2-year-old daughter, Caylee Anthony. A person who had spent time in the Anthony household described Casey's parents and brother as having to walk on eggshells around Casey, out of fear of the way she might react.

According to the Urban Dictionary, an emotional terrorist is *"any person (usually a female) who uses seemingly subtle or inconsequential text messages, body language, or short tone of voice to begin a surprise emotional attack against a boyfriend, girlfriend, husband, wife or Ex. The attack usually results in catastrophic relationship damage."*

When anyone creates an environment that leaves you fearful of their reaction, that is the highest form of manipulation. Someone, whether male or female, who might 'cut you off' from feeling and receiving their love as a form of punishment for not doing what they want you to can hold your emotions hostage in order to get what they want.

Terrorist is a strong word unless someone gets hurt or, in this case, someone loses their life. Let's find a moment of emotional tranquility in order to receive a whisper from an angel on this subject:

When a relationship becomes unhealthy, dysfunctional components begin to filter through the bonds of love. Unhealthy cords from negative attachments to ideas, beliefs, behaviors, people and material things can rob your energy in a manifestation known as fatigue. Some people are taught to believe that unconditional love means operating under another's free will to keep in order to keep that person happy at all costs. That path creates distance from personal integrity.

It is difficult to see where the smallest support for another person's ability to manipulate and control your behaviors can manifests into broken relationships. It is equally difficult to stand firm against someone you love, even when they are demanding such action from you. Their demand may come from within an energy of extreme anger or from the sweetest form of passive aggression. A healthy boundary is the only defense, for that boundary is generated from respect and love. Do not trick yourself into believing that unconditional love overrides your responsibility to stand in truth and become a teacher, leader, and an example for healthy behaviors.

When an emotional terrorist takes you out of your character, a teaching becomes present for you. In that teaching is the opportunity to speak courageous words of love so that your voice is not only heard, but answered and honored. The price to express your truth can be high, but the rewards are endless if you are willing to inventory your life through the eyes of love. For it is through those eyes that you release judgments by opening a sacred space occupied by your heart.

Call on help from the angels for support in these situations, and you will find the language that clearly mirrors the courage, strength and vitality found within Divine Energy, as it rolls off your tongue with grace and ease.

Have you ever felt carried away by your emotions or wished you could have responded more out of logic than feelings? ***Emotions*** are defined as *a mental state that arises spontaneously, rather than through conscious effort, and is often accompanied by physiological changes. A feeling or a part of the consciousness that involves feeling* can also be a way to define emotions.

As multi-faceted creatures, we live in an emotional body that can rule our actions or at the very least influence our decisions. The need to find balance in every aspect of life arose in conversation several times over the weekend, and definitely applies to the emotional issues we all face.

In my energy work, I have found that emotions can play a trick by masking the real issue and thereby creating a distraction from the truth. I believe this occurs when we repress our true emotions, allowing another response to surface. Let's gain control of our emotions (tee hee) long enough to tune in to the angels for a whisper on emotions:

The layer effect of emotions you mention could represent the way energy moves and connects the spiritual body with the physical body in order to create emotions. The contrast offered by the human physical experience would appear more like some sort of aimless chemistry experiment, without the energy that connects each person to the world beyond the five body senses.

From this connection, humans draw the passion that fuels love, art, creativity and the unlimited journey of the soul. Emotions are a blend of energies creating a response that directs and guides each person to the lessons and experiences that were chosen by each person's journey.

When emotions reach extreme levels, the soul is crying out in resistance to accepting things the way they are. The emotional response that is without the fuel of passion can come from fears created and attached to outcome. In other words, self-fulfilling prophecies can undermine the balance of energy needed for the individual to take the desired actions.

It is common for the emotional body to make sacrifices in order to shoulder the responsibility of others. This leads to disharmony and sometime illness, so it is important for each person to discern the proper emotional response through periodic cleansing of the mind, body and spirit. Forgiveness, releasing that which no longer serves, conscious awareness of your body, positive affirmations, acceptance, faith and the infusion of loving energy, will manifest the greatest balance of the emotional body.

Energy is at the essence of every cell in the Universe. Each cell in the body has a negative and a positive charge that occupies the outer layer. This allows for a constant motion that moves in harmony with adjoining cells to create change. This change that occurs is a back and forth exchange of positions producing energy.

So our bodies are made up of millions of cells; each one producing energy. Our soul can move and produce energy at incredible levels. It is our body mass that slows this energy down as a controlled creation of life, so we can stop and smell the roses.

The body has several points that are intersecting lines of energy. The Chinese identified these intersections as areas that are the best to treat all areas of the body. This is known as Acupuncture.

There are also energy points that exist in the etheric body which lie 1-2 inches outside the body. These energy centers are known as Chakras and they occupy the surface of the body in our Electro Magnetic Field (EMF) that is also known as our Aura. The seven main chakras exist in the front of the body in this etheric field.

Several things can affect our energy centers such as physical or emotional stress that has disharmonic effect on the body starting with these energetic fields. Unhappiness, trauma, and loss are a few examples of things that can trigger this state.

This is why energy work is more and more prevalent among our society. It takes a movement of energy to eliminate stagnant or disharmonious energetic vibrations. Let's get a whisper on this.

It is always interesting to see the different ways that man creates energy. Often in sporting events, the winner has displayed a burst of energy through channeled anger. This is the result of a mental exercise that has developed a technique that allows the player to dig deep into the self to gather all energy possible.

It is the positive and negative poles working together that allows for the purest form of energy. The light and dark always work together to produce a charge that is maximum strength. People often make the mistake that one can exist without the other, when it is the harmonious balance between the two that produces energy

When you have a situation that is draining your energy, there is a balance that is missing. An example is when you try to apply your energy to a resolution that is not desired by the other person. As you increase your energy in this area, and the person that you are trying to help increases theirs, the energies collide in an unbalanced form. Clearly knowing how you can help this person with an agreement from all sides is the way to balance the energy.

When your own energy is out of balance, often this means that you need to release energy that no longer serves you, to allow for the natural and divine balance to occur. This is the way you travel the path of the enlightened soul.

\

A reader wrote these words and asked for a whisper: "How do we give to others when we believe their pain is where they need to be? I can't tell someone 'I am sorry' for their pain because I think they either chose it, or there is a really important lesson for them to learn."

I can relate to facing situations that leave you speechless on some level (grins). When a person is crying, I try to not interrupt by attempting to make them feel better. The release of tears is just as important as the energy leading up to that expression. Yet, I do want to comfort them in some way.

According to Alan Melah (from the *The Innerwords Messenger* newsletter), part of following a creed that helps you reach an enlightened perspective is to *realize we don't come into the world to be good, we come to be better.* In an attempt to be better (tee hee), I will ask for the enlightened perspective held within a whisper from an angel:

It's all about the language, perspective and the process of analyzing a situation. Being sorry for another person's challenges indicates that something is out of order, which creates descending energy. Your sympathy is not called for, but your compassion is. You can support someone through their pain without becoming entangled in that energy.

Your resistance to offering regrets is telling you something about the way to handle yourself and what words might best fit the situation. From the perspective that defines the serving nature of the experience, your discernment can become focused on what you can say and do in the moment that is helpful and high-vibrational, even if that is simply lending a compassionate ear without trying to fix anything. Giving compassionate energy is often wordless recognition generated from the heart and communicated through the eyes.

Your spiritual energy can support others through their hardships with an upward movement, provided you do not attach to their outcome. When choices are made from the higher perspective rather than from the lower energies of shame, regret, guilt or pity, you can help ease the burden of others. Have compassion for everyone involved, including yourself, for having gone through the lessons that allow you to clearly see things from an elevated viewpoint.

On the stage of life, you are a performer who writes your portion of the script. Use energy and language that express compassion and love in the midst of sorrow and pain, and you will be called to appear in many rewarding encore performances! Angels never weep, for within sorrow is a greater opportunity to share love.

This word gets kicked around so much that it may have developed some negative connotations in the minds of some people. People can speak of their enlightenment with an elitist attitude, which doesn't help the cause. But what does it really mean?

Enlightenment broadly means wisdom or understanding enabling clarity of perception. However, the English word covers two concepts which can be quite distinct: religious or spiritual enlightenment, and secular or intellectual enlightenment. This can cause confusion, since those who claim intellectual enlightenment often reject spiritual concepts altogether. In secular use, the concept refers mainly to the European intellectual movement known as the Age of Enlightenment, also called the Age of Reason, referring to philosophical developments related to scientific rationality in the 17th and 18th centuries.

The Age of Reason sounds so inviting, hopeful and enlightened! I now see that this word is similar to other confusing terms like New Age, Lightworkers and Angel Therapist® (tee hee). These words sometimes represent ancient ideas that are resurfacing in today's world and are being met with fear, judgment and misunderstanding.

"If I could define **enlightenment** briefly I would say it is 'the quiet acceptance of what is" is a quote by Dr. Wayne Dyer that I personally like. But this one by Jack Handy made me laugh: "If you ever reach total **enlightenment** while drinking beer, I bet it makes beer shoot out your nose." It's time for some enlightenment from an angel in the form of a whisper:

The origin of most words emanate from a feeling, which is then expressed through the use of letters or symbols. The ancient civilizations were building language using symbols in much the same way as today. When a word is misused, misunderstood or attached to judgments, the original intended meaning can become diluted. I hope you have just become enlightened to the fact that you can be persuaded to follow the vibrations of judgments and misuse if you allow that.

Now is the time when greater awareness is placed in the hands of the individual in order to make conscious choices around the evolving world of today. Words have even greater meaning as communication expands to reach all corners of the globe. Enlightenment speaks to this raised awareness on many levels, from the extremely personal and internal, to the consciousness of an entire species facing issues of survival.

Your personal journey speaks to your enlightenment while conveying energetic meanings to your family, friends, and neighbors. The choices you make carry a consequence into this circle, so choose your path carefully. Like the experience of traveling through the darkest night, some light will help illuminate the truth of your journey, and somewhere along the way you may shine that light on another human being.

The brightest light in the Universe transcends visual definition while finding its way to your heart in order to ask the questions: What does your heart desire? What does your soul need? Where do you find comfort? Will you choose to stand in the light? The answers are found within your essence.

One thing I can say without doubts regarding my own personal journey is that as I reach for different levels of spiritual growth, I experience one epiphany after another. Each one raises my awareness around a subject that might be considered somewhat removed from the spiritual realm, yet the cumulative effect definitely raises my consciousness.

Epiphany originally defined *the twelve days after Christmas as a celebration for the visit of the three wise men to the infant Jesus.* Epiphany today gives meaning to *a sudden realization or a divine manifestation.* John Milton once said, *"Gratitude bestows reverence, allowing us to encounter everyday epiphanies, those transcendent moments of awe that change forever how we experience life and the world."*

I must admit that living in gratitude contributed to my experiences over the past few years and so do these Whispers. An epiphany a week is almost guaranteed with my commitment to this process (lol)! One of my biggest epiphanies is that we are always connected to the highest power in the Universe, unless we choose to limit ourselves from that reality. In gratitude, I await a divine manifestation delivered as an Angel Whisper on epiphany:

Growth comes through a series of realizations about the life process followed by integration of those thoughts into the act of living. By choosing to expand your awareness, epiphanies help solidify your place and purpose on the planet as the human experience joins the spiritual journey to create learning.

Even if you are feeling closed to the spiritual aspects of life, your epiphanies will lead you to a heart-opening in one form or the other. By making clear choices with consideration for the purpose and integrity of the soul, epiphanies appear to provide a road map that further illuminates your path.

One moment of awareness can easily alter the course of your life and change your direction forever, so validation of thought is important. Your mind is as fragile as any part of the human body, so it is wise to guard it well. Seeing the difference between truth and illusion is a necessary function of the human experience; so too are epiphanies as a tool to break down and release old paradigms.

Meditation, daydreams, prayers, and movement offer many opportunities for the realization of truth to provide a platform that launches your action steps. You can save time and stress if you take a moment to ask Spirit for help and for answers to the questions of life as you receive divine moments of insight. Then it is simply a matter of trust and finding resonance with the vibrations in an epiphany to align with your core being.

Mental, spiritual, emotional and physical health issues can find resolve in a single epiphany. One epiphany a day keeps the doctor away, so choose your spiritual food carefully!

There is a science that relates to consciousness which has defined the esoteric bodies. According to the website called 'The Esoteric Science', *Man is deeper and broader than a physical body stimulated by mere chemical and biological reactions. Man is body and Soul, and in between lie many components or invisible vehicles of consciousness that form the lower self and the higher Self. All are vibratory in nature and in perpetual movement like the Etheric field around the body (Aura). These Esoteric Bodies constitute, with the physical body, the seven dimensions of consciousness in one's being, and these are as follows:*

1- *The Physical body: the practical application (sensation)*
2- *The Etheric body (aura): the nature of the physical (presence)*
3- *The Astral body: (feelings)*
4- *The Thought and Intelligence body: (mind)*
5- *The body of Love: (knowledge)*
6- *The Will body: (the will)*
7- *The Wisdom body: (the Soul)*

The study of various bodies is an essential component in the life of an energy practitioner, as it relates to such things as healing, ascension, manifestation, life itself and even death. Gaining an understanding of life-force energies and the form they take can provide a beacon that illuminates the path of a rewarding and happy life. Allow me a moment to listen for a whisper from an angel on the esoteric bodies.

The human is a multi-dimensional being living in a complex vehicle that can be broken down in various partial systems. Each part provides a piece of the whole, and it is that whole system which most people see and experience. The physical body is anchored in the sensory experience, which usually dominates a person's perception and focus.

The mental body combines the thoughts formed in the brain with intelligence which has penetrated the energy body and therefore resides in the spirit or soul. Purification or spiritual cleansing should begin in the mental body, starting at the top and following a spiral descent into the darkness or shadow side of an individual.

The etheric body, or aura, holds the energy, vitality and vibration of consciousness, providing a space where your emotions meet your consciousness and form a response to life's situations. Talk therapy is one method used to purge disharmony from the mental body, as is movement with intention.

The astral body is an energetic body that projects the life-force energy into the Universe to meet with other vibrations that align the human consciousness with the Cosmic Heart, thereby forming a direct connection to the light of the Creator.

The body of love is the energy from within that moves freely without form, as it knows love and searches for experiences that help to create loving moments. This body craves inspiration, drawing forward and co-creating the lessons of love that you will synthesize into wisdom. The wisdom body integrates those vibrations into a unified and cohesive framework that essentially defines your current incarnation and your intentions for this lifetime.

The will body holds the mystery and excitement of the unknown. The phenomena and super-human experiences are generated from this body, and there is no power in the Universe that can usurp the will body.

In the search for understanding, I often reduce things to the very essence or the heart of the matter. It is interesting to me how my immediate response in thought forms around the word *essence* went straight to the heart. My focus on this word emerged from a moment of deep internal perspective on life and what we call death.

Essence is used as a noun that means something that is, or exists; entity. The essence is that which makes something what it is; intrinsic, fundamental nature or most important quality (of something); essential being. In philosophy, essence refers to the inward nature of anything, underlying its manifestations; true substance or the indispensable conceptual characteristics and relations of anything.

During a moment of stillness, I tried to connect to the essence of who I am, and in the process began speaking directly to my spirit or soul. Who or what am I without the physical body? And is that an energy that forms my essence?

In a fate-filled moment, the essence of one of my relationships turned on a dime, only to create several opportunities for myself and others. This required a shift in my psyche to be able to not only see, but to embrace my opportunities. Without that shift, my beliefs might have held me back from forming a deeper bond in this relationship. No matter how I define it, the result touched me at the core of my essence

George Bernard Shaw once said, "The worst sin toward our fellow creatures is not to hate them, but to be indifferent to them; that's the essence of inhumanity". Maybe the essence of an angel will deliver a whisper on the subject:

Everyone is tuned to a different frequency and that determines many aspects of their essence. With each group of like resonance, there are colors, vibrations, sounds and movement patterns that somewhat determine the core traits of the individual and help form compatibility with others through familiarity. This serves as a foundation to community.

As each incarnation offers growth opportunities, the physical experience communicates levels of development and ascension to the essence. This illuminates a path filled with experiences that offer spiritual awakenings to reach the deepest level of the soul or energetic essence until a completion of attunement has been reached.

The body, mind and spirit can work in harmony to bring peace to the essence when judgment becomes understanding, forgiveness becomes commonplace, when love finds no conditions, when grief becomes acceptance, when enemies become brothers and sisters, and ultimately when there are no barriers between you and the Highest Power.

To taste the essence of your life, simply allow joy, love, happiness and the highest vibrations to move throughout the body like the tides of the ocean. Know that an ebb and flow represent balance and wholeness around your experience as integration into your essence and as a reward for your efforts to embrace your place in the world today.

I went deep into thought around an interesting subject on Sunday, and the line of thinking was directed at memory and how it relates to the journey of the soul. My personal experiences as a medium indicate a type of remembering occurs in the spirit-world.

Then there is déjà-vu, a hard-to-define concept that almost everyone has experienced. A type of remembering that occurs in the present moment. Future predictions come to a person in the form of images or a movie that plays in the mind's eye. Is this a type of remembering of the future? Some dreams carry prophecy to a whole new level (tee hee) and could explain the phenomenon of déjà vu.

But beyond the physical examination and for those who believe in the spirit or energy having eternal life, what about memory from beyond the veil? Can memory take on another form that is beyond the physical sense and the human mind? I believe there is intelligence in the spirit world which mirrors the human mental process. This would imply that our spirit holds intelligence that is completely separate from the brain.

In this moment, I am feeling like a mystery within my being has been spotted, and awareness will only deepen the eternal memory of my soul. I will kindly ask the angels to whisper a message that my soul will never forget.

The body is the vehicle by which energy travels in order to experience love in a dimension, where everything slows down. The human journey in simple terms is the manifestation of the soul taking time to smell the roses. Information contained within this reality becomes an imprint on the essence of the soul with specific needs being met.

You are walking in the footprint of lifetimes past, present and future. You walk because you remember, but not on a conscious level. If you exposed memories during your physical incarnation of all your experiences throughout eternity, your system would become overloaded with the minutia of details surrounding the way your soul arrived with a teaching in place.

As the soul aligns beyond the need for a physical incarnation, energy that is eternal will hold an engrained pilgrimage in the sacred light of love. Inside a collection of fond experiences, there lives a vibration that lifts the Cosmic Heart of love into the most elevated perspective to ultimately become one with the Universal energies.

There is a moment where time seems to stop as a flavor or taste triggers a memory. This type of experience can emit from the intelligence of the soul as it transfers information from beyond a conscious memory.

Many thanks to Georgia for sending in a word suggestion for this week's Angel Whispers. I was looking for a fun word connected to joy, and here it is in my email inbox! I am feeling very connected to this precious word that gets such little attention.

Exuberant: *1. extreme or excessive in degree, size, or extent. 2. joyously unrestrained and enthusiastic. 3. produced in extreme abundance .*Wow, joy and abundance in the same meanings makes this my kind of word.

What comes up for me immediately is the idea of a 'motivational speaker.' The motivation usually comes from inspiration with their story or delivery of an idea. In the end, it is their experience and not yours. But exuberance is infectious and I am sure that most of you have experienced a speaker that believed in what they were saying with such enthusiasm that they somehow moved you with their words. I would love to be known as an exuberant angel reader and speaker!

In Doreen Virtue's *Ascended Masters* Oracle cards, the Power of Joy card says "of all the emotions, Joy has the highest energy vibration. Joy has the power to remove all obstacles and attract all your needs." Exuberance feels like the passion behind the joy and the motivation that keeps you searching for it.

I wonder about the translation that the angels make when you are vibrating with exuberance. I would have to think that love and a zest for life come through with that message of joyous vibrations to the Divine. I now wait in extremely joyous passion and anticipation of an Angel Whisper on the word *exuberant*:

Angels pick people with exuberance to spread the words of truth, light and love. In the highest vibrations of the Prana, there exists a seed of light that grows with the Human Spirit. In this seed lies the Power of the Divine to spread joy through exuberant expressions of love.

To find your exuberant Self, you must first release the negative judgments about who you are and why you are here. The exuberance of a child comes from the clearing of the soul and a life with the layers of a social structure that are removed. The pure essence of a child is exuberant joy and love without obstacles. Setting an intention to experience the joys in life will help you return to the child essence and the core of your existence.

You can train your body by introducing the wisdom of knowing exuberance. By closing your eyes and thinking of anything that you are passionate about, you can message your body that these are the vibrations that enhance joy, beauty, love and life itself.

Feel the excitement that fills the body with joy and be a witness to the passion of the soul. This will release the Higher Self to seek and experience joy without obstacles, love without fear, forgiveness without anger, and passion without attachments. Like everything you face in your life, the choices are made with your free will and the freedom of the mind, body and soul.

This word appeared in last week's *Whisper* and then took me away into deep thoughts on my morning bicycle rides. To me, this is a state of beings that your mind cannot support all alone. It takes the body or heart to support and hold this emotional response to life. I have been 'building' faith for the past few years. I've always had it, even though I might have misplaced it from time to time.

I went on my own spiritual quest at the age of sixteen, first going to bible studies followed by attending different churches. I ended up in the First Baptist Church of my small hometown. During that period of my life, I attended a rally at the local football stadium to hear Billy Graham speak. I was 'saved' that night by the inspirational words.

I set an intention right then to try to live my life like Jesus. I soon found that I didn't really resonate with the fear-based teachings of that particular church. My last day there was when the minister hurried through his sermon and ran out of the building, saying he had to get home for the Dallas Cowboys' game. As I came out on the steps of the church where we were usually greeted by this spiritual leader, I heard tires burning rubber. I turned to see the smoke of spinning tires on his Cadillac as he drove from his special reserved front-row parking spot.

So I left the church. I became a big Dallas Cowboys' fan as I worked and watched football on the weekends. I soon became a carpenter, and did remodeling and restoration on old houses for the next thirty years. I tried to be honest and treat people with respect as I strongly adhere to the 'Golden Rule.' Then this last year, I started creating my new life as a healer. I started my 'encore career' as an ATP© and crystal healer.

Recently, I had the epiphany that decades ago I set the intention to live like Jesus and now I can say that I tried the best that I knew how. I have carried the faith from those days forward to today. I may have misplaced it at times when I made mistakes, but I never lost it. *Faith: 1. a believing without proof; trust; confidence; reliance.* Will you join in faith on this week's whisper?

Faith is the true power of Source. The belief in the unknown is a power that mankind has used for centuries to achieve great wonders on the Earth. Faith can move mountains. Mountains can inspire faith. Do you see the circle of energy that is created?

Faith is a key ingredient to life. Do not allow expectations to color your faith. When this happens, you have enabled your ego to take the place of your faith. This will take a mountain of faith and reduce it to rubble very quickly.

When you carry faith in your heart that the positive aspects of life are here for you, then they will be. The same goes for faith in the negative. The bubble of light that you surround yourself with is the energy connected to your faith.

When you make faith a building block for your life, you will weather all storms. When you make faith your foundation of life, you are a pillar of courage and strength. This is the power of faith when held in the serving light of the human spirit. Handle with care!

My thanks go out to everyone who responded to last week's whisper on 'overglowing,' a word that I made up (lol). The different words that each person shared from their invented vocabularies were quite entertaining, like Pam's 'fishmeckled' which means "out of sorts." Of course it does, Pam!

*The alternative word **fall** is now mostly a North American English word for the season with traces to old Germanic languages. The term came to denote the season in the 16th century, a contraction of Middle English expressions like "fall of the leaf" and "fall of the year." **Autumn** is nonetheless preferred in scientific and often in literary contexts while the word 'fall' can have several meanings as a verb or a noun.*

In my November travels, I witnessed the glorious fall season in Kona (Hawaii), Tulsa (Oklahoma), Dallas, Waco (Texas), Ruidoso (New Mexico) and of course Austin. Each time zone brought a particular beauty to the eyes with its own unique perspective. I can honestly say that in the month of November, I was lucky to witness the vibrant colors that are always found in these nature showcases in the fall. From the deep blue ocean filled with canary yellow angelfish against a black lava rock, to the burnt orange sunset that illuminated the pink and purple clouds on the distant frontal wave, the colors of the fall of '08 left lifelong impressions with me.

I will now gently and with gratitude ask the angels to let a whisper fall into my ears with love and profound meaning in order to color our lives like autumn leaves:

The harsh situations that are always with you on your life journey can raise filters of protection for those that choose to limit their view. Filters can be serving, yet they can detract from the human experiences. With eyes fully open, the colors of nature and fall can impact the soul in ways that are unimaginable. This speaks to the power of free will.

Every season brings great reminders and knowledge about change and the acceptance of movement. With every ending, the completion of a cycle heralds great new beginnings. This is a benchmark for life itself. The new leaves of springtime are a return to new life and abundance after a dormant period that follows the loss of foliage. The dormant period is time for the land to rest and the seeds of time to be sown into the stars.

This moment in the history of man could be referred to as 'fall' in more ways than one. In the depth of wars, anger, persecution, global pollution, poverty and disease, there is a growing unwillingness to accept these as a conscious choice. This is the way that social structures shift and purge to bring in the new thoughts and ideas.

The strongest tree on the planet began as a seed in the soul of Gaia. If you can believe that the Mother Earth is a single growing and moving organism, then seeing the vibrant colors of fall through the lens of pure love becomes a way of life. In this light, the painter and the painted become one in the landscape of art, where there is no imitation needed, regarding the prospect of life.

The other day, I was leaving a parking lot near downtown Austin. I drove to the end of the alley to enter a busy street. On one side of my vehicle was a man who appeared to be homeless. He wasn't very clean, he had a large pack on his shoulders and he looked like he had consumed a few drinks. Let's call him John.

He looked across the hood of my truck and started waving at a man on the sidewalk to my left. This man looked very similar in nature. Let's call him Jack. John crossed in front of my vehicle and went over to Jack and gave him the biggest bear hug that I have witnessed between two men in a while. It warmed my heart.

Traffic was heavy, so I had time to observe the reunion of the homeless souls. It was getting a little frustrating to wait so long to get onto the busy road, but then it happened.

In the blink of an eye, Jack waved goodbye to his friend and stepped off the curb to cross the street. He never even glanced to his left at oncoming traffic. Terror struck me as I thought I was about to witness a life changing event.

A car was racing up so fast, that there was no way he could stop. As Jack's life flashed before my eyes (LOL), John grabbed Jack's backpack and pulled him back to the sidewalk. Jack nearly fell over backwards from the sudden shift of momentum. They both stood there laughing. I don't think Jack even realized the danger. He may have reasoned that John wanted another hug. From my perspective, John had just saved Jack's life. Time for a whisper:

Fate is the overlapping energy that makes up your free will. Your chance meeting with someone is therefore, your fate and no coincidence. What you call future events, are determined by the moment to moment choices that make up the completion of the circle or wave form that is set in motion. Wherever these points intersect, is the climatic conclusion of energetic channeling through free will and choice.

What can be a collision course, can also be a once in a lifetime moment of sharing complete love and harmony. The meaning of life is to experience unconditional love at the primal level of your existence, the eternal soul. This is your fate.

If you want to control of your fate, you must surrender the thoughts of others for those that are yours. This is how your inner voice will guide you down the path of light. In this light, you will discover that you have very little control over your fate. Yet, you will also discover that there is a flow of energy that surrounds the living light. Here you will find Source and connect with the true nature of your fate.

When you release the fear of the unknown such as your fate, you surrender yourself to true faith. This faith in a Divine Order of life is inherent in all of mankind. It is up to you to evolve as a people holding this faith. If this message is unclear, stare into the eyes of a child or listen to their laughter and you will receive.

Maybe some of you experienced this on Friday night. Some may have even paid for the pleasure of experiencing fear! Even beyond Halloween, there are several areas for all of us to focus on that bring fears. Then we get into controlling fear and a good follow-up to last week's whisper on 'control.'

Fear is an emotional response to threats and danger. It is a basic survival mechanism occurring in response to a specific stimulus, such as pain or the threat of pain. Psychologists John B. Watson and Paul Ekman have suggested that fear is one of a small set of innate emotions. This set also includes joy, sadness, and anger. Fear should be distinguished from anxiety, which typically occurs without any external threat. Additionally, fear is related to the specific behaviors of escape and avoidance, whereas anxiety is the result of threats which are perceived to be uncontrollable or unavoidable.

It seems like our world has turned to fears for motivation, blame and control. When I was younger, there was more emphasis on hope, integrity and determination from the leaders of that time and within our society as a whole. Currently actions and reactions out of fear seem to fuel a worldwide energy that rules the decisions of entire countries.

Fears attach unhealthy cords that can lead to emotional and health problems, so it is important to reject fears with an unwillingness to carry them forward. Maybe we can get more insight into this primal emotion with a fearless attempt at an angelic channeled message that I call a whisper:

Fear is an emotion that can bring balance to your state of mind and this is why you have probably heard the expression 'a healthy dose of fear.' Think of the human experience without fears and you will better understand the meaning to which I playfully refer.

You have witnessed incredible acts of courage throughout the history of mankind that illuminate the accomplishments that are possible when you momentarily suspend thoughts of fear. In these moments of conscious choice, it is faith that draws you into the actions associated with overcoming fears.

If you want to master your fears and build faith with intention and purpose, know that everything is Divine and give away any concerns to the Highest Power. Acknowledge any fears with honor to your heart for bringing focus and serving your soul. As you take a moment for acknowledgment, you lay the solid foundation for the rejection of that which does not serve.

Turn the energy of fear into the excitement of opportunity to grow and experience something that is bringing clarity to your existence. Fear is the gateway to faith, courage, love, understanding and everything you desire to be in life. Without fear, there is only an opening into the mystery of your soul, the mastery of your life and the everlasting energy that turns seeds of inspiration into your dreams.

I find out when I am asking people to forgive, they are usually quick to say they can carry out such a simple task. But often they return with "I don't know how to forgive, can you show me how?" It seems like forgiveness is something that should be in the most basic teachings, maybe first grade (LOL). But in fact, the dictionary can't even describe this one word. 'The act of forgiving' is the Thorndike-Barnhart description, and when you go to forgive you will read 'give up the wish to punish or get even with'.

When the focus turns inward toward you, it gets even more complicated. I usually get "I don't know if I can forgive myself" as an answer to this question, so I usually follow with "that is a good honest answer". This was my answer to the same question when I went down the path of healing.

Each of us knows the difference between right and wrong. So when we commit an act that our soul has determined is wrong, the reaction is usually one of two things; we justify the action in an attempt to make it right or we bury it away in the depths of our existence. So to forgive ourselves feels like we are making another assessment of the right or wrongness of the action.

Actions are unforgivable and this where we get stuck. People that commit a murder for example are sometimes forgiven immediately by the victim's family. I believe this is due to the fact that there is no gray area in this scenario as far as whether the action was right or wrong. You either have the power to forgive the soul or you don't.

I needed more of a shout than a whisper with forgiveness;

You hold the world in your hands and you have been shown this to be true. You are a child of God and worthy of forgiveness, especially from yourself. Could you forgive a child? See the footsteps of the jogger in the sand on the beach. They line up with one step in front of the other. That is you and your journey of life. You are all alone in this journey, just like the footprints in the sand, yet you are one with the Universe.

Last night you danced on the beach as you raised your arms to the heavens. You formed a hole to look through with your hands and one by one you framed the stars as a witness to the glory of your world. This glory can be found in the act of forgiveness.

Forgiveness doesn't condone the actions of another. It just means that you are no longer willing to carry the painful and toxic anger within your body and mind. It is your decision whether or not to free yourself of the weight of the forgiveness burden. In this way, the people in need of your forgiveness are your greatest spiritual teachers.

When you invalidate a wrongful act by simply ignoring the problem, you have just affirmed it as one of your problem. Through discussion with others and talking through the issue, you will be better able to forgive yourself and others.

Don't forget to ask for help with forgiveness, the angels are really good at this!

Freedom is the quality or state of being free or the absence of necessity, coercion, or constraint in choice or action. Independence can speak to the quality or state of being exempt or released, usually from something onerous such as freedom from care. Bertrand Russell once said, "Freedom in general may be defined as the absence of obstacles to the realization of desires."

In the past few months, a recurring theme has been key poignant moments that define freedom. I am sure that everyone is interested in some type of freedom, such as financial freedom, freedom form worry, freedom from pain or freedom from those nagging voices in your head (tee hee)!

Sometimes I wonder if I would know true freedom enough to fully recognize the energy and feelings of independence. I am thinking that maybe freedom is felt below the surface of other emotions and therefore difficult to discern. The feeling of relief might be one of those surface emotions that you just feel as positive and move past the conscious association with being freed from a situation or belief. Once freedom is felt, I am sure it is hard to give up and therefore may create several lessons on the path to freedom.

Let's see if the angels have insight to be found in a whisper on freedom:

Most people who feel separated from feelings of freedom or trapped in a situation are really expressing difficulty in seeing the truth. Truth really can set you free, if you are willing to create freedom in your world. Life presents a whole matrix of tricks which gives everyone ample opportunity to find the contrast they need on their journey to freedom. Your willingness to see the truth and to feel the love that is available to you is all you need to position yourself in the various avenues that lead to freedom.

Freedom from attachments can define a healthy lifestyle and does not eliminate compassion, respect and deeper feelings of love, but instead firmly anchors those feelings in the essence of your freedom. From that position of detached love comes a Divine flow of energy that allows a release from control, shame, guilt and illusions. At your core is the highest form of spiritual freedom, and when your spirit feels free, you can soar on the wings of your heart and fully express and experience love in the world.

In the depths of your soul, there is a yearning for the feeling that propelled you into this life. Complete freedom to choose an existence that is in your truest alignment is a vibration that your soul knows well. Don't limit yourself in any way that might form a separation between you and your spirit; instead, create a flight that soars in the vibrations of freedom. Self-love, love for your fellow human, love for the Earth and love for life itself all converge in a space that contains your highest measure of personal freedom and a stream of light between you and the Highest Power.

On the breath on freedom, your story of never-ending truth is communicated as a gift of acceptance to the Universe.

Okay, so this is two words, but they are used together quite frequently. I had a reading this week where the ideas and thoughts behind these words propelled me into deep thought regarding their meaning to me and others.

Some spiritual scholars will have you believe that our destiny is predetermined right down to every minute and every action. I guess I believe that to some extent. But what if you get off your path? Can your destiny be altered? Or can someone's free will interrupt another's path? I have a hard time believing that it is someone's destiny and life path to have their life taken by a drunk driver, or be in the path of a tsunami.

Free Will: 1. the belief that a human being's choices are or can be made freely without external constraint. Today, Beckie and I made several decisions in a fifteen-minute span that had profound effects on our path. It all started over our free will to go to lunch. Instead of eating at home, we decided to go to a favorite place on the east side of Austin. This had us driving in that direction.

We needed to get a letter in the mail and as Beckie held the letter; we turned down a street and by chance spotted our mail carrier still in the neighborhood. We circled the block and gave the letter to our mailman, who was still in the same spot talking to a worker in the front yard of a neighbor's house. He smiled as he took the letters and then the man behind him walked up to the car. The worker that our postman was talking to was a long-lost friend and someone that I had hired for a job fifteen years prior. We had the best conversation that resulted in some interesting spiritual exchanges. Then we traded phone numbers and in effect reconnected.

Our free will led us straight into this chance meeting that was an analogy for 'it's a small world after all.' The entire event could have gone in any direction. Now I will use my free will without any constraints to receive a message from an external source that I call a whisper:

Mankind is one of the only groups of beings in the Universe and across the Galaxy that has been given the gift of evolving with free will. This creates a resistance to ascend into the loving beings that lie in the soul of man.

Free will places an uncertainty in the face of destiny. There is a roadmap to each life path that is determined in the moment. Therefore your future is determined in the present by the choices you make.

In the absence of free will exist an uninterrupted flow of energy that leads to the Divine. By receiving the gift of free will, man has chosen the path of greatest resistance, making the life experience full of drama, uncertainty and challenge beyond the realm of knowing.

When you control free will and ego with the use of Divine Source, the flow of Prana (life force) quickens by dissolving fears and expectations. This leads to ascension into the light of love through acceptance and understanding.

The word *tithe* is derived from the Old English word *"teogoþa"* meaning tenth, and refers to a voluntary contribution, or a tax or levy given to support a religious organization or clergy. Specifically, this was an amount set at ten percent of one's annual earnings. Today, tithes (or *tithing*) are normally voluntary and paid in some form of currency, whereas historically tithes could be paid in kind, such as agricultural products.

Some interpretations of Biblical teachings conclude that although tithing was practiced extensively in the Old Testament, it was never practiced or taught within the first-century Church. Instead the New Testament scriptures are seen as teaching the concept of "freewill offerings" as a means of supporting the church.

I like the sound of that expression much better, probably because it feels more attached to the Soul than the Church. I believe in tithing or freewill offerings as a way to give and enhance the flow of energy around me. Maybe the angels are playing a trick on me to write about giving at a time when there is so much focus and fear around the economy! Oh well, I will go along with it (tee hee).

In my attempt to keep a well-defined and healthy perspective on freewill offerings, I may have over-analyzed. Because I work with energy a lot, I believe my offerings are more in the vein of agricultural products. In other words, I give back some of the energy that I have farmed in the back space that I lovingly call my Sacred Room. I freely give a portion of time, energy and money to my family, friends and community in order to have that experience in my world. I will now ask the angels for a freewill offering:

When you stand in the image of creation, your nature is to give. This is your spiritual connection with everything that is Holy or Sacred in your life. This feeling of giving has a direct relationship with joy, love and happiness.

It is important for you discern tithing for yourself. An unbalanced flow in the area of giving can lead to or re-enforce blocks in receiving. Without balance in life, inner peace and harmony can seem illusive, energy levels can drop, relationships can suffer and the Lower Self has a voice in an area where there once was none.

Self-imposed rules about freewill offerings are nothing more than the voice of the Lower Self building paradigms. The slow evolution into these structures creates barriers that will take a conscious effort to remove, therefore it is important to review this area of life on a regular basis.

A freewill offering of energy can take place in the blink of an eye with wide-ranging effects, so don't underestimate your power in this area. The ultimate source of movement of energy through tithing comes in the mirror as a reflection of God, Divine Source and Universal Oneness. This is where true balance occurs and the richness of life is felt at a Soul-satisfying level. As you look into the mirror, the eye becomes the window to your Soul, and inside this landscape you will find the essence of your freewill offerings.

Friendship

To all my friends, this word study was sparked by a situation that developed with a client, so just relax. I was amazed at the words that were examined by thinking about friendship: Trust, love, manipulation, honesty, jealousy, balance, needs, expectations and a plethora of emotions. Wow, a row of whispers!

I work with several people that tell me they have no friends, and this is a social statement in itself. Everyone is so busy with life that there is less and less time to develop a friendship and keep it in balance.

With friendship comes intimacy, which is something that I crave in all of my relationships. True love and intimacy sometimes seem as elusive as community and a society in harmony with our very existence. If you have two people, and one is a taker and the other one is a giver, it is just a matter of time before that relationship is out of balance. Yet a true friend is one that stands beside you no matter what, right?

Doreen Virtue, one of my greatest spiritual teachers, told a story during my ATP® training about one of her friends. Every time she saw this friend, she would pour out her problems to Doreen in a way that felt as if she was expecting a fix. Doreen started to avoid her until one day she ran into the woman at the grocery store. Doreen had to tell her that she could not be her friend, in order to maintain her own integrity and speak the truth. As she tells it, this friend was a little shocked at the realization that she was doing something that was crossing boundaries.

Friendship is a state of being a friend, and according to the dictionary, a friend is a person that likes another and who favors and supports that person. As we move into this new age of Aquarius and find ourselves in the 'decanate' (first 10 degrees), we are being forced to look at ourselves to see who we really are. Therefore as friends, we become a mirror, which can easily trigger all the words in the first paragraph along with this whisper:

Friendships are the basis for all relationships. Even as an infant, parents should know who the child is first. It is the balance between friend and parent that determines the depth of true intimacy. Understanding without judgment is a quality of friendship.

If you will strive in all relationships to be a friend first, you lay down a foundation that serves mankind and begins the ebb and flow. As in all of life, it is this flow that will emerge as peace for the planet and create a community.

True friendship is a dialogue that leads to communication between souls that you refer to as enlightenment. It is because of this aspect of human development that you have made the connection with the new age.

Instead of allowing yourself the freedom to simply turn off this connection, speak the truth from your heart and strengthen the relationship. As in nature, there is a season for everything. Now is the time to see how deep you can go and who your friends really are. Don't abandon them; just have clear boundaries that build trust, respect and balance. This will feel soothing to your spirit as you find out who you are instead of mourning for the loss of what could have been.

Yoga for Body, Breath and Mind: A Guide to Personal Reintegration, by A.G. Mohan with foreword by Shri T. Krishna-Charya, describes **functional integration** as *something that exists when the energy flow in one's system is in order. When our energy is focused we become centered and integrated. We can affect the state of this energy flow through what we eat, our personal disciplines and habits, the behavior of our senses, particularly through our breath.*

Part of my life involves empowering people with messages of love from the angelic guides, designed to bring awareness and illumination around truth. This can lead to reflection, release, shifting paradigms and psychological integration of beliefs. The idea that breath plays a key part in functional integration might be something that some of us can easily overlook. Yet the release of old thought patterns, addictive and destructive behaviors, structures of belief systems and toxic emotions begins with awareness in the body that surrounds the basis to all of life found in each breath.

I often witness an initial struggle emerging with change and the functional integration of energy that is in true alignment with the body, mind and spirit. In most cases, making big changes in life requires a slow and methodic removal of layers of resistance formed over a lifetime. Without the complete integration of the energy that helps us function at our best, the mind can become disturbed. Disharmony in the body and breath can result in the absence of this energy. Let's integrate a word from the angels on this deep internal conversation between the body and spirit:

If you can say that things aren't going well for you, this could be your signal that there is a need for discernment and awareness that will reach the deepest levels of the body. At the cellular level, there exists a need for energy to flow in harmony, and this could feel disruptive on the surface.

Illusions and focus with an attachment to outcomes can rest on the surface and form a comfort zone that supports your belief. Resistance to change can mirror beliefs that there is safety in complacency and heartache waiting for you outside stagnant energy. When you integrate feelings of love, joy and happiness into the basic functions of your essence, a truth will shine and illuminate the heart.

The challenges of life exist for your growth and development as a way to heighten the experiences of unconditional love while allowing for your free will, dignity and respect to stay intact. The satisfaction that evolves through your personal journey creates the energy of strength, resolve and true love for the Self.

As you expand your lungs and breathe in every experience in life, you are choosing the beliefs that you will hold on your path. When you decide to make changes and aspire to discover the highest vibration of your being, you may be required to release the breath of past illusions, social beliefs, the thoughts of others placed upon you, and any resistance to receiving Divine love and light.

Many of you may think that I ask the angels a burning question that I or the other Whisperees (tee hee) have proposed. That does happen occasionally, but generally I get direction from angelic energy. If I choose a subject that doesn't fit the times or the moment, I just don't 'feel it' in the writing process. It is definitely a partnership that opens a channel, similar to dialing up a radio station to find music that draws you into movement.

The subject today is one chosen by the angels and delivered to multiple clients, which got my attention! So without further adieu, let's get a whisper on this wild future!

The future holds variables that are challenging to forecast, which makes it easy to intuit fear when facing the future. What might be defined as a difference in today's world is that mankind has reached a level in the evolutionary process where mapping is giving way to individual creation in the formation of new and uncharted pathways to love.

Energy from Source is currently in a state similar to that held by the responsible parent. The child has grown to maturity, and the knowledge has been handed down like a precious gift. It is time to let go and see how the child does on their own, knowing that supporting features remain true and viable within a bond of love that can never be broken.

You are now firmly in the director's chair as you orchestrate the movie of your life, and the choices you make will have an immediate consequence as you move from scene to scene. You get to create happiness through choices, love through expression, energy through movement, healing through art, and completion of a life process through intention.

We use the word 'wild' so that you may understand the guidance for flexibility, for cutting unhealthy ties to outcome, for finding humor and irony in the transformational changes that everyone will face, and for the love from Spirit that is eternally present. How you prepare for the future will lay the groundwork for your experiences, and the way you view life will allow you to align with the higher levels of Consciousness needed in a future so wild.

Personal responsibility and integrity of the soul will be your springboard into the coming flight. If you were a bird, would you refuse to fly? The world is your gallery and the Universe is your doting Cosmic parent! Feel your future by living in the highest vibration while loving the human experience at the deepest level of intentional living, and your future will be wonderfully wild!

In many human societies, the act of mutually exchanging money, goods, etc., may contribute to social cohesion. Economists have theories regarding the notion of a gift economy.

A **gift** or **present** is the transfer of something, without the need for compensation that is involved in trade. A gift is a voluntary act which does not require anything in return. Even though it involves possibly a social expectation of reciprocity, or a return in the form of prestige or power, a gift is meant to be free. By extension, the term **gift** can refer to anything that makes the other more happy or less sad, especially as a favor, including forgiveness or kindness.

When I read this definition, I think of the natural feelings that occur when someone gives us a gift and we have nothing to give in return. I don't ever feel like I am giving something in expectation of receiving a gift in return, yet that feeling exists. I think most people are basically the same and enjoy giving.

In this season, a lot of attention is focused on giving. What would people say to a note or card that expressed a gift of forgiveness, understanding or love? I personally wish that the attention to the retail sales aspect of the season would disappear and be replaced by the gift of cookies!

My gift to all of you this season is my thanks and my love for your support and kindness in 2007. With this I also include my blessings and best wishes for the upcoming year. May we all be contributors to the spiritual gift economy. And now I will receive and pass on the gift of an angel whisper:

When you give a gift without attachments, you are then able to receive the same. This is the mark of balance in the individual and spreads through society. A gift from Source can be accepted in this way. There need not be any bargaining.

To give is the ultimate mirror of creation and the eternal expression of life. The gift of forgiveness is returned many times, even when the reception is less than your anticipation. There is a ripple effect that reaches everyone who is willing to acknowledge it.

Remove all ego judgments from the process and you will open the full measure of your gift. Those who reject a gift are allowing the ego to interfere with the life process. Be gracious in all aspects of giving and receiving so you will truly feel the effects.

A gift in the moment of need is the Divine energy that moves the human spirit. Pay attention to Nature and witness the way gifts are given and received to fully realize the true essence that exists. Then you will feel the gift of Source and the joy of life itself.

Goals or Intentions?

One of my readers asked the question, "What is the difference between goals and intentions?" She is such a beautiful person I was lured into the curious world of wonder around the words and language we use. Plus I'm married to her and thought I had better get on it (tee hee)! Besides, it is the time of year when we focus on our resolutions.

Intention might be defined as *an anticipated outcome that guides your planned actions and forms new patterns.* While goals could be defined as *the state of affairs that a plan is intended to achieve and that (when achieved) terminates behavior.* According to Diana Scharf Hunt, "Goals are dreams with deadlines."

My thoughts around this discernment are that goals can focus on physical manifestations while intentions are connected to your spirit. The way we position and carry ourselves as we reach for our goals or the purpose behind the goals might speak toward the intention.

Obstacles might slow our achievements or prevent us from reaching our goals, yet our intentions stay intact and in some ways may guide us. The action steps taken toward reaching goals can be influenced by our intentions, like staying on a path that keeps us in integrity. Let's set an intention to receive information from the angels and reach for the stars that are sprinkled amongst the goals:

Your intentions should bear little focus on the outcome as the journey is more in the spotlight than the destination. Intentions connect you with your spirit in a way that can guide you with respect to action steps around reaching goals. There is a lot of information available that might lead you to believe that you can simply close your eyes while sitting on the couch and attract everything you need. In truth, it is your total participation that attracts those things you wish to create in life and fulfills your goals.

The best approach to this creation is having a range of goals and intentions that include small and large benefits or, better yet, that build on each other to create a higher possible outcome and benefit to others. When your goals are attached to what others believe and if you are basing your projections on how others might receive your actions, then you are vibrating with the lowest human denominator. That is why clarity and vision are essential aspects of setting goals and intentions that fit you and your needs.

If you include serving a higher purpose in your thoughts of goals and intentions, you elevate yourself from the mind that fills with questions around how you might reach that resolution. By clearing away past hurts and false judgments that have supported perspectives that tend to focus on failures, you can break old paradigms and release obstacles that are standing in your way. Integrity will align you with your goals and intentions while bringing peace and contentment that feed the soul. If you must measure your success, be present in the conscious assessment of your reality while simultaneously connecting with your spiritual truth. Take a leap of faith that contains energy with a message that says you need not suffer or sacrifice, then accept that things are really very simple. Teaching only love is the best way to learn!

There is a movie titled 'Doubt' that is a story about a Catholic nun (played by Meryl Streep) who has suspicions about the conduct of a priest (played by Philip Seymour Hoffman). One scene that had real impact on me involved a lesson given to a nun who had fueled some rumors. She was instructed to go up on the rooftop of her building with her pillow and a knife, slash and stab the pillow multiple times, and then return. The visual in the movie was that of thousands of goose feathers filling the streets as they drifted from the rooftop.

She followed the instructions and when she returned, the young nun was told to go out and collect all the feathers from the pillow. "But that would be impossible," she replied. The lesson was to compare the release of feathers to the way gossip spreads, making it impossible to retract.

That evening, Beckie and I watched as a bird lost a feather in flight. The feather drifted to the ground and just before it hit, a small gust of wind lifted the feather back into the air. We watched as the feather took flight and slowly climbed the mountain behind us, until it disappeared over the top. Let's ask the angels to create the flight of a feather with a whisper on gossip:

Like the feather analogy in regard to gossip, you might create a practice that enables you to see gossip as energy. Where does it go and what is its serving nature? Are you spreading energy that will influence another with incorrect information or incorrect thinking, directing energy toward another?

At times, issues need to be addressed and you may need support in your actions. This could require talking to another about the actions of someone who is not present. If this is done with purpose and integrity, motivation becomes supported by the containment of energy. It is always important to get information from the source before coming to any conclusions.

Looking at energy and identifying the leaks as things that do not serve your Divine life-purpose will lead you toward a higher consciousness. Once a person's reputation has been altered, there is great difficulty in restoring the perspective to others. Your discernment around energy is needed to lead others into the light of Oneness.

How you treat each other today will lay the foundation for generations to come. Taking responsibility for yourself creates more freedom than you can imagine. Freedom brings unconditional love, peace of mind, alignment of energies, and integrity of the soul. Breathe deep and be like a feather that climbs the mountain!

Thank God! Thank you for the beautiful day, friends and family, nature and animals, angels and archangels, and everything in the Universe. There, does that cover it? *Gratitude* 1) kindly feeling because of a favor received; 2) desire to do a favor in return; 3) thankfulness. These dictionary definitions seem to fall a little short in the full description of this emotion. Can't you be thankful for things that aren't a favor?

As I studied this feeling, it occurred to me that people who thank God have a central figure to direct their feelings toward. Whereas those folks who believe 'all is one' or that there is a Universal force that drives our existence might be a little challenged about where to focus their giving of gratitude. This is just a guess, but my point is that focus and clarity seem to be big part of the delivery of this package.

The giving of gratitude is something that appears to be a lost art these days. I say that because of my own personal experiences. It seems that teaching your children to not only feel gratitude, but to express it, can be difficult to do, and this may be a social statement.

I know of parents that are teaching their children the art of gratitude. Every Christmas before opening their presents, the children must write a little note to thank their friends and family for bearing gifts. This is not a difficult teaching, so why does it seem like an ingredient that is lacking for so many people?

A close friend taught me a valuable lesson about gratitude. In a moment where the outcome of an event was unclear, my friend stopped and gave thanks to his creator for what he was about to receive. He decided to 'pay it forward,' so to speak. My lesson was complete when he received what it was that he was giving gratitude for. Since my friend is more than twenty years younger than I, the lesson was two-fold in the sense that we can all learn these lessons from each other. Thanks for all who teach me these valuable life lessons. And thank you for the whisper I am about to receive.

Gratitude is the way to honor yourself and others as well as your Creator. When you give gratitude in advance, you have just honored and increased your faith. When you give gratitude in a tough situation, you have just felt a deeper love.

When you give thanks on any level, this is a vibration that emanates from the brain in the same way that prayer does. You have made a conscious decision that allows more room for Spirit to work and help you in your life, and you made it a gift of the heart.

As you travel through the journey of your life, make time to stop along the way and acknowledge your gratitude. If you make amends in this manner, you are allowing a completion of a heart circle that you will no longer need to carry with you.

If you are seeking to bring balance to your life, the act of gratitude is a giving and receiving that brings harmony and love as a gift to your soul! The greatest gift that you can bestow on an individual or Source is the gratitude that you feel.

Last night, I attended a memorial service here in Austin, and I am still processing from that event. I guess that's part of my guidance to write the whisper of guilt. Hey, wait a minute.........you see my typo? I was talking about *grief* and in popped *guilt*. Guilt and grief are so often partners in the range of emotions that surround a loss.

But what I witnessed during last night's display of closure was a spiritual teaching from the parents who were laying their beloved son to rest. The two of them led us through a soulful journey into the life of this young man. And they did it in a way that created space for all of us to open to the love that surrounded his beautiful life experience, and beyond.

Instead of the typical sadness and ceremony that often accompany a tragic event like this, there was a feeling that this spirit was now being set free to dance around the room. And I think he did just that. As a medium, I was getting my own strong messages regarding his dance of the soul last night. What surprised me was the number of people who came up to me with their own messages from this young man. Everything from "he is thrilled" to "this is the way he wants it" was said to me by perfect strangers.

Grief: Deep sadness as that caused by bereavement: sorrow. In some ways this word was redefined for me last night. I'm not saying there wasn't or won't be sadness, but the sadness last night was somehow coated with love and a celebration of life as unique and special as this young man. Bittersweet! Angels, a whisper please:

Everything that you ever wanted to say to someone can still be said. The unspoken can become a part of the guilt that holds the grief. So for you to truly honor those that you love, you must turn pain into joy, sorrow into acceptance, guilt into forgiveness and life itself into love without end.

There is a reason that you possess the sixth sense. This is so that everyone can communicate without the spoken word. Sometimes this is the purest form, because it emanates from your feelings and therefore the heart.

The mystery surrounding the journey of the soul is part of the dreams and inspirations of men and women, while the essence of the meaning is without doubt. You truly know another soul when you carry them in your heart. Simply allow them to reside there.

To heal grief, first remove all judgments of self and others. Remove all guilt from the past and present. Then, invite the soul that has crossed into your heart for an exchange of communication. Ask for the answers to all your questions. The message you receive is the true nature of your love and loss delivered from Source. You will then know how you can support this soul and yours as you journey together forever.

This is a word that demands attention, and I am surprised that I don't already have a 'whisper' on its meaning. My job is to help people with their guidance and I often give affirming information with some Divine assistance. I also work with several people who are guided in unusual and inspirational ways to fulfill a life mission.

Guidance means something that provides direction or advice as to a decision or course of action: the act of guiding or showing the way. According to Buddha, "Just as treasures are uncovered from the earth, so virtue appears from good deeds, and wisdom appears from a pure and peaceful mind. To walk safely through the maze of human life, one needs the light of wisdom and the guidance of virtue."

There are usually two sides to every coin and I think guidance is no exception. Ego can affect our inner guidance and lead us astray if we are not careful. Yet Divine guidance is always empowering to the individual, and this feeling can help discern where the information is coming from.

Visions can guide our actions, even if an illusion is being presented, and in this manner we can learn lessons of love and life. I was once guided on a thirteen-mile hike which had several thousand feet of elevation changes. Had I known the truth about the difficulty of the task, I might have declined the invitation, but in the end I was forever changed for the better. Let's tune in for some guidance in the form of an angel that whispers:

Mankind has been guided from the beginning of time in order to arrive at this moment in time. The trials and tribulations of reaching this point in time are not without merit, so judgments on the nature of following guidance do not always tell the story.

Guidance requires an individual to 'tune in' to the vibrations of the body in order to discern the truth around what is serving. Complete resonance with a thought or idea provides energy to move forward in the direction of your divine path. Feeling your way around the truth determines the need, or lack of it, to create action steps around your guidance. In other words, there is no need to repeat the experience if you have already learned the lessons.

In the absence of faith, guidance could lead you on a harsh and painful journey. Therefore, the best guidance is offered inside faith as it teaches you to place the 'how' in the hands of the Highest Power while surrendering to the illuminated truth.

Nearly every aspect of your spiritual life offers opportunities to grow beyond the limits of the mind. Guidance can be affirmed by the Universe when you are not clear about your path or if you are unsure about moving forward with the information that you received. The ancient civilizations used the elders as a source of affirming knowledge, and modern times should present no difference.

What a glorious sound this word has. Definite, confident, even filled with a truth of conviction, yet mysterious and elusive. Some would agree that the meaning of life is in the feeling of this word or emotion. I watched 'Living Luminaries,' last month's featured Spiritual Cinema movie, and the entire film was dedicated to answering the questions that surround this one feeling.

It seems that the consensus among our spiritual visionaries is that true happiness is found in the present. Also, that it is a choice we all make as to whether or not we will let circumstances alter our own state of mind. In order to achieve happiness, we must decide to focus on the positive aspects of our world, live in the moment, and accept that we don't always get what we want out of life.

One of the challenging things about this for me is that when there is silence around me, my mind wanders into one area after another, usually starting with the past. I also find that where my mind tends to wander is toward the painful experiences rather than the blissful, happy moments of the past. If I manage to turn off the past, the future comes to mind. It's no wonder that I feel challenged to live in the present, with so many self-induced mental distractions that I lovingly call 'my thoughts.'

One of the featured experts in this movie is a man who spent two years of his life sitting on a park bench all day every day. By doing this, he trained his mind to turn off all distractions so that he could be totally present with the 'now.' Only then was he able to experience true happiness in the surroundings and events that were outside of his own being, yet part of his existence.

I am trying to achieve true happiness without the dedication of time on a park bench, so I will find other ways to become connected with the happiness in this moment. Swami Beyondananda closed the movie with his words of wisdom and contrary to everything said: "I live in the future, that way I am always one step ahead of everyone else." And now the whisper:

Happiness is part of the reason you are here. The more your spirit feels this emotion, the higher your capacity for love. When you look around at the beauty that fills your world, you will know this to be true.

In the silence of nature there exists a spiritual realm that is filled with happiness. If you seek this, you will find all the answers. In the quiet of a bird's flight, that soul is flying. In the pure happiness of this flight, there is a message to your soul.

As you give gratitude for your life, ask for happiness. If you truly wish to be happy, you must make this a clear focus of your existence. The goal is reached by all who seek. Then you will find the success was in the journey instead of the destination.

The creation of life itself was to receive and reflect the joy, beauty and loving light that reside in the purest essence of mankind. When you look in the mirror and discover happiness, you have just discovered the gift of love from Source. Amen!

What an illusive feeling in our modern world—even the sound of the word seems to illicit a calm voice and spirit. Feel free to speak the word out loud and see what I mean (tee hee)! Even as I start writing, I get the feeling that the angels will straighten me out on this one.

I want harmony in my life, but waiting for the world to bring harmony to me could be a long process that requires a lot of patience. So that thought is telling me that I must create harmony in my life if I truly want to feel and experience peace.

__Harmony__ means compatibility in opinion and action or in the structure of music with respect to the composition and progression of chords. It can also be defined as a harmonious state of things in general and of their properties (as of colors and sounds) or an agreement of opinions.

It all sounds so agreeable, so my new definition might induce me to be in agreement with everything in order to be in harmony with the world at large. Now I am sounding like the ultimate 'yes' man. I think I need a quote to bring balance to my thoughts on harmony. *"Love is the __harmony__ of two souls singing together"* by Gregory Godek gave me the warm fuzzies. How about some more warm fuzzies from a whisper on the sound of angel wings:

Finding harmony in life requires a process of discernment about core truths that are found in every person. Layers of guilt, fears and judgments create a separation from the vibrations of true harmony, so it is up to each person to make choices to better define their solitary path to peace.

If you are out of harmony with the action of others, then you might need to focus on acceptance and self-love as a way to release the negative emotions that hold you back from the flow of life. Being in the flow gives you the greatest chance at finding truth and harmony. Some use meditation, while others use athletic abilities to release that which no longer serves. It is important for you to find resonance in a method of release, for when the body is lacking harmony, illness can manifest.

You might define harmony as something that exists in the energy of love, so one sure way to reach harmony is to find love in all aspects of life. Even if the initial response to a person or situation is not love, you can create change that will illuminate the chance for love to be discovered. Within the darkest emotions of mankind there is a seed of light, so you must find this blessing or at least acknowledge it is there. This will shift the focus to the highest potential and the possibility of the most positive outcome.

Harmony is something that you create. In every storm there is a center filled with peace. Find that center within yourself and make that the foundation upon which you build your life. Don't let others take away your chance at a harmonious and joyous life. Be willing to shine, even if it threatens those around you, and you will become the master of harmony.

Isn't it interesting the way words affect us and to what level a single word can impact our lives? From the literal translation to the self-imposed and sometimes subtle meanings, the effect of words can vary within the interpretation. In addition, other factors like the tone, the look and the feel come along with the word's delivery.

This word is one that I have struggled with from time to time, and so I wanted to get a whisper on the word "healer". A healer could be described as *someone who is skilled in a particular therapy or practice*. Healing is *a natural process by which the body repairs itself.* My interpretation is that the healer is a type of facilitator of that process.

The curative effects of a healing modality or practice can depend on many factors, such as the environment, a person's belief, comfort level with the healer, vibrational energy and trust. My only issue with the label of healer is that it can imply that one person has the power to create or harness a healing energy that in some ways negates any individual's natural ability to heal.

Maybe I need to get over it and accept the aspect that speaks to my abilities to partner with spirit and another person in order help them connect with that natural ability each person possesses. I'm calling all angels to help heal my perspective on healers (tee hee) with a process that I call angel whispers:

Everyone possesses the ability to heal and to be healed. It's not a matter of power or gifts, because there is a natural energy that can occur. The truth is that each person has choices to make, and it is through those choices that you find balance, harmony and an energy that some define as healing.

This awareness that may present itself as the first step toward healing with a downward spiral of energy that is followed by an upward flow. This upward direction of consciousness is treating beliefs and limitations that have been drawn up from the depths of the sub-conscious, and it is that energy treatment that is sometimes facilitated by a healer.

One person's experience with healing energy spreads within a type of global communication, or vibration, to help mankind understand their position in a fast-paced, evolving landscape. The energy of the times is demanding that each person assume their role in evolution, which illuminates individual responsibility toward a global outcome.

If you believe that you are incapable or undeserving of this knowledge and ability, then it will be so. If you accept your role as a healer, then your path will become littered with experience and a witnessing of the greatest time to be alive. Your simple task is to make a choice, and what appears to be the path of least resistance might be a matrix trick that leads you into the school of hard knocks.

I looked at both of my desktop dictionaries and found only heal, which means to make better or to cure. So I would say that healing is the act of making better or the act of curing. Fortunately my own healing arena is filled with people that I can turn to for help and guidance. This in itself has removed the fear and trust issues for myself.

In the search for understanding, I have a new appreciation for the healing qualities of the crystal. I have adopted techniques for using the crystal and different healing modalities from the teachings of Doreen Virtue, Marcel Vogel and my own angelic guides. So I have witnessed several varieties of healing experiences that include my own. Marcel Vogel wanted to teach us to view healing as a normal part of our existence, not as some sort of miracle or extraordinary occurrence.

For the crystal treatment, there are three things that are essential to successful healing. One is a belief in God or the acknowledgment of a Higher Power. Second, healing yourself is possible and supported by your belief system. And the last magic ingredient is love, it's magic because you can add all you want and never spoil the recipe!

The middle ingredient is where some people struggle. I had a client that wasn't totally sold on the concept of healing the self, and this was the beautiful whisper that resulted:

If you had a cut on the arm that was deep enough to draw blood, would you think for one moment that your arm would never heal? Just as your skin can heal the wounds of the flesh, your heart and soul can heal spiritual and emotional wounds.

If you nurture that cut and add your love or the love of others, the healing power is greater. This is true of all healing. When you decide that your healing is no one's business, you slow down the process. It's not until you open up to the process, that healing energies are performing at optimum levels.

When prayer, meditation or similar vibrational activities are engaged, the body can then locate and tune the areas that are in disharmony. As you quiet the active mind, the inner voice is then able to be heard. This brings clarity, trust and insight into the framework of true healing.

When the healing light appears, simply walk the path that is illuminated. Only then in the rainbow of colors, are you walking with the angels and archangels. Emerald green is the spectral color of Archangel Raphael (he who heals). Visualize this light in any area that needs healing and feel the power of the conduit of energy that exists in the realm of the divine. In this manner, you are messaging the body with your intentions of healing

Healing is sending messages to the heart and mind that says you are ready to receive the gift of nature. While the divine gift of nature is your ability to heal.

With everything that I know, my mind seemed reasonably prepared for the eventual outcome regarding my father's death. But my heart was not prepared for something that was obvious to the mind. So how could I prepare my heart? My feelings of the heart encouraged me to release many times in the elevator, restrooms and in my vehicle over that last few months, which must have prepared me on some level.

So maybe it is a trick with a cosmic design that teaches us like children throughout our lives. The only separation between me and my heart comes from within, and that statement could be applied to dreams, truths and my relationship with a Highest Power. Man has made up all kinds of excuses and ideas that evoke a myriad of ways to find limitations, when really we are unlimited in our potential.

The human body is an amazingly complex chemistry system that challenges the best minds on the planet in their understanding of how it works. There are many ways to care for the heart, and I am learning for the sake of my body, mind and spirit. And now a whisper from the heart song of an angel:

The energy of the heart is the most powerful unseen force in the Universe. There are many ancient and modern symbols that represent the heart and the energy of love, togetherness and sexual energy, some that might surprise you. Being in the center of the torso, the heart represents the center of the Universe and the natural order of love.

You will discover that the collective movement of love from each individual is the connection that binds everyone together. The heart energy contains the mystery that life presents, like the unseen force of the Highest Power. This gives freedom to each person to decide the best way to handle their heart. Some need firm boundaries around the heart, while others can be more open to love without fear of judgment.

It is wise to be cautious with matters of the heart, so know your heart well and learn from lessons of love. Those teachings will provide an opening for every aspect of life and give you the expanding experience of self-love. Love, forgiveness, joy, acceptance, understanding and freedom are good for healing the heart, so engage in those regularly.

If you teach only love, you will become the best student of love. When you engage the heart in a balanced way of entering into all your decisions, you will find the loving peace that is part of your Divine inheritance on Earth. Searching to find whatever sings to your heart will illuminate the pathway to upper ethers otherwise know as Heaven.

It is interesting the way each person looks at the future and then connects that view to thoughts and ideas. It is hard to know how to respond to another person or your own views when offered the worst-case scenario as a possible outcome to your ideas and dreams.

There are many professions and lifestyles that require special attention given to outcome, such as gamblers, day traders, developers, tightrope walkers (tee hee) and so on. If a professional gambler went to work each day with thoughts that they were going to lose all their money, I am sure they would.

On the other hand, if we connect with the ideas around experiencing the highest potential from our action steps, then we have directed energy toward manifesting something desired or dreamed about. But how do we resonate with the highest potential without anything short of that appearing as lost opportunities or shattered dreams?

Rusty Berkus once said, *"There comes that mysterious meeting in life when someone acknowledges who we are and what we can be, igniting the circuits of our highest potential."* Let's ask the angels to ignite some of our circuits with a whisper on reaching the highest potential:

Within every stream of energy there is a vibrational resonance with the highest possible potential to any given situation. Free will, the environment, social oppression and limiting thinking create a reality that manifests the perfect energetic response from the Universe. This illuminates a path of higher learning and growth that can be supported by all areas of the human experience.

Projecting the highest potential is serving beyond understanding, as it embodies the ideas and principles around faith-based initiatives. When you allow your body to feel the vibrations associated with the best-case scenarios, you are manifesting or messaging the Universe this desired outcome. Regardless of the outcome, daydreaming or imagining the highest potential gives the feelings of joy and happiness. Repeated offerings of this vibration fulfill the dreams on an energetic level, giving the individual power to accept any physical outcome.

If you are going to the worst-case scenario with every effort, you are denying yourself the true feelings associated with the dreams that you were born to carry. This negatively affects faith through placing obstacles generated by the mind that is supported by ego judgments and limiting beliefs. Faith challenges us to see that everything is in Divine Order, which is realized through your perspective on life.

Would you rather live in the low vibrations around defeat or take flight in the higher vibrations of joy and happiness? It takes only one thought to start vibrations and messages that begin the manifestation of your dreams, intentions, goals and visions of your life. Within every life there is a seed that grows and blooms in the perfection of the highest potential.

The world stage was set for the Verizon Heritage Championship Golf Tournament being played at Hilton Head, South Carolina, and at stake was first prize, worth more than a million dollars. Brian Davis was playing the first hole of a playoff with Jim Furyk to determine the winner. When Davis' ball landed in a rough area, he made his shot and then called himself for violating the rules.

When a PGA official reviewed the video tape of his shot, it was confirmed that Davis had touched a single reed on his backstroke. The result was a two-stroke penalty, which cost him first place and more than $400,000, the difference between a first- and a second-place finish! Although the touch to the reed was almost indiscernible except in slow motion, Davis did the right thing even though he wasn't completely sure of what happened.

The sport of golf is built on the premise that people officiate themselves, and in that light there was nothing unusual with this situation. But to thousands of young people, this man displayed a sense of honesty and honor rarely witnessed in the world today. Some school students claim to have never seen such honesty from an adult!

Role models have let our children down repeatedly over the last few years, and it does the heart good to see a model for honesty. I have to believe that Brian Davis will reap the rewards of his choice many times over for standing in the light of a single moment of truth. Let's see what an angel might whisper on the breath of such honesty:

The world needs examples of truth, integrity, honesty and conscious living. The truth is always known by the heart, and any betrayal of those emotions solicits a response from the Universe. Have you noticed that Karma seems to be instantly delivered in this New Age?

The children of today are bright and clear channels that easily read emotions; therefore, you cannot hide things from them. They will know truth on an energetic level like never before and in a framework that does not allow for compartmentalized justifications. There are no more grey areas, only a chilling barometer that accurately meters truth and lies.

Honesty shines a bright light in a day and time where the truth has gotten lost in a maze of interpretation that spins story after story lacking essential truth-giving information. It is the children who will bring focus on truth and integrity, so engaging in lies and empty promises will have consequences giving way to the larger meaning.

Be honest with yourself and refrain from building illusions. The truth can support a freedom to experience the joy that life has to offer. Honesty begins in the quiet space of your inner self and expands into the Universe with increasing momentum that offers a voice that speaks to the Higher Self and to the process of evolution.

Evolve and ascend on a single beam of light known as your truth, in order to experience the deepest levels of love found in simply being present.

Honor comes from the Latin word honorare and means the evaluation of a person's trustworthiness and social status based on that individual's espousals and actions. It can be viewed as natural that honor is as real to the human condition as love, and likewise derives from the formative personal bonds that establish one's personal dignity and character.

The island traditions are steeped in time-honored practices relating to people and nature. One trip to the airport to head back to the U.S. sure shifted that energy! It seems our culture has lost ground when it comes to respect and honor, compared to the ancient beliefs.

Beckie and I spent time at the "place of refuge" in the National Historic Park named Pu'uhonua o Honaunau, where there are the remains of a thousand-foot-long lava-walled area. According to tradition, if you broke the laws of the culture, which were dictated by the family, you had to swim through the 'bay of sharks' to the place of refuge. If you made it, you were forgiven your misdeeds and allowed to return to the tribe with a 'clean slate.' If not, you were 'recycled,' as the natives put it.

This sacred ground was a small part of the teachings on honor that I received this last week. I might have to write another whisper on this incredible journey, but for now I will unpack my luggage and ask the angelic guides for some insight into the word honor:

Honor is connected to the energy of love. When you honor yourself and others, you bring into focus the sanctity of life on many levels. As you honor yourself, you are better equipped to share your loving energy with others through respect.

To feel honor, simply recognize there is a divine light that shines in everyone and connects you with the Oneness that surrounds you. Meditation, ceremony, singing, dancing and movement of energy are all ways that you can feel honor in the physical. When you honor yourself and others, you are better able to set aside judgments based in ego, and that builds your auric field. This is one of the easiest ways to spread light in the world around you while forming a barrier of protection.

If you want to teach love, start with the basic need that exists within the human experience. How many times have you heard the word love followed by honor in ceremonies like weddings and memorials? This is more than symbolic as it brings to the surface emotions like respect, dignity, forgiveness and a world of positive feelings.

Honor can heal the wounds inflicted by all others, including yourself. Connecting with the Highest Power with honor can soothe the soul, open your heart and bring peace to the planet while connecting to the Universal rhythms and vibrations shared by all of life. If you have lost respect, you can easily find it with honor without swimming through the shark-infested waters of the past.

This has been a buzz word since the last election, and now I see it used everywhere, but what does it mean or suggest? Having heavily engaged in this energy of hope over the past few weeks with respect to an illness in the family, I believe there may be a deeper meaning than mere wishful thinking or positive daydreaming.

Hope can refer to a sloping plain between mountain ridges or a small bay; an inlet; a haven. But hope is generally thought to mean a desire of some good, accompanied with an expectation of obtaining it, or a belief that it is obtainable; an expectation of something which is thought to be desirable; confidence; pleasing expectancy.

Those words 'pleasing expectancy' makes me ponder my own feelings around hope. It is not necessarily healthy to engage in following an illusion, but is there a difference between an illusion and pleasing expectancy? And what is the alternative to feeling hope? I found this quote from Josh Hartnett: *Hope is the most exciting thing in life, and if you honestly believe that love is out there, it will come. And even if it doesn't come straight away there is still that chance all through your life that it will."*

I think we all need and want hope because I believe our fathers before us had to have a lot of hope and courage for all of us to arrive at this moment. *"Perhaps they are not stars, but rather openings in heaven where the love of our lost ones pours through and shines down upon us to let us know they are happy"* is an Eskimo proverb that speaks to the soul and elicits a whisper from an angel:

Manifesting desires, intentions and even miracles comes through the vibrations of hope and the resonance found within the positive projections of the future. The most positive energy of hope springs forward from the depths of your faith as past civilizations held great hopes in the midst of even greater unknowns.

As information has become more available through technology and science, humans have a tendency toward limiting hopes due to what they think they know. This can lead to a breakdown in faith and beliefs, which can create obstacles on the path of illumination. Depending heavily on the mind to find all the answers to life can remove the heart from feeling an unseen truth, causing separation from hope.

Hope can sustain life on a global scale, but it begins with the individual before falling on the society as a collective whole. People can naturally lose hope in the face of challenges, and that is why it is important for the community to help bolster the hope of individuals. Collective hope, joy and love can be spread throughout the society without total agreement on all fronts as long as there is a space held with honor and respect for the views of everyone.

Children are the catalyst for the highest levels of hope and impetus for change. In the eyes of children, your heart can feel hope, your mind can find hope and your soul can express hope. Return to your own childhood essence and you will find that same energy of hope.

Ann McMaster writes in her blog *Life As It Is* regarding the word 'hopium'. "Hopium - a mental drug that dulls down everything I don't want to see and brightens up the least little detail that affirms what I DO want to see; and if there are no clues, I make it up to suit my best-case scenario.

"Symptoms include asking friends what they think; harboring secret doubts, but not telling anyone; defending myself/others to everyone else; exaggerating positive traits, excusing bad behavior, etc.

"Example - I knew in my heart of hearts that this man was Mr. Right Now, and not Mr. Right (for me). BUT, he was so much of what I wanted in a relationship, and I was ready for The Relationship. My Reticular Activating System was true to my visualization and kicked to the curb all data that contradicted my fantasy.

"When hopium wears off and can no longer repel the relentless invasion of reality, there is usually a crash into utter despair, complete with accusations of being a fool, stupid, naive, etc. Then the usual fatal predictions of never having what I really want; and now I can't even have second best, etc."

Well, thanks for that insight, Ann! Is anyone out there addicted to hopium (tee hee)? Maybe the angels can share some insightful energy with a whisper on hopium:

Even faith can override common sense and rational thinking when balance is lost, allowing an unhealthy attachment to outcome to gain a foothold in your energy. There is a fine line that draws the contrasting lights between heaven and earth. On one side of the rainbow are the layers of lower human energies, and just beyond that line are the upper vibrations of heavenly manifestations.

The challenge in making distinction between the two provides many opportunities for you to be tricked into a school of thought. So don't be too hard on yourself. With upward movement of energy, there are always plenty of blue skies mixing with Source energy to create positive motivation. The more you can resonate with the highest potential, the more success you will experience.

The realities of reason are deeply embedded in the matrix of energy in a way that can be easy to overlook. Staying grounded can help with any attachments, but the mental process of knowing the Divinity of every moment rests in the energy of gratitude. Being a gracious receiver of every aspect in the present moment assures the happiest outcome. Support your every move with an underlying current of gratitude, and you will swim in the river of light offered within your reality. When truth prevails, love brings peace.

The *100th Human* title by Chris Fenwick is a play on the 100ᵗʰ-monkey experiment performed in 1950s' Japan. The experiment suggests that if enough beings within a species change behavior, that change becomes available and can be adopted by the rest of the species, no matter the distance between them.

This novel claims that there is one person who can save us from the 3Ds (doom, disaster and devastation), but it isn't necessarily Jesus, Rama, Buddha, Superman, or even the next president of the United States – it's you. As the Hopi Indian Elders say, "We are the ones we've been waiting for."

"The 100th human" puts the responsibility of diverting the worst-case doomsday scenarios squarely on each human's shoulders, and then arms them with the things that are necessary to make it happen. As Chris Fenwick puts it "There are many others out there who are already taking on the role of hero in their own lives, and collectively, I believe we make a profound transformation together."

This week I was a witness to several people saying very similar things. Fears and concerns around our future are manifesting in the form of similar consciousness between people who don't know each other and are separated by great distances. If we are the ones that we have been waiting for, then what do we do? I am going to raise my consciousness and ask for an angel whisper:

It is the role of the individual to take responsibility for their actions while standing for the rights of the less fortunate. As you become the master in your reach for the Higher Self, your example will shift the views and perception of others. By shattering the paradigms of the past, the unity of the future becomes the present reality in the form of hope.

The Christ Consciousness created an energetic shift in the Age of Pisces. Your Higher Consciousness will bring these teachings into an expanding wave of energy that will bring completion to a cycle of human development. Many of you feel this energy in vibrations similar to standing in the Ocean and feeling the water pull you away from the shore, followed by a wave that crashes on the beach, pushing you back. Learn to swim in the ocean of your breath.

A single strand of energy can guide you, protect you, empower you, love you and give you the gift of being at peace with yourself. The Universe is filled with these strands of light, and your connection is the essence of manifesting dreams, desire, intentions, and everything that is found in the kingdom of the Earth.

Divine moments are the stepping stones from one loving strand of energy to another with an opportunity to learn in the space between. In every person there is an Avatar waiting to be revealed in their Divine moment of destiny.

Living a life in the energy of faith, hope, optimism, passion and love is the greatest form of preparation for any outcome.

Would you believe that illusions are often helpful in our lives? Well, maybe this isn't always the case or even the norm, but I have been getting lessons on the illusions that we create and co-create as well as those that others create and the role illusions play in our lives.

*An **illusion** is a distortion of the senses, revealing how the brain normally organizes and interprets sensory stimulation. While illusions distort reality, they are generally shared by most people. Illusions may occur with more of the human senses than vision, but visual illusions, optical illusions, are the most well known and understood. The emphasis on visual illusions occurs because vision often dominates the other senses.*

The term illusion *refers to a specific form of sensory distortion. Unlike a hallucination, which is a distortion in the absence of a stimulus, an illusion describes a misinterpretation of a true sensation. For example, hearing voices regardless of the environment would be a hallucination, whereas hearing voices in the sound of running water (or other auditory source) would be an illusion.*

By that example, I am living an illusion or a series of back-to-back hallucinations (tee hee). I truly hold a belief that supports me when I hear my inner voice, the voice of Spirit or the voice of angels. Maybe we can clear up some illusions with the wisdom and voice of an angel in the form of a whisper:

In order for angels to communicate, it is sometimes necessary to use illusions such as dreams, visions and what some might consider a phenomenon. This alone is the reason to co-create the illusions that become part of the human experience. Without the illusion, the human experience might become predictable and without the willingness to change or experience growth through challenges.

It is in the dreams of others that you will find illusion, yet that is also where you find passion. Inside the energy of love you will find illusion and truth constantly coming together in ways that could not have been expected. That is why we co-create with you even if the illusion is completely false. There is an unknown element that nurtures your future with something that warms the heart.

An illusion that holds you in a paradigm and prevents change is the unhealthy form of illusion. When something is clearly without truth, the illusion is only serving the ego. If there is a glimmer of truth, the shine will make the illusion appealing and possibly serving. If you open to this process, it can bring understanding, forgiveness and love into greater awareness in your life.

What about God, the angels and all that is Divine? Isn't this some form of an illusion by definition? Look at the way an illusion serves mankind to find the truth, and remember it is always the feeling behind the illusion that you can trust regardless of your circumstances or events. This is where you will find the knowledge to move beyond the illusions of life and into the full spectrum of love as you travel the rainbow bridge that takes you beyond your present reality and into your dreams.

In Yoga teachings, the *kleshas* are any of the five hindrances to enlightenment, which are ignorance or *avidya*, egocentricity, attachments, aversions, and the instinctive will to live. Avidya also means incorrect thinking, so it is often referred to as the 'Great Illusion'.

According to Sundara Yoga Therapy, *we usually learn or recognize mistakes through retrospect. To truly perceive, we must know something for what it is not (the impure as pure, unhappiness as happiness, non-self as self). If the mind is in a state that does not allow us to see or accept reality, we may take steps that lead to some form of suffering for us and those who surround us.*

Some people come across as having it all figured out, with every aspect of life in a neat little compartment. This might be to create a feeling of security or safety, for those things may exist in our minds and any departure could signal fears.

Now that I am aware of the kleshas and especially incorrect thinking, I can become enlightened (tee hee)! Did I just form an illusion? Let's see what a whisper from an angel does with the kleshas and incorrect thinking:

Mankind has reached a critical stage in the process of evolution. This process will create the greatest shifting ever experienced in the history of human development. Currently and in the future, species development will not be dictated by governments, countries or corporations. The new paradigms will be created at the individual levels through raised consciousness and awareness that shines light on what exists in the shadow realm.

Through these shifts and changes, an understanding that you are all connected with energy as one will emerge gracefully. The separation that mankind has created supports suffering. Suffering is no longer on the path to salvation, and the need to suffer no longer resonates with the souls that have realized Oneness. Opening to the abundant life that you were born to live is blocked only by incorrect thinking and the projection of an ego-based energy.

With incorrect thinking comes guilt, lack of acceptance, misunderstandings, anger and illusions that separate you from the truth. When you separate yourself from reality, you distance yourself from faith, hope, love and Source energy, God or the Highest Power. The separation that is created as a result of incorrect thinking evokes feelings of being on an island, all alone and without the supporting energy that is available at all times.

When you look at life through eyes of love and without illusions, you are connecting with beauty, joy, correct thinking and every nurturing energetic component that the Universe has to offer you.

Have you ever reached that point where every little decision seems to become monumental or even confrontational? When I was in the housing restoration business, my clients sometimes became affected by what I referred to as 'decision overload', which is the result of making several important commitments in a relatively short period of time.

There are times when some of my previous decisions have me feeling unsure or unclear about moving forward with confident action steps. At other times, maybe I don't think I have enough information to make the best choice. Could some of these things that I have brought up be ways to feed resistance or fears?

Indecision is an adjective defined as hesitant, irresolute, inconclusive or lacking definition. William Arthur Ward once said, "The optimist lives on the peninsula of infinite possibilities; the pessimist is stranded on the island of perpetual indecision." I am usually on the peninsula with the optimists, so how do I end up on the island? Well, let's see if there are some gentle winds that can guide us in a whisper from an angel on indecision:

Most decisions, be it large or small, require a response from your analytical mind and your heart, which then solicits intuition and patience as you engage both sides of the brain to get an answer. When you are out of balance in any area of life or during times of increased stress, decisions seem to be much more challenging. If you think back on times when you made smooth and easy decisions, these might be a reflection on the way things were flowing during that period.

Life flows in cycles and rhythms that can bring forward an increased awareness regarding your current state of affairs. Moving forward with confidence and conviction comes from knowing when to put your best thoughts forward with patience.

The best approach to any decision is to remain open to all possibilities, including those that seem remote, with the intention of being guided into the best one, regardless of your past experiences. You might allow yourself the opportunity to experience your own spiritual growth in the making of today's choices and decisions as you witness shifts in patterns.

Truth always illuminates the path that leads you to choosing your rightful place in the Kingdom of the Earth. Keeping alignment with your core being, standing in the light of your integrity and coming from a place of love for yourself and others will serve your spirit and bring the energy of content in all decision-making processes. Indecision can be a conscious choice, so consider your indecision carefully.

The term **Indigo Children** *originates from the 1982 book "Understanding Your Life Through Color," by Nancy Ann Tappe, a self-styled mystic and psychic, who claimed to possess the ability to perceive people's auras. She wrote that during the late 1970s she began noticing that many children were being born with "indigo" auras. Today, she estimates that 60 percent of people age 14 to 25 and 97 percent of children under the age of ten are "Indigo."*

The Indigo Children are believed to be warrior spirits that have lived many lifetimes and therefore have highly developed gifts. They are often referred to as gifted and psychic with a specific soul purpose to help create change in the world. The largest influx of Indigos came in the mid-seventies with the soul of a volunteer and the heart of the warrior. They have a unique and personal spiritual connection with the Divine and rarely seek knowledge in this area from a religion or structured teaching as Indigos often find their spirituality in nature or Earth-based vibrations.

Generally speaking, Indigos don't fit into the structure of our society. They are here to disrupt and change our current social framework. This is intended to create a worldwide shift in our consciousness as a species and to blaze the trail of conscious change. Indigo children are often diagnosed as ADD or ADHD because of their disruptive behavior.

One of the pitfalls for Indigo Children is addictive behaviors that range from drug use to staying on the computer for hours at a time. They will argue their point to the bitter end, even if they are wrong, as their focus becomes the battle instead of the point. On the other hand, they are leaders and eternally connected to the Crystal and Rainbow children. Indigos can often feel overwhelmed with their individual powers and their large life purpose to literally change the world. I will now listen for the universe to whisper a truth about the Indigo Children:

Archangel Michael is working with the Indigo children to help usher in the Age of Aquarius. For a paradigm shift to occur for mankind, special leaders with great courage are needed. The fight for your species to move up into the next level of ascension depends on the unity of Indigo, Crystal and Rainbow children.

Keep things simple for the Indigo and they will focus on their strengths. You can support them without the struggle by simply understanding who they are and why they are here. The power of the Indigo is as strong as the power of Nature with all the Divine energy they channel from the Earth.

Teach the Indigo love through acceptance and help them change the world. Show them the power of surrender and your ascension will become a balanced movement of cohesive unity. Your gentle loving guidance will be heard and felt by the Indigo above the roar of any battle. A lion doesn't kill in anger as she is acting out her natural instincts for survival. Since the beginning of man, Indigos have walked the Earth. The Indigo brothers and sisters are your partners in evolution. When they plant the seeds of love in the land of change, a new vision emerges within the realm of the human energy. Follow this spectrum of light and you will witness the ends of the rainbow.

One thing I personally regard as a paradigm shift in energy around the close of the decade is that my actions and choices seem to have an immediate response from the Universe. Some might call it instant karma that is specific to me, but from my view it seems to be affecting the masses in much the same way.

In a recent experience, I held back from speaking my truth. The response was immediate, intense and could have been lethal. As someone who helps others follow guidance, I couldn't help but wonder why I didn't give myself the opportunity to voice my feelings. The answer I heard was, "I made up a story about how my voice might be received and that held me static in making the right choice." Remember obstacle illusion (tee hee and ouchy)?

The only way I can hear my inner voice is to silence the meaningless mind-chatter, forget the story, pay attention and really listen! In the moments of decision-making, it seems a little too easy to give up the power that resides within me. This could translate into an unwillingness to leave my comfort zone by dishonoring my true inner voice. I will now place myself in the comforting arms of an angel who whispers information about my inner voice:

It might be important to bring focus to the many voices, besides the one you want to hear from. Each body of energy has a voice. Your physical body holds wisdom and your mind has a voice that sounds throughout the entire body, so accessing the deepest level of your soul takes a focus that transcends thoughts and emotions.

Your higher self is the bridge between the soul and the Divine. The language spoken on that 'bridge' is the most powerful voice in the Universe, speaking from within that space where your true self communes with the Divine. Sacred geometry, music, sound, visions, breath, movement and repetitive thoughts are all words of the same language.

The magnetic field which surrounds the physical body holds the integrity of the soul, and when you invalidate that energy through emotions, thoughts and actions, the bubble that is defined as your aura is disrupted. The disharmony, no matter how great or small, sends a message to the Universe that might signal a call for learning. In order to avoid repeating lessons that do not contribute to your journey, you must proclaim that you are no longer in need. Make this proclamation your clear communication to an energy vested in your best interest.

Listening to the voices from within your field of integrity, following the song that lives in your loving heart, finding the true voice that lifts your breath, surrendering to the wisdom of the soul and finding the center in the present moment are really simple and effective ways to be efficient with your energy.

Speak your truth in the voice that you and others can trust and believe in order to make it your reality.

My friend Craig and I experienced a night of inspiration recently. I discovered the results in the writings of my new book that I am working on, as well as in the writing of my whisper about Discipline. Craig found it when he went home and wrote a beautiful song. Less than a week later, we were performing that song on the steps of the State Capital building for several hundred people. It was a perfect melody with a divine message tailored to that moment. We played it three times for the crowd!

Everyone has experienced an inspirational moment, but how many times have you failed to act on it with such lightning speed or even at all? Once the inspired event has passed, I find it harder to go back and be re-inspired. This is not a judgment as much as a reflective observation on my part.

I was truly inspired to start writing these Angel Whispers, and when I focus on that moment of inspiration, I realize that if I had allowed my analytical mind to take over, nothing further might have happened. *I don't have the time. No one will be interested. What about the expense?* These are just a few of the thoughts that might have stopped me from going ahead with something where the outcome is obscured.

The retrospective on my choice to follow this inspired moment is that I have received several emails and phone calls regarding Angel Whispers. The rewards from just one of these messages have made it all worthwhile in the sense that you never know who will be inspired by one word, one note in a song or even by actions that your analytical mind might see as insignificant. *Inspiration*, a divine influence directly and immediately exerted upon the mind and soul of man.

I am finding that I am inspired by my friends, family and the world around me like never before. Maybe I am seeing things in a different light or maybe inspiration is infectious and ripples out around you in unforeseen and mysterious ways. Maybe a night of conversation can create a change of Universal proportions. And just maybe, inspiration can be as subtle as a whisper:

The fate of mankind has often hinged on a whisper of inspiration. The divine language is universally spoken yet rarely understood. The traps inside the mind can misplace or misguide inspiration. It is when the inspired moment reaches the soul that the true message and motivation are received. Those that feel the inspiration can quickly act on it while others are still thinking about it.

Therein lies the connection between inspiration and faith. Like all divine teachings, the areas of space that hold inspiration, faith, truth and love are often fused together in a way that, when connected, form the foundation of life.

If you want to experience inspiration at the raised vibrations of the divine, then you must open your heart to your own powers of creating change and speaking the truth.
Inspiration lights the pathway to the travels of the soul and can forever change the landscape for mankind.

Admittedly, I am feeling completely inspired these days. There is some connection between opening your heart and receiving this precious emotion that seems to ripple out into the Universe for everyone to grab onto. I often get wonderful email messages from some of you who receive the 'Whispers,' expressing beautifully inspired thoughts.

I love those moments with friends where one of you has an idea and, as it goes around the room, it turns into a life-changing seed of visionary projections. Certain people, music made by some of those people, and random unexpected acts of kindness committed by people, are all inspirational sources for me. There is also that delicious shared experience that happens to an entire group of people, like this week's Hilde Girls® performance where audience, singers and musicians all reveled in the inspirational collaboration and collection of hearts.

*Inspiration can refer to a person who is an idol or someone who has a skill that is desirable. Artistic inspiration can imply sudden creativity in artistic production. An **inspirational revelation** is an uncovering or disclosure of something hidden via communication from the Divine.*

Wow, I just found my first definition of a 'whisper.' That is so inspiring! It must be part of our journey to be inspired and to inspire each other along the way. In some ways it seems like life is an inspiration quest. I am feeling waves of inspirational energy simply by focusing on the subject. Now that's what I call an epiphany, and I will take that as my signal to ask for a whisper of inspirational revelation:

To discern your inspiration while in the midst of a harsh environment requires a willingness to focus on the subtleties of life. Watching the butterfly draw sustenance from a flower will show you the passion that exists in all of nature. In one faint windswept moment, you can breathe in a mystery that will inspire you.

Inspirational revelations are like fuel to a fire. By filling your soul with inspiration, your life force is gaining the energy and vibrations that resonate with the Divine. The source of inspired energy comes from the Highest Power and is filled with light.

Inspiration, passion, and a willingness to believe are some the building blocks that support love. These are gifts and can be received by those who tune into the frequencies of joy, purpose, creating and serving beyond the self. The Entire self is fully present during the full opening of the heart when God and the angels are asked to enter.

If you are walking the enlightened path, let inspirational revelations illuminate the way. The truth that you seek can be found in the space you hold for inspiration. The life you were born to live resides in your heart and occupies the soul waiting to be released. Touch the loving essence of your being with inspiration to know Divine peace and harmony in the Universe. To know love, know inspiration.

"You really are what you think" were the words used by Dr. Marcel Vogel as he concluded a talk in Canada. When I listened to these audio cassettes that are now more than twenty years old, I gained an understanding of how integrity is relative to my life.

It is common knowledge that our brains send electrical impulses to all parts of our body to achieve everything from basic motor skills to deep reflective thought. Every thought that we generate sends an electrical charge to the cells in our body so that they work in harmony to accomplish the intention of this thought. When this thought is out of integrity, the impulses sent to all parts of our body are out of harmony.

Our world is filled with energy from every molecule and every cell that we encounter. It is our personal integrity that dictates how these energies integrate with our being. The more integrity that we have, the more integrated we are, the less these outside energies can affect us. When a person is out of integrity with themselves repeatedly, they are weakening their Electro-Magnetic Field (EMF) to the point that a bombardment of energies is allowed to enter.

Integrity: 1. strict adherence to a standard of value or conduct. 2. Personal honesty and independence. Even the dictionary alludes to the independence from other energies through integrity. The higher the integrity, the less effect the thoughts, energies and actions of others can have on you and me.

Some people even set themselves up by doing things like spending the energy to get a handicapped parking permit. Then every time they use that parking permit, they are ensuring that someone with special needs will not have access. This may seem like a small thing, but I use it as an example of how easy it is to walk the path outside of integrity. The smaller the action, the easier it is to justify. The whisper:

There are major life lessons that each of us must learn. One is integrity. This value is essential in creating a society that lives in harmony. The teachings behind the story of Noah's Ark and the great flood are related to a society that was so far out of integrity that many people lost their lives so the world could start fresh again. One aspect of this story tells us that nature is never out of integrity. So many animals were saved, while entire civilizations perished.

Mistakes in this area are forgivable, but intentionally acting outside of integrity puts the forgiveness on a soul level. There are many gifts of knowledge, including the clear knowing of what is right. There are no guidelines or rules that dictate your measure for this action. Only a willingness to discover the self and therefore the divine, will yield true teachings.

In the purest form of love, you will find truth. The truth holds a space for your integrity. If you seek this space, you will uncover a light that illuminates the higher self. Love for yourself emerges from integrity as a conscious choice that you made in this lifetime. Once you embrace this choice, part of your journey is complete for there is no going back.

The energy that has descended upon the planet this year appears to revolve, to some degree, around integrity. From the deepest levels of personal integrity to the various ingredients that make up corporate and state-level integrity, the ones who are not aligned with their integrity seem to be making headlines on a daily basis.

My work in the spiritual realm has provided somewhat of an eye-opening experience regarding the numbers of people who are in loveless marriages and unions. The angels often say "refuse to commit to an absence of love," and that makes me wonder about the meaning of integrity as it relates to the most primal emotion known as love. Staying in a relationship out of a sense of duty to the family, to faith, to a religion or ideal, or any reason for that matter, brings up the issue of who or what is being served.

If I am going to align with my own integrity as well as helping others with that alignment, then it seems like love is the place to start. Finances, relationships, careers and all that other junk might have to wait their turn (tee hee)! Let's get a whisper from an angel on the integrity of love:

The mysteries of life and the illuminated truth forge a partnership to create the energy that drives the human spirit. On one hand, there is light. On the other, darkness. The bridge that connects the two is love. If that connection fails to hold a balance, there is a loss of energy. That is the simplest expression of the integrity of love.

Being responsible for yourself, your thoughts, your actions, your precious body and your entire being places a weight on your shoulders. But this weight is not a burden; instead, it acts as a counter-balance that supports you in the energy and integrity of love and loving yourself. Trying to shift this weight away from you can set you on a circular path, much like a ship that lists in the water due to an uneven load.

There is an integrity of the spirit that holds a light in order for the soul to clearly see the path ahead. There is service to the Divine that rewards the sacrifice made for the greater good. And there is a balance to create between integrity and sacrifice in order to serve the greater good of everyone involved. That creation must be orchestrated from the sounds that emanate from the heart.

To know the integrity of love, you must listen to the heart. That is where you will find the voice of reason and the reason you have a voice.

Last week's whisper, titled 'The Eternal Memory,' still has my curiosity working overtime. I have an outspoken love for the way science supports our spirituality, and a little blurb from an article drew my interest, sending me right back down the rabbit hole (tee hee).

According to an article by Robert Lanza, M.D., scientists carried out an amazing experiment in 2002 that showed that within pairs of particles, each particle anticipated what its twin would do in the future. Somehow, the particles "knew" what the researcher would do before it happened, as if there were no space or time between them. In a 2007 study published in *Science Magazine*, scientists shot particles into an apparatus and showed that they could retroactively change whether the particles behaved as protons or waves. The particles had to "decide" what to do as they passed a fork in the apparatus. Later on, the experimenter could flip a switch. It turns out that what the observer decided at that point determined how the particle had behaved at the fork in the past. Thus the knowledge in our mind can determine how particles behave.

So if our bodies and spirit are made up of millions of pairs of particles that hold intelligence, the subtleties around gleaning that information must be escaping a few of us because according to the dictionary, *intelligence* is limited to an umbrella term describing a property of the mind's comprehending-related abilities, such as the capacities for abstract thought, reasoning, planning and problem-solving, the use of language, and to learn. It must be time to ask for a whisper from the angels that better defines us as intelligent beings:

The truth is that humans have become increasingly impatient and lazy at the same time. Instant gratification rules for many. Spiritual guidance comes from a resonance vibration that combines emotions, intelligence, heart, and connection with a higher power. All of these energies exist beyond the veil. Intelligence can be intuitive!

The mind and body can trick you into feeling a false sense of control by helping you build illusions around your source of information. By validating a path of pure logic, you invalidate the wisdom held within energy. You numb your psychic senses with a total dependence on physical manifestations. With all the information that is available to your fingertips, when does your spirit get to assimilate the rest of story?

Create a space for intelligent energy at a soul level to gather and give voice to that which is deep within your being. The information brought forward through prayer, meditation, movement, contemplation, silence and heart openings contains wisdom that is truly cosmic in nature, divine in source and Universal in law. With this knowledge, all possibilities are met with faith that manifests miracles.

The collective intelligence possessed by mankind can bridge the gap between the mysteries once held as sacred and the light you hold as truth. Simply open to your higher intelligence as you would embrace reading a good book.

This is such a powerful yet underrated word, to my mind. It was only recently that I realized the significance of this word and activity. For me, it has been overlooked, much the same as 'asking' for what I want. Setting an intention and asking Source and the Universe for my true desires never occurred to me in my first fifty years (ha ha).

An intention is performing an action with the specific purpose of reaching the end or goal you aim at or intend to accomplish. Whether an action is successful or unsuccessful depends at least on whether the intended result was brought about. Unexpected consequences (negative or positive) of someone's acting are called unintentional. Intentional behavior can also be just thoughtful and deliberate goal-directedness.

In all the healing modalities that I have become involved in, this could be the single most important aspect. Setting an intention to heal your body is using the power of thought to send a message to your physical, emotional and spiritual body that you intend to resolve an issue. Merely making this statement can often heal without any other action, even though we all need help from time to time.

My last week's whisper on resolution alluded to the power of intention, so I wanted to follow up with this word in this start to 2008. I am a little slow to set goals and intentions for the next year and multi-year cycles, for one reason: I want to be clear on my wants and needs before I set those intentions, due to my recent epiphany that equates to "watch what you ask for." I guess I have faith that I will receive everything I intend. Now for an intentional whisper:

Intention is a like a cord that wraps around you, your family, your friends, your planet and your Universe. It is a bond that connects all. The integrity around your intentions determines the power that is ultimately connected with Source.

You were given free will to determine your path and how it relates to the path of others. Intention is part of the thought process that leads up to the free-will response. An unintentional action that turns out to be unfavorable is often categorized as a mistake.

With intentions comes the clarity of your path. When this becomes illuminated, it is easier to see. It is the same as lighting a dark alley, and brings that same comfort level. The greatest leaders of all time have known this to be true and have used this to create their path.

Pure Source is intentional, so when you raise your awareness and focus on intention with integrity, there is a Divine movement of energy within. This can unlock the Kingdom that is before you and wash away the tides of despair and hopelessness while filling the soul with light, love and true understanding of your life purpose.

A friend once made the statement that everything ever written or spoken was that person's interpretation and therefore it is possible that all the facts and truth written around the history of mankind could be slightly skewed. Things like 'how a war was started,' 'who was the main character of a historical circumstance,' and 'who said what and when' could all boil down to the discernment or perspective of the individual.

How many times have you witnessed several people come away with completely different takes on the same event? What about the circle game, where you feed a rumor to a starting point in the circle and then laugh as the story is translated from the last person in the circle with far different details? If you cannot find the absolute truth in anyone's interpretation, then where do you find it?

I think it comes down to vibrations felt by the heart. The vibrations of truth are without intellect or judgments, therefore you could bypass the words as you search for the truth held by the body and validated by Spirit. In my work as a medium, messages from the other side are often given in the form of symbols. In some cases the meaning is obvious, while in others cases it is a trick by the ego leading you down the path of mistaken meanings. Careful discernment with an openness to discover true meanings is the best way to interpret any situation. That can take time and intention to see things in the truest light. With that thought, I will engage in the interpretation of an angel whisper:

The discernment you refer to is something that exists on many levels. To apply it to only one and then to regard that one level as the absolute truth would be a disservice. It is the application of interpretation to all levels of the body, mind and spirit that will illuminate the highest level of discernment.

People often make the mistake of interpretation from the surface, and while connecting with the Clair senses could provide some great answers, it is always wise to look a little below the surface. In this way, you are allowing yourself the greatest depth of the experience.

Do not allow the interpretation of others to lead to judgments, unless you feel a need for some time in the lower self energies. It is the opening to Spirit without judgments in the light of obtaining help with discernment and being willing to see the truth that serves you the most. Staying within the energy of interpretation can color the views of change.

Interpretation at the highest level is a reflection of love and joy manifesting by taking the time to discern your challenges and resistance. Interpretation to see the truth can be compared to the analogy of a stone that skips on top of the water to reach the other shore instead of sinking under the weight, as logic would dictate. The intellectual interpretation makes it impossible to rationalize while the spiritual interpretation combines the energy of play and joy to turn the experience into a miracle.

I get to spend parts of my days interacting with people and their intuition. It is always fun to exchange intuitive energies with people, especially when it comes as a surprise. I hope I never grow to expect an experience of intuitive communication to appear completely common place. I think it is fun to explore the fertile ground that intuition opens up inside the heart.

__Intuition__ is apparent ability to acquire knowledge without a clear inference or reasoning process (My friend, might call this inspired lunacy…tee hee). *It is "the immediate apprehension of an object by the mind without the intervention of any reasoning process". Intuition, by definition, has no objective validity. However it is extremely widespread as an apparent phenomenon. For this reason, it has been the subject of study in Psychology, as well as a topic of interest in the supernatural.*

"Intuition is a combination of historical (empirical) data, deep and heightened observation and an ability to cut through the thickness of surface reality. Intuition is like a slow motion machine that captures data instantaneously and hits you like a ton of bricks. Intuition is a knowing, a sensing that is beyond the conscious understanding — a gut feeling. Intuition is not pseudo-science." Abella Arthur

This is what I love about my research with the 'Angel Whisper', the unexpected twist and turns that take me deep into the study of our language. One statement like the comment by Abella Arthur can take me into deep thought and activate the philosophical mind to look at life with broader perspective.

I think everyone has intuitive abilities, so it comes down to a matter of trusting those abilities enough to expand and breathe with total acceptance. The hardest thing for me to do when engaging with the intuitive practice is to get my head out of the way and let my heart lead. I will now attempt to cut through the thickness of surface reality with intuition and a whisper:

When you view the world through intuitive eyes, you are inviting spirit to interact and gift you with the mysteries that are outside your realm of experience. The intuitive guide is working with the vibrations of desire, free will and survival to help you know what is right.

The process of evolution is dependent on the ability of mankind to express through intuitive creativity. The greatest spiritual teachings are gained through intuition and can be specifically guided to fit your situation.

Intuition can be compared to a recording of your life where you have the ability to reverse or fast forward. In this way, you are 'bending time' to feel the vibrations that are outside the moment. The Higher Self will bring this into focus to get the attention of the Lower Self and offer an action to the free will of Spirit.

The pure essence of the human experience is dependent on the connection with the Soul through intuitive powers. When the physical realities of limitations are presented, the intuitive nature can connect with Divine energy and circumvent all expectations of the analytical mind through faith, love and an opening to the Angelic light.

I was doing some research into the Ute tribe for an upcoming book and discovered details about several encounters with Jesus as described by different tribes of Native Americans. Some of them were dated prior to the arrival of Columbus and his 'discovery of the New World,' which is also the time we associate as the Native inhabitants' introduction to Christianity.

One described encounter with Native Americans involved Quanah Parker, who is credited as the founder of the Native American Church movement. Parker adopted the peyote religion after reportedly seeing a vision of Jesus Christ while suffering from a near-fatal injury on the battlefield. Peyote is reported to contain ingredients which act as potent natural antibiotics, so Parker was given peyote by a Ute medicine man to cure the infections of his wounds. During the experience, Parker claimed he heard the voice of Jesus Christ who appeared to him dressed in a white robe and told him that in order to atone for his many killings and misdeeds, he must forsake a life of violence and conflict and take the peyote religion to the Indian peoples. Parker's words and teachings comprise the core of the Native American Church doctrine.

Parker taught that the sacred peyote medicine was the sacrament given to the Indian peoples by the Lord Jesus Christ, and was to be used with water when taking communion in a traditional Native American Church medicine ceremony. Parker created the "half-moon" style of the peyote ceremony. The "cross" ceremony later evolved in Oklahoma due to Kiowa influences introduced by John Wilson, a Kiowa Indian who traveled extensively with Parker during the early days of the Native American Church movement. The Native American Church was the first truly "American" religion based on Christianity, outside of the Latter Day Saints.

Parker's most famous teaching regarding the Spirituality of the Native American Church: *The White Man goes into his church and talks about Jesus. The Indian goes into his Tipi and talks with Jesus.* I wonder if they are talking about a whisper:

Jesus mastered ascension and rose from his grave to walk among the people once again. His teachings were showing mankind how to ascend while on the Earth plane. Jesus is open to all, regardless of their beliefs.

In order to bring a higher consciousness to the minds of man, a powerful message had to be delivered, one that would carry and last forever in the hearts and minds of all who could believe. Jesus delivered such a message with kindness and dignity.

As a conduit for Divine energy, love and forgiveness became the benchmark for the healings and teachings of Jesus. Without judgment, Jesus helped everyone regardless of their belief and continues that tradition today.

If you walk in the Golden light of the Christ Consciousness, you will find truth. If you trust in this truth, you will feel the faith that vibrates in all of life. In Nature lies your ability to know GOD, feel love, experience joy and witness life with open arms, open hearts, open minds and open spirits. Jesus offers freedom in the journey of the Soul.

What a simple and short yet expressive little word! I get this loving message quite a bit from the angelic realm and have been delivering it with more frequency: "Go out and find some joy." I notice that the importance of finding the joy in life is often mentioned in the Abraham-Hicks *Daily Word*. Some of us need a daily reminder on this subject, especially if it is not on the conscious or sub-conscious agenda.

I recently received an email from a client with the inauspicious subject line that read 'last year on earth.' Inside was the single, thought-provoking question: `If this were your last year on earth, how would you spend it?` My mind started racing through several different scenarios before I put on the brakes in an attempt to stop the next book from popping out (tee hee). Besides a twenty-thousand-word answer might take me months to return!

After clearing my mind and asking for clarity and focus, I went back into my office and answered my sweet client with these words: "I would go on a quest for joy to experience what life offers in that area. I'm not even sure where that would take me, but I think the answers would come from deep inside, like passion, love, bewilderment and all those deep emotions."

As I wrote those words and sent them, it came to me that the right answer to my client's question should have been, "I would do the same thing that I am doing now. I wouldn't change a thing." I am living my dream every moment of every day. Sure, there are setbacks, drama, tears and laughter, along with every other human emotion. But isn't that where the joy of living exists? So the quest for joy should start right here and right now.

Joy has an equally short and simple definition. The feeling of joy may seem to be more elusive than the definition suggests. But to me that is a teaching in itself. Joy is an emotion of great happiness, as defined by the dictionary account. Now from the angelic realm where the definition lies in a whisper, let's listen together!

Look into the eyes of a child and you will witness joy. Babies come into the world with a natural ability to experience and give joy. If you could talk to someone who has crossed, they would describe joy in very simple terms. It is not complicated.

The joy that is found in your daily existence is exhibited in Nature. There is no doubt in the ways that joy and happiness exist in the kingdom outside the human realm. The psyche is programmed early in life to accept certain things as being true. When the programming is done in nature, the effects are without false assumptions.

With clarity and truth come acceptance and understanding. When you forgive yourself and others, pure love is manifested at higher levels into your being. When you surrender to the Divine Source that fills the landscape of human existence, you will find the joy that is in your essence.

The seed of creation gives you choices to make that will ultimately form your environment. With that seed comes innate ability to feel and experience joy, starting at birth, so you can know love and joy at the soul level. Choosing the path filled with the most joy is not only divine, it is essential to the ascension of the human spirit.

Karma in Sanskrit means act, action or performance that gives birth to the concept of our actions or deeds as that which causes the entire cycle of cause and effect. Through the law of karma, the effects of all deeds actively create past, present, and future experiences, thus making one responsible for one's own life and the pain and joy it brings to him/her and others. In spiritual beliefs that incorporate reincarnation, karma extends through one's present life and all past and future lives as well.

Amma says that in our past lives we place this karmic energy in the bank and then spend part of this lifetime withdrawing karma until it is no longer an influence. It is my involvement with reading the past lives of others that has helped me begin to understand karma as energy. I believe that we shouldn't have to relive past lives, but I discovered this week that there are always exceptions as I witnessed a digression of epic proportions into the healing arena of transmuting Karmic Energy!

Yet in another case, angelic guidance created a situation where my client was able to gather all of her relationships whom she shared a Karmic Energy and attachment. In this moment she experienced beautiful healing, love like you find in a fairy tale, profound visions and incredible details a about family abuse issue. Their faith, willingness, courage and determination contributed to inspiring Karmic resolution and this weeks whisper:

In gratitude, you will find the energy of healing. With intention and Divine Energy, you can remove that which does not resonate. In ceremonious meditation you will find integrity of the Soul. In reverence there is acknowledgment of Divine Power.

Light a candle as you hold onto symbols or representations of the person that shares your Karmic Energy. Place stones, jewelry, photos or mementos of your loved ones in your circle as ultimate expressions of support, love and courage as you combine the elements of intention, ceremony, love and gratitude to the Highest Power.

Evoke the Highest Power, Angels, Archangels, Saints or Ascended Masters to assist you with your intentions. Ask your Higher Self if your karmic path is to find completion in this lifetime. Accept the answer with faith. Focus on the people in your present, past and future lives as you discern your karmic destiny. Make amends to any and all that you have wronged and send this energy in every direction of time and space.

Visualize yourself wrapped in red ribbons, red is for the past and the ribbons represent the Karmic Energy. Then bring to mind the one that shares your Karmic Energy as you ask their soul if you can be released forever. If they refuse, ask them what you can do to help resolve the Karmic issue. Offer them forgiveness or help with the forgiveness issues as you and the Angels gently persuade them. Anyone that is unwilling to communicate resolution must leave your healing circle.

Ask the Archangels to cut the ribbons and release you from the Karmic Energy. If your karmic journey is complete, the release will occur. If not, then find the peace in lessons of life that become the teachers of the heart and soul. Merging into the flow of Divine love with intention and purpose fills your essence with the vibrations of good Karmic Energy.

Laughter is a part of human behavior regulated by the brain and is sometimes seemingly contagious, taking only one person to provoke laughter from others as a positive feedback. The study of humor and laughter, and its psychological and physiological effects on the human body, is called gelotology, which has led to new and beneficial therapies practiced by doctors, psychiatrists, and other mental health professionals using humor to treat a variety of physical and psychological issues.

We have all heard the saying "laughter is the best medicine", but I like the statement by the French philosopher who went by the pen name Voltaire, "The art of medicine consists of keeping the patient amused while nature heals the disease."
The effects of laughter's releasing hormones and endorphins in the human body can build the immune system, lower stress and provide a distraction to the serious issues that life and illness can present.

I laughed my way through the research of this whisper as I discovered different therapies built around laughter, such as Laughter Yoga and Laughter Meditation. I became hysterical! So enjoy a good laugh today to feel the effects of bringing joy and healing vibrations together with a chance to simply lighten up. In the energy of laughter, let's take a moment to engage in a whisper from the angels:

The human experience offers many wide-ranging opportunities to explore the deep mysteries of life. Due to the challenges presented in the physical and material world, laughter can be overlooked as the gateway to your joy, love and happiness.

One's ability to laugh at themselves presents everyone with an opportunity to subdue the voice of ego, bringing clarity and in some cases illuminating the truest light of a situation or circumstance. Bringing balance through laughter can facilitate a profound release of thought patterns and paradigms, resulting in the removal of obstacles that may be preventing or blocking you from your Divine life-purpose.

If you can find ways to infuse the energy of compassion combined with laughter into difficult life issues, your perspective can be altered to assist you in finding alignment with the true nature of your essence. The path to unconditional love and acceptance is found in your joy and purpose. Laughter illuminates that path and allows your guardians and guides to communicate nurturing messages.

The healing energies of the Mother Earth and the benefit of partnerships with the angels are fortified by the physical relationship between humans and Divine Source. That physical thread of connection is anchored in breath with strength and courage generated in the depth of meaning within each exhale and inhale. Exhaling the breath of laughter brings forward the gift of passionate joy, forming a bridge between spirituality and the vibrations of the Cosmic Heart.

The phrase **Law of Attraction,** *although used widely by esoteric writers, has a variety of definitions. Turn-of-the-century references conceptualized the law of attraction as relating to physical structure and to how matter develops. A more modern consensus says people's thoughts (both conscious and unconscious) dictate the reality of their lives. Essentially "If you really want something and truly believe it's possible, you'll get it,", but putting a lot of attention and thought onto something you don't want means you'll probably get that too.*

Widespread popular interest for the law of attraction reached its peak after the release of the 'The Secret.' After the film's release, the book, Law of Attraction: The Basics of the Teachings of Abraham, *by Esther Hicks and Jerry Hicks made* The New York Times' *Best Sellers list, drawing more attention and interest to this topic. In 2007, Oprah Winfrey began a series of interviews during her talk show on the law of attraction.*

I think it is noteworthy to mention that the Hickses had their names and association with that film (*The Secret*) legally removed. My understanding is that key aspects of the teachings were omitted from the final film product. I personally think that the movie over-simplifies the roles that we play in attracting what we want from life. For these reasons, I can understand the criticism and the empowerment behind the Laws of Attraction. Let's see if we can attract an angel for a whisper on the subject:

It is sometimes amusing for the angels to witness the way humans move through intellectual processes to find comfort in the heart. Of course your thoughts and vibrations attract a resonance with you and the world around you. But you must keep in mind that ingredients that make up your life are wide and varied. Some are within your control, and for those you can accept responsibility. Some are outside of your control, and for those you should not attach blame or victim beliefs.

The way to attract the things you want in life starts in your willingness to view the truth about who you are and where you are going. Inside that light is a space that holds a vision for your dreams and desires. When you are nurturing that truth, true meanings about what you want to attract are what make your dreams a reality.

The strongest energy in all Universal Laws is in the form of love. Love can attract the abundance of the divine kingdom on all levels of body, mind and spirit. With love feeding the soul, the search that most of you are going through becomes complete and without the need to define what lies in the peripheral.

The basic laws that govern life as taught by the spiritual masters on Earth are describing the actions that serve your life, such as living by the 'Golden Rule.' When you find peace in your heart among the chaos of perceived destinies, your life purpose finds focus in joy, love, laughter and living in each moment that life has to offer. It is your choice in the perception of what life has to offer.

Left Brain versus Right Brain

<u>Funderstanding</u> describes the two sides of the brain thus: *"The theory of the structure and functions of the mind suggests that the two different sides of the brain control two different 'modes' of thinking. It also suggests that each of us prefers one mode over the other. Experimentation has shown that the two different sides, or hemispheres, of the brain are responsible for different manners of thinking. For example, the left brain deals with the logical, sequential, rational, analytical and objective, by looking at parts. While the right brain looks at the random, intuitive, holistic and synthesizing, by looking at the whole."*

My thinking around this area came through an observation of my clients' thought processes. Skeptics seem to live out of their left brain, wanting proof or validation for the logical mind. I also see those who rely heavily on their feelings to maneuver through life. I immediately analyzed my Libra-self as balanced in my thinking, so I took an online <u>test</u> to determine which side of my brain was dominant! Out of thirty-two questions, I answered 16 with the right brain and 16 with the left. I wonder which side made me take the test (tee hee)?

Like every other aspect of life, I am sure the trick is to find balance, and that is what I am constantly seeking. Maybe I should rephrase that to say that I am 'casually seeking' a whole brain response (lol). Let's receive a whisper from the angels that both sides of the brain can easily agree upon:

The balanced union of the mind, body and spirit is largely dependent on the use of both sides of the brain. Your body and spirit feel your experiences with a natural analyzation that gives wisdom in the form of energy and represents an integration of vibrations meant to bridge the right and left sides of the brain.

If you are coming from dominant left-brained thinking, you could be discounting the miraculous wisdom that lives and breathes within your energy body. If you are coming from a dominant right-brain style of thinking, you may find that Universe seems to trick you into forming illusions around perceived outcomes.

The completely open mind creates a flow of energy that uses several pathways of light to move energy through the brain. This can be compared to driving: When you are stuck in traffic, you look for an alternative route that will take you around the obstacles and deliver you safely to your front door. Limitations in your thought process are a direct result of the choices that you are making with your journey.

Take the time to nurture your thoughts by giving choice and voice to the intelligence found within the spiritual body. This body is grounded in the light of truth meant to bring balance to the mind. Your future is anchored in the wisdom of your past which is feeding the choices of the moment and creating the path that you will travel.

To find balance in the mind, infuse love into every thought.

It is hard to witness events like the ones unfolding in Japan, while dealing with the human emotions that continue to surface. We are experiencing the most gripping of human dramas, with real-time communications and in breathtaking detail.

When Kaycie (a *Whisper* reader) and others expressed questions regarding the deeper meaning of theses events, I watched the struggle the Japanese face raise many questions with everyone around faith, mankind and the future of the planet.

As I searched the Internet, I followed a thread that led me the way birds and fish move in unison with the presence of epithelial wound-healing cells known as keratocytes. This movement of cell structure might be released in a moment of experiencing trauma or evading danger. What do we release in seeing such images as those coming out of Japan? Compassion, heartache, fear, depression, love and a full range of emotions release in a way that joins us all.

As I searched my heart and soul, I turned inward to hear the voice of silence that whispers knowledge in the form of an angel.

The wounding of the planet brings heightened awareness to the need for healing energies, coping skills, alignment shifts and evolutionary changes. As multi-dimensional beings supported by the Earth, you have a responsibility to uphold the integrity with every aspect of life as it relates to your being and the environment. The vibrations from deep within the core of the planet are a reflection of every living organism to some degree.

Birds fly in unison as a result of an emergent energy that comes from moment-by-moment decisions. This form of unison creates a continuum that includes instantaneous agreements from the whole. Those agreements involve sacrifice and surrender of personal agendas so that the group may survive as one. Mankind is learning that a maneuver wave, or learning to move in unison, is an essential ingredient in the process of evolution, ascension and survival.

Man has learned how to crawl and how to walk. Now it is time to run or move quickly as one. An event, like the one in Japan, is the Earth telling you to place differences aside if you want your species to survive. The Earth has the power to communicate what is necessary on this path of awakening, especially for those who would not yield to any other force.

The rumbling of the Earth clearly states that awakening energy is at the core of your present incarnation and situation. You are no longer a toddler in the energy of the soul, but an advanced student with a strong spirit that has come to break down the outdated structures with motivation and purpose to create the new paradigm for Ages.

Mankind must follow the Cosmic Heart of the Universe in order to find the collective human unconsciousness of movement that will usher in profound peace.

Thanks to Danielle for the suggestion to create a whisper on the word trust, a sometimes elusive feeling amongst a vast landscape of opposition (lol). I am merely referring to the challenges with trust, whether it is with your faith, other people or with one's own self. By definition, *trust means to have confidence or faith with reliance on the integrity, strength, ability, surety, etc., of a person or thing.* But what if that trust connects with optimism to form illusions?

In my quest for answers, Google held 300 million possibilities (tee hee). But here is what I found at ChangingMinds.org: *Trust is both an emotional and logical act. Emotionally, it is where you expose your vulnerabilities to people by believing they will not take advantage of your openness. Logically, it is where you have assessed the probabilities of gain and loss, calculating expected utility based on hard performance data, and concluded that the person in question will behave in a predictable manner. In practice, trust is a bit of both. I trust you because I have experienced your trustworthiness and because I have faith in human nature. We feel trust. Emotions associated with trust include companionship, friendship, love, agreement, relaxation, comfort.*

If a person who is trustworthy commits an act that displays the opposite, does that mean we should no longer trust that person? And what if that person is looking back at you in the mirror (tee hee)? My brain is hurting, and that is my sign that it is time for a whisper from an angel on trust:

In the grand scheme of things, trust is an essential ingredient to the enjoyment of life. Like anything else that appears to be lost, trust can be found in the most unlikely places. If you are lacking trust in general, that could indicate the need to address issues relating to self-worth, lack of faith, the fear of failure or some sort of limiting belief about yourself, your environment, or the world in general.

You are constantly bombarded by a variety of energies that individually may be very subtle, but in unison, these energies can create feelings around the distrust in the world. It is important to separate yourself from actions that manifest distrust. Second-guessing yourself, seeing the world or the human journey as being without hope, living with damaging and negative emotions, or belief in an ideology that does not align with your true essence can support the emotion of distrust.

Building faith, supporting your spiritual growth, self-forgiveness, surrender to a higher power and a willingness to let go of things that do not serve are all ways to build trust. Giving through sharing always builds trust by spreading throughout the world like ripples of water across a pond. If you could elevate your heart to extend trust to someone who might not have earned it, you are teaching that person the value of trust. In order to accomplish this act and then feel the rewards, you might view it as sharing your trust, and in that way you are not giving up a part of yourself as much as you are moving loving energy through the Cosmic heart!

Learn ways to trust yourself first in order to experience trust with others.

I received a response from last week's perspective on truth and that is the impetus of this week's angel whisper regarding the word *lie*. One of my readers wrote: "I have never held others to the standard of truth, mainly because I know I don't tell it sometimes when I think it might hurt someone's feelings. And I believe I don't get told the truth at times, whether because of the person's consideration of my own feelings, or deeper reasons of wanting to hide something from me. Let's say I'm a pretty permanent skeptic, but I don't hold it against people because I have such a low expectation.

*A **lie** (also called **prevarication**) is a type of deception in the form of an untruthful statement with the intention to deceive, often with the further intention to maintain a secret or reputation, protect someone's feelings or to avoid a punishment. To lie is to state something one believes is false with the intention that it be taken for the truth by someone else.*

Lying is typically used to refer to deceptions in oral or written communication. Other forms of deception, such as disguises or forgeries, are generally not considered lies, though the underlying intent may be the same; however, even a true statement can be considered a lie if the person making that statement is doing so to deceive. In this situation, it is the intent of being untruthful rather than the truthfulness of the statement itself that is considered.

OMG, the truth can be a lie! It's time for a whisper:

A lie is an illusion. This illusion is usually created by the psyche to allow the individual to remain in the comfort of a paradigm. A person creates his lie in the same way that he creates his truth and is then free to form a resonance of an illusion. Living in the illusion of a non-truth is the mind's refusal to illuminate purpose, integrity and service to a Higher Power.

Lying with intention to deceive can open one to the darkest human emotions and remove the power of an individual. The aura provides a protective bubble that shields the body, mind and spirit from the bombardment of energies. When you engage in lying, this protection is compromised. Repeating this action is a repression of the Spirit and dilutes the capacity to love and live in the moment.

If a 'white lie' does no harm and has no significance, then why not speak the truth? If it is intended to spare someone a hurt, you are back to living the illusion. The truth causes pain only when that is what the individual chooses to create. So the choice to lie is your ego making a judgment about the receptivity of another.

In truth there is light, while in a lie there is darkness, and between them is your choice. When you choose truth, you are expressing love for yourself and others, respect for a higher power, compassion for those that are misguided and tolerance of life on Earth. Choose peace, teach only love and stand in the light to feel the vibrations that are the essence of Creation.

Would you believe that I could not find this word combination in the dictionaries that I use? I found it ironic that the meaning of these words could be so elusive in definition as well as our evolution. *What is my life purpose?* is a question many people are asking the angels.

Rick Warren's book titled *The Purpose Driven Life®* has taken some criticism over certain perceived omissions that involve the Book of Revelations. More specifically, questions were raised about the role that sins and repentance play in our life purpose. I'm not sure how valid these points are, nor do I see the correlations. I may not agree with everything that Warren says, but he does make several key points that I think are true and helpful in understanding our purpose.

The bottom line is that I believe we all have a life purpose and that our passion and drive revolve around that. But I also think the ideas about our life purpose are somewhat linear, which makes it even harder to identify and act upon this enigmatic energy force that lives and breathes in each of us.

I did come across this quote that I found really tasty. "Everyone has a purpose in life, a unique gift or special talent to give to others. And when we blend this unique talent with service to others we experience the ecstasy and exultation of our own spirit, which is the ultimate goal of all goals." - Deepak Chopra, author.

While blending my talents with service one day, I did receive a profound angelic message around this subject. It went something like this; "Don't worry about your life purpose, my child; know that you have lived a purpose-filled life". That is certainly a whisper that has inspired me in pursuit of purpose. In that pursuit, I find a whisper:

The purpose of life is found at the essence of your existence. It is an imprint of knowledge that forms an energetic pathway. In this pathway you will find the vibrations of love and joy at the highest level. The flow of Spirit reaches maximum fluidity in the alignment of purpose.

In the absence of focus in this area, there lies an opening of vulnerability that can be damaging to the Lower Self. Denial of purpose leads to living an illusion regarding the Highest Power. A detachment from purpose is disconnecting from Divine Source. In love, there is always purpose. In service, there is always love. In purpose, there is connection to love and service.

Life purpose can be analyzed for mental affirmations to a degree, but the true test comes through the heart. In this purpose, you will find enough passion to illuminate your path and the path of those around you. This is where you find truth at the core of transcending evolution.

If you want to understand life purpose, you must understand life. The limitations placed on this meaning of life also limit your ability to define purpose. It might serve you to think of it as a Soul purpose, without beginnings or endings. Whether you are on the physical plane or not, your purpose remains at the heart of your truth and never-ending story.

I was at Whole Foods, eating lunch on their outdoor mezzanine, when I realized that I needed a napkin. At that moment a woman jumped up and started chasing her napkin in the swirling wind for about thirty feet before she gave up. I watched the napkin dance in the wind, as it tossed and spun itself into the center of two boys playing. The sight made me chuckle as the boys screamed at the leaves and napkin moving in a circle around them. The napkin slowly made its way toward me as I wondered, "Is this a coincidence, manifestation, happy accident or living in the present?"

Maybe it was a lesson on being present and paying attention, but that term is hard to wrap my head around. What does *being present* mean? I hear people say using this term in a way that seems to imply that we are not doing something important (tee hee). During a conversation, the mind can wander off into thought, so does that mean I am no longer present? Do thoughts of the past and future mean that you have left the present or are you being present to those thoughts?

Abraham Maslow once said, *"The ability to be in the present moment is a major component of mental wellness."* Oh great, now I am wondering about my mental health (lol)! Maybe living in the present is an indicator of our overall well-being and the impetus for releasing and healing the past, without attention to the future or outcomes. Let's see if a whisper from an angel can bring us to living in the present:

Living in the present should be viewed as a conscious state of being with focus from an elevated perspective. Life offers many distractions and constant decisions around how you will approach each situation. Some people are firmly rooted in the present with one foot in the past and one in the future, while others seem to get stuck in the past or the illusions of the future to the point of being distracted.

Follow the order of your ideas and patterns to better understand and discern your own ability to live in the present. Within each choice you make, there is energy that defines the influence from past experiences or the uncertainty of your future. You can maintain presence while acting upon the lessons of those influences, because there is a higher truth that always speaks to those who listen.

Ascension leads to living in the present at the highest levels and the free will of choice gives you the freedom to make conscious decisions. Belief in a Higher Power gives freedom to the individual and releases the pressure to control outcomes. That is why faith is such an important aspect of the Divine life path.

Nature provides a theater of presence in the moment as the animal kingdom perfectly displays the purpose-filled life. Play, sing, dance, laugh and love as a way of living in the moment, and you will return to the conscious state of being that is the rightful inheritance of your inner child. Do not allow others to dictate the life you were born to live. Set intentions around the love for life. Follow your heart to light the path of love. Feel, speak and teach love to know true presence.

Thanks to all of you who responded to the whisper on Shame, and to the one reader who went deeper in their emotions to write with this comment: *"Meanwhile, the topic is loneliness / the deeper problem I think is security, which is tangled up with lack of trust. It's a basic human need (to feel secure/stable), that I think many of us have to 'work' to feel secure. Is there any angelic insight on the connection between loneliness and security?"*

Good question and thanks for trusting that I have, or can get, an answer, Tiffany (tee hee)! But I do think loneliness is an issue with a lot of people. Maybe some have been hurt and are not open to relationships, while others may be waiting for just the right person to show up. I am sure there are others choosing to be alone who never feeling loneliness.

Loneliness is defined as: *1. The condition of being lonely; solitude; seclusion. 2. The state of being unfrequented by human beings.* Most of the people in my world who express loneliness are frequented by human beings, just the wrong ones (grinning). So maybe the security issue plays into that assessment, along with some other energies.

The state of listening to an angelic communication can be as solitary as a ride on the breath of a whisper on loneliness:

Timing, energy, readiness, your Divine path, and the lessons contracted for this lifetime all combine in a common thread that weaves its way through multi-faceted dimensions in order to reach your state of awareness. Surfacing at times in your life, like a bubble of air gently rising to the surface, the current issues you face are bringing opportunities for transmutation.

Loneliness might be showing up in your life as an issue demanding your attention, so that you may create efforts toward a completion, a resolution or an energy shift. Your perspective also determines the action steps you create. Are you sad because you are lonely, or are you lonely because you are sad? Have you made a choice that the Universe is supporting due to a perspective that only you may hold? Is there something missing in your life and are you under an illusion that it is a person? Have you imposed rules on your life? Perhaps it is grief that created a disharmony. From a position of love, loneliness might be simply considered an attachment.

It would be natural to feel lonely if you are feeling insecure, without trust or unsafe in some way. Vulnerability can be a lonely feeling. So you see, there lies great potential for illusions around anything you have defined as the emotion of being alone.

The repeated reminder to find ways to love yourself is really a way of jogging memories around following your heart. Following your heart leads you to find peace, joy and happiness, not in a place, but in the existence that you create with your time on Earth. Breaking free from old paradigms, expanding your consciousness, accepting who you are from a spiritual perspective, and finding the deepest measure of love can evoke a feeling of loneliness on a path where few travel. But that time is limited as you will soon discover a state of Oneness.

This whisper is dedicated to my good friend and beloved community icon, Danny Roy Young. The outpouring of love was inspirational at his memorial service yesterday with 1111 (his street address too) people in attendance. After a year of writing these whispers, I was a little surprised to see that I had never asked the angels about love.

During the ceremony, the three ministers each spoke and broke into tears as they talked about this incredible human being. Even people from the congregation remarked that they had never seen that reaction from these individuals. They compared Danny to John the Baptist as well as other saints.

If you Google *love*, you will find more than two billion entries! But as I looked at some of them, the definitions fell short of my expectations. They should just post a picture of Danny to explain the word (LOL). This man taught more people how to love than anyone I have ever personally known. Danny would call you up just to say, "I love you" or "I miss you" or "Get by here so I can love on your neck."

Danny did not regularly attend church but he spent a lot of time there as a youth advocate and was very engaged with the church leaders. He had other passions that could be characterized as the 'simple things in life,' and he made the expression of love feel simple. "Danny was a gift from God" was spoken more than once as he was eulogized.

As a speaker, I found it challenging to express words that felt like a complete summary for this man in a few short minutes of time. But one thing was very clear: This man embodied the word love. I will now try to capture the same essence in a few short lines from the angels that I call a whisper:

Love is the energy of the Divine. It is like all of the unseen things that man tries to explain with words. In every corner of the Universe, you can know love if you are willing to make the choice to feel what you cannot see.

The energy of the angels is something that if you express it in words might sound like super-love or an extra large. That is why angels are dedicated as guides during the human experience, so that you can know that love is all around you in a big way.

Think of the most joyous thing that ever happened in your life and rest in that energy for a moment to know love. If you set an intention to experience love in any situation you will find the source and the ability to alter the psyche. People like Danny are sent to Earth as a teacher of love through exampled living.

The souls or essence of mankind is a complete reflection of love. To remove layers that block your love, forgive yourself and others, expand your thinking to have more loving experiences, build your faith on the energy of joy, and say the words "I love you" as many times as you can. The best place to start is in the mirror. The most powerful wave of love is found in single moments of reflection.

A few years ago, in the fall of 2009, I was acting as a caretaker for my father, who was in his final days. Spending many nights in his country apartment, I would sleep with the windows open in my room. One evening, the cows in the pasture that adjoined the property bellowed all night long. I kept waking up to the unusual sound that became somewhat unnerving.

The next day I asked a local rancher about the cattle sounds. He told me they must have taken the calves that day. "The herd will search the field throughout the day and night, looking for one misplaced calf," he explained. The herd continued to voice the loss for the next few nights, until we left for the hospital one last time.

At my father's apartment, I could hear the trains as they rolled through the Central Texas corridor. Big Russell passed on Veterans Day (11.11.09), two days after his 80th birthday. Even knowing that he is in a better place does not completely balance the feelings of missing his physical presence. As I ask for a whisper tonight, a train blows its horn in the distance. I suddenly feel like I am getting a big hello (grinning)! Let's see what the angels might whisper about loss:

When you observe nature, you are witnessing raw emotions being expressed in the present moment. There is nothing to stop a process of releasing energy that is triggered by the light of truth. Humans can find ways to deny the energetic release that could bring balance to an experience.

In nature, the needs are reduced to the most simple measure necessary for survival. Something you might not witness in nature due to the subtle expressions is gratitude. In gratitude, you can overcome loss because you will bring focus to what is found. What you find within a loss offers the reward of freedom, freedom to love without attachment.

When people or things fall away, a type of birthing occurs. An energetic shifting happens within a Divine Matrix that Cosmically connects everyone to the Tree of Life. Your past and your future are exported to other dimensions as you operate from a present reality grounded in the physical.

In order to know the light, one must know the darkness. To move into another dimension, birthing occurs to facilitate the movement. You enter a body and are born in this dimension, and then you leave the body to be born into another dimension. What falls away needs to fall away.

Don't deny yourself the full expression of your feelings captured within the experience of an event horizon.

"Do you believe in magic …?" Isn't that an old Lovin' Spoonful song? We could all use a little help from time to time, and when something feels or appears as magic, it can just make you smile and feel good. Miracles might be viewed as magic, and everyone loves a story that contains the unexplained or supernatural.

Magic *could be defined as any art that invokes supernatural powers or an illusory feat considered magical by naïve observers.* *Magic* *can possess or use characteristics normally associated with supernatural powers such as "charming incantations,"* I am not sure if that definition works for me, but I like what Johann Wolfgang von Goethe once said: *"Magic is believing in yourself. If you can do that, anything is possible."*

David Blaine, the magician, held his breath for more than seventeen minutes to set a world record and defy medical science. After Blaine failed many attempts, his doctor offered a simple suggestion on how to accomplish the feat. He told him, "You are a magician, aren't you? Then use magic." Even though the act was monitored and witnessed by many, skeptics still discount the fact that he really accomplished the extraordinary challenge.

Magic could be one of those words that we each get a chance to personally define. I will go on record today as a naïve observer who not only believes in, but loves to believe in magic, as I become still in order to receive a magical angel whisper:

There are many ways that the human body is capable of having experiences with feelings generated from beyond the body senses. In this age, people have well-developed analytical minds that can easily discount anything that defies logic. It is those who seek and acknowledge the expansive possibilities in the Universe who are open to the supernatural.

Even if you place magic under the heading of entertainment, you can still see the joy and connection with Spirit that unfolds in an illusion. If you are actively co-creating that illusion, then maybe you are drawing magical energy with an invitation for unexplained events to come into your awareness.

Science, religion and technology can support magic or not, depending on the perspective. There is no logical data that would support a jet airplane with no engine thrust landing in the Hudson and floating while everyone escaped, yet it did happen.

If you are truly creating your own reality, as some science might suggest, then you are making the choice to accept certain possibilities that might not be supported by the analytical mind. Empowerment, enlightenment and the willingness to embrace the mystery that is part of the make-up of the world will lead you into magical experiences and the ability to set aside anything blocking you from knowing that your life is everything but void of magic.

You are a master of illusion, so go out and make some magic! As you spread joy through magic, your soul feels the vibrations of a spirit in service to love.

Unlike setting intentions and goals or saying prayers, making a wish feels like a completely different energy. As a young child I couldn't decide on the wish that I was making on that shooting star or from tossing that coin in the fountain. Could that be a sign of contentment and satisfaction?

This last week, I decided to gift myself with making a wish, and in that moment I felt an internal shift. What possible resistance could a person have to making a wish (worthiness, too many choices, wouldn't want to get hopes up)? But eventually I became clear, and this was my wish:

I wish to feel secure and safe with myself and my abilities. Within that security, I wish for the courage and strength to live my life with resolve to follow my dreams and to find the joy and blessings in every possible outcome. I wish for the contrasts of life to feed my soul with the same satisfaction found at the end of a delicious meal with family and friends.

My thought and inspiration around this writing were partially driven by the vision of everyone reading this email, followed by each reader's taking a moment to make their wish. Socrates once said, "Be as you wish to seem." I hope you take a moment to make a wish and feel the vibrations of the truth as you cross the bridge into your own imagination. I will do that same thing by asking for a whisper from an angel:

Your vision rarely becomes the truth without the energy first passing by you. If you grab that energy enough to make a wish, you are sending out love and inspiration with clarity that carries a certain level of faith. Those high-frequency vibrations are surrounded by great power, angelic strength and God-like healing energy.

Healing energy comes through those with hope, and making a wish can provide that glimmer of hope. To glimmer, something must be shiny, and to be shiny it must be filled with light. Your wishes for yourself and others send out enough light to penetrate the darkest surfaces, and that is why someone without hope is inviting the darkness to bring experiences and knowledge. If you let self-doubt and worthiness issues separate you from your wishes, you are merely choosing to take a path with more challenges and lessons.

Your choice in making a wish is important because in order to find that wish, you must illuminate your deepest thoughts and ideas around a happy and joyful life. One should make wishing a daily practice without attachment to the outcome. Simply find the joy that dwells with your own inner child and feel the freedom to express your deepest essence and your highest capacity to love.

In the angelic kingdom, your wish is heard loud and clear with acceptance, like children receiving a gift. The 'gift' of your wish is felt as a freedom of thought without expectations that allows us to open certain channels of direction for your expressed energy. In this way your wish becomes our wish for you, like thousands of voices that join in singing the same heart song in order to spread abundant hope and blissful joy.

This is a word that we hear a lot about today, from movies like 'The Secret' to books, CDs and seminars. There is a real buzz around this word. It appears to me that there are several layers of meaning around *manifestation* though it has such a simple definition: **Manifestation** is a way of making thoughts reality.

This is what one reader wrote: *There are fundamental particles of matter and energy (some out there and specifically, Dr. Francisco Rosero call them adamantine particles). These particles require 'power' to build the other particles and atoms. There is only one type of energy that is compatible with them, and this energy is the magnetic power of Love which holds every galaxy, star and planet in its place. In the presence of love, patterns of beauty, perfection, harmony and efficiency are able to manifest spontaneously. Love is not only the most beautiful feeling, it is the power which forms and directs these particles to manifest into the physical.*

My reader went on to write about her personal meditation that she has created to assist in manifesting. A large number of the population are looking for this magic ingredient of life, and who doesn't want to manifest their dreams, desires and intentions into reality?

A few things we commonly hear about manifestation: Build a story-board with pictures of the things that you desire to manifest; visualize your life having already received these things; don't think of the things you don't want; keep the faith that these things are coming to you. Something tells me there is a lot more to it. Let's see what the angels have to say as I manifest a whisper:

Think back on a time or occasion in your life when you had a happy heart. That is how you manifest your dreams. The vibrations of gratitude that the heart sends in this moment of bliss are connecting everything that your soul wants for this lifetime. Finding complete resonance with the feelings of love, hope, faith and happiness can create the space that holds the basic keys to your life in love.

Some people are using manifestation to acquire material things in an effort to find happiness. It is true that the Kingdom of the Divine can bring satisfaction, but who is being served by this? If the end result is completely self-serving, achieving true happiness then becomes dependent on the Self.

Manifesting a life of joy, purpose and limitless love can create an elevation of spirit that opens the door to freedom. The feeling of freedom from fears, worry, guilt, anger and many toxic emotions can bring balance to life and unleash the creative energy of manifestation to epic proportions.

When you observe nature, you will see that in the balance of all of life there are Universal Laws that must be adhered to in all manifestations. As you become aligned with these Universal Truths, you can then illuminate the co-creation of your destiny as you ride on a wave of pure love. On every breath, there is energy of passion that surrounds you with every footstep into the mysteries of life. It is your free will that decides where to draw your next breath.

My first book is named *Mariposa*, which is the Spanish word for butterfly as well as the name of the street on which I live (tee hee). I have written songs, poetry and chapters dedicated to this unusual creature in our world. Some believe that the butterfly represents transformation with an ability to move between the spirit world and the physical.

One reader writes in response to the last whisper: *"I exited the tub, dressed in my pajamas and plopped on the couch to watch TV. Russell, the program was on the Monarch Butterfly and it told of how it takes several generations for the butterflies to complete the journey from the northern US (and Canada) to Mexico and back again. One butterfly makes part of the trip, breeds, then dies and the offspring continue the journey and the process repeats itself over and over again. So here is the whisper: This lifetime is only one leg of a journey."*

In this light, you can start to understand the role that the generations preceding each of us plays in our current lives. The special connection and journey we share with our ancestors lives and breathes within us as one building block stacks upon the other. Let's see what the angels say about the word *mariposa*.

Nature provides many answers to the questions of life, and the butterfly is no exception. Facing incredible and life-threatening odds, the butterfly is undaunted with a zest for life that inspires the journey of a lifetime. Then with style and grace, this fragile-winged creature displays a love for life that is unmatched in the world.

The mariposa represents the vivid colors and beauty available in the world, even to those with short lives. Both the sweet and the bittersweet aspects are presenting a duality that requires the whole-hearted participation of the soul with every flight. The butterfly illuminates the partnership that exists between the nature world and mankind in a way that focuses the need to understand and accept certain truths in life.

The abundant earth provides the opportunity to accept that all your needs will be met if you are willing to have faith that over the next horizon is sweet nectar and a peaceful, nurturing environment. There is also an opportunity to honor those that have supported your journey as a way to propel you into the future, riding a stream of love that once found momentum from the birth of a single seed.

Allow the mariposa to display the deepest form of love for life as one example of the building blocks for the soul. The understanding gained from the movement of air found in the wings of a butterfly is all you need to connect with nature and a Higher Power. Beyond that, start each day with an open heart, a willing mind and wishful soul as you create discoveries in the deepest levels of love for life.

There is so much information out there about meditation and the benefits as described by Eastern and Western cultures, that I felt drawn in many directions. I personally don't do well sitting in a dark and quiet room, waiting for thoughts to come to me. I like to go to the Source in the way of a 'moving meditation,' which is also called 'Dynamic Meditation.' You apply the same principles involving meditation to an activity like yoga, walking, running or bicycle riding to experience similar results.

The word *meditation* comes from the Latin *meditatio*, which originally indicated every type of physical or intellectual exercise, then later evolved into the more specific meaning 'contemplation.'

The gift of learning to meditate is the greatest gift you can give yourself in this life. For it is only through meditation that you can undertake the journey to discover your true nature, and find the stability and confidence you will need to live, and die, well. Meditation is the road to enlightenment. - Sogyal Rinpoche, The Tibetan Book of Living and Dying.

Dr. Marcel Vogel describes the 'Alpha' state of mind in one of his many talks about the science of the human body. He explains that when we reach this state through meditation or a similar activity to 'quiet the mind,' we are reaching a stage of openness that allows for a wide range of channeling opportunities.

As a method of stress reduction, meditation is often used in hospitals in cases of chronic or terminal illness to reduce complications associated with increased stress, including a depressed immune system. The relaxation response measured in meditation includes changes in metabolism, heart rate, respiration, blood pressure and brain chemistry. The result of my relaxation response can be found in an angel whisper:

When you engage in a practice that silences the mind, you can open up to the sounds that often escape the awareness of the conscious self. Through meditative practices, you are tuning into a frequency that opens a channel to anything that you seek.

Meditative states increase the tone of resonance that vibrates from within and expands your thoughts into the welcoming Universe. A deeper understanding of Source energy can be found in this state of being, while messaging the Divine becomes clear.

In a moment of meditation, you can unlock the doors to the mysteries and magic that surround the angelic realm and beyond. This knowledge can ripple in all directions of space and time to create a healing benefit to all who know you, and even those who do not.

It is in the moment of contemplation that humans find the meaning of creation and therefore experience the feeling shared with God. Meditation is a mirror for love, faith, truth, beliefs, hope and anything that is considered positive. The fruits of your thoughts are preceded only by the seeds planted by your heart and soul.

Here is a word that has many different levels and layers when it comes to each individual's view of the world around us. I think we can all agree that the nation and world witnessed a miracle past this week. I am not talking about Obama's being our new president, even thought that may qualify in the minds and hearts of many.

I am talking about the story of birds taking out two engines on an Airbus over New York City, and a pilot landing the airplane in the frigid waters of the Hudson River in a way that allowed everyone to escape a certain tragedy. That, my friends, is a miracle!

Some define miracle in the simplest terms, while others place it on a level of impossibility, to the point of standing behind the belief that there is a rational explanation for everything in the Universe. I think I am somewhere on the simpler side (tee hee).

A client this week shared a story of healing that clearly demonstrated a connection with the Highest Power, Angels, Ascended Masters and loved ones on both sides of the veil. The result was the manifestation of fulfilling lifelong dreams, abundance, healing, ascension and a deepening of relationships, all with the feelings of destiny with guidance. It was literally jaw-dropping in the description of events that were well beyond explanation and deep into the mysteries of life and how it works.

One of my heroes, Dr. Marcel Vogel, who was a spiritual scientist, often said something like, "There are no such things as miracles, only your ability to connect with nature." This statement holds great meaning, and I am not sure whether he truly believed that or was using the statement as a way to teach us about manifesting miracles by changing our views. It's time to ask for some angelic insights in the form of a whisper:

Miracle is a word that does not adequately describe the energy that exists in the perception. The feeling of being a witness to a miracle is the raising of vibrations through joy, love of life and a connection with the Divine Source.

If you want to manifest a miracle in your life, clear way old hurts, release toxic emotions, engage in movement, eat healthy, nurture the heart, experience joy and give gratitude. You will raise your vibrations to a level that lowers the energy of control, expectations, ego judgments, old thought patterns and anything else that is standing in your way of creating heightened joy in your life.

If you want to define a miracle, first define your faith. Your faith supports your belief in a process that allows for Spirit to show you miracles on a regular basis, but first you must be open to the possibilities through the path of your truth.

By releasing all attachments to outcome and raising your vibrations to discover truth and clarity, you can redefine miracles in a way that makes them inclusive in your life and opens the door to receiving. Whether it is found in a sunset or a seemingly impossible outcome, miracles surround you and exist in your aura of love and light.

I have been hearing this word a lot lately, so I went to the Wikipedia definition to find out more. The word *monad* has Greek origins with the word *monos*, which means alone. According to the Pythagoreans, it was a term for God or the first being, or the totality of all beings. Monad, being the source or the One, meaning without division.

I believe that bringing balance to the body, mind and spirit is dependent on a connection with the energy of love, or what some refer to as Source energy. Maybe the meaning of monad holds some information around how we bring that balance.

In functional programming, a **monad** is a kind of abstract data-type constructor used to represent computations. In music, a monad refers to a single note. I love a word with all these meanings (tee hee)! Let's tune into a single note that springs from an angel who whispers on the word *monad*.

The duality found in the words aloneness and oneness can help demonstrate the monad, each feeling dependent on the other for true meaning. Without the back of the hand, there is no front of the hand. Polar opposites can exist without division and work in harmony to produce positive energy without conflict. When looking through the divine lens, there is no visible division of energy. Simply put, there can be opposing patterns that occupy the same space, like partners holding a common purpose.

You can choose to view man as one single organism or as several organisms combining to make one man. Yet another perspective offers that man is a part of the organism known as planet Earth, one of several parts that make up a Universe. You must determine your place in the Cosmos that you hold close to your heart and honor as your perspective of truth.

When facing opposition, the elevated perspective would allow you to be present and engaged during divisive moments. This not only opens your energy, but opens those who hold the opposing viewpoints. You are then creating an energy with purpose, true meaning and upward flow as each voice is heard and respected.

Meaning without division, direction without resistance, faith without question, love without condition and life without end describe the energies that are programmed in the monad of the eternal soul.

I was reading a biography that described an eight-year-old having the personal experience of committing a mortal sin. You know me (tee hee), I was all over the dictionary trying to understand the meaning.

In Roman Catholic moral theology, a **mortal sin** *must meet all of the following conditions at the same time: Its subject must be a grave (or serious) matter. It must be committed with full knowledge, both of the sin and of the gravity of the offense (no one is considered ignorant of the principles of the moral law, which are inborn as part of human knowledge, but these principles can be misunderstood in a particular context). It must be committed with deliberate and complete consent, enough for it to have been a personal decision to commit the sin.*

It was slightly shocking to read the definition and apply it to this person as compassion filled my heart with thoughts of a child making this determination. How his life must have been affected by the mere notion of one's fate being defined in such a way. Let's get a whisper from an angel in hopes of finding peace with the idea of committing a mortal sin:

In simple terms, committing a mortal sin represents 'wounding' the essence or the soul. Willful and conscious acts that go against the moral fiber of an individual help to create a path of assimilating information for the purpose of spiritual integration. Some may view this as the 'soul contract'.

Each person has a moral barometer or an internal gauge that measures the belief system both consciously and unconsciously. When someone intentionally crosses the line of their spiritual belief, they are inflicting a 'wound' to the self. The ego can partner with free will to create a conflict in order to experience the contrast that usually invokes a teaching on some level, which is determined by the nature of the act.

Some who commit mortal sins are manifesting a 'wound' that forms a personal barrier or distance from God. Descending into a personal darkness represents suffering, which can be an influence of Western religions that teach suffering as a way to salvation. Do not pity those who choose to go in to the depths of their darkness, for their path to ascension is a dramatic and profound soul experience beyond understanding.

In the moral fabric of society, each thread needs to weave the energy of personal responsibility and integrity. At the crossroads, where the ascending individual meets the descending souls, you will find an energetic vacuum that lifts each heart into the stream of Divine love and gentle Oneness. The journey is a sacred and shared experience.

It doesn't take a rocket scientist to see the great movement happening in our culture today (tee hee). Technological advances are making it easier to move about the continent from the safety of your own home or by taking off on a great adventure!

Time seems to be speeding up with 'real-time' news reports available to everyone, thanks to social media, technology and the courage of some select individuals. Even the movement of spirit seems to be instantaneous, and that could be the result of a heightened awareness available to all and sweeping the country!

Maybe you are considering a big move, and this has landed in your mailbox as an answer to your prayers (grinning). It is very possible that I was a hunter/gatherer or some type of nomad in one lifetime, as I get the movement bug every three years like clockwork.

And maybe it's simply time to move the body and some energy, whether it takes the form of micro-movements created from stillness, or giant leaps and bounds of faith-filled flight. Let's move an angel to the point of whispering a vibration that ushers in some form of movement!

Movement reflects the essence of spirit, and that is why people turn for guidance during periods of shifting energies. Whether it is moving the body for fun and exercise or moving across the globe, change is embraced in energy that has motion. Even in stillness, there is movement of breath, blood, electricity and energy.

Your divine path echoes the sentiment of movement with an illuminated path that beckons your involvement. In a moment of silence, spirit whispers direction and offers a source of support for extreme movement. That is often referred to as courage. But sometimes people get bored with silence as they fail to recognize the voice that comes from the great void with an offering of warmth, comfort and support for the journey ahead.

The exhilaration that comes from the feeling of moving fast is a remembrance of the joy and love that fills the soul. Those feelings evoked from a fast ride are helpful in awakening to movement, but you don't need a carnival experience to fulfill that Divine spark. You simply need to anchor yourself in the light that shines from within in order to have a knowing that spirit is with you.

Move your body, seek symbiotic relationships, move light from within, move beyond self-imposed constraints, and you will move with ascending energy. Within the spiraling ribbons of color and light is a place that is safely yours to call home. Come home through movement, and find what you have been searching for.

Music   *Sunday June 12, 2011*

Thanks for the Whisper request and all the fine editing work you do for me on the Whispers, Jen! In the same way that you and I occupy the space of these rooms and structures, it is said that angels occupy the space of sound, music and breath. Like angels, music is hard to define, and that definition has been a source of debate throughout the ages (tee hee).

I happen to believe that vibrations have to be included in the definition of music, but vibrations also define the essence that makes up the structure of our Universe. Stringed instruments are tuned with focus on vibrations. Horns attune to the vibrations of human breath. Drums are tuned to the pressure and tightness of the skin or head as it relates to vibration. Voice is tuned to the vibration of the heart.

As some of you know, I use singing bowls for healing and manifestation. These instruments tune and relate to specific energy centers of the human body. The bowls are known to bring the human mind to an Alpha state, which might explain the euphoric feeling that some people get when listening to music.

These Angel Whispers are received through vibrations and a type of listening to the feelings transmitted in a moment of resonance. Let's listen to the sound of music made by an angel to create a whisper:

When vibrations follow form and that form expresses passion, music is born. Mankind has always created a sound that becomes movement in sync with the rhythms of life. Ancient human life listened to heartbeats of nature in order to define the Universal rhythms, and then mimicked that creative energy.

The repeating patterns found in music define the beat that resonates with each generation and their part of the human existence. Tribes repeated that pattern through the Ages to passionately describe their own personal journey and as a way of honoring their earthly beginnings, as well as feeling the energy of those who came before them. Music became an integral part of ceremonies for this type of honoring, leaving song and rhythm as an indelible mark on every culture.

Today, music is the glue that holds the people of the world together. The song of each heart offers a bridge to peace for those willing to listen and hear the voice of truth. Your resonance with music reminds you of your home and place in the world and gives you that remembrance in no uncertain terms. Open your heart to sound, vibrations, breath and music to better hear the passionate stirrings of your heart and soul.

In your heavenly afterlife, music will connect you with the Divine stream of love that awaits everyone. For in music, Oneness is present and available, openings are created, spirit feels closer, love rises to the surface, creating a new paradigm, and the greatest opportunity for transformation exists. Angels love music!

In our modern times, we are constantly challenging our belief systems as science, medicine and spirituality come together to enlighten us with a vast expanse of knowledge. Belief in the unseen world can cross boundaries on a daily basis with ideas around energy, God and the meaning of life itself.

The process of writing the Angel Whispers provides a daily intersecting at these borders, and the word *nadis*, plural for *nadi*, is no exception. Nadis first appear in Sanskrit teachings in the 7th and 8th centuries BC. In these writings the heart was said to be the center of the 72,000 nadis.

Nadis are not nerves but rather channels for the flow of consciousness. Just as the negative and positive forces of electricity flow through complex circuits, in the same way vital force and mental force flow through every part of our body via these nadis. These channels are all over the human body, yet cannot been seen or detected like blood vessels and nerves.

Doctors and scientists are currently working with ideas around repairing the human brain using light to connect blocked channels or to correct the flow in nadis. The injection of fiber optic strands into the brain of mice shows remarkable results with hopes for immediate cures around illnesses such as Parkinson's disease.

Using the power of uniting energy flow by connecting the meridians or intersecting points in the human body is part of the evolution process. All the Saints and Divine incarnations who came on this earth advocated knowing this power which is the ultimate truth. And now for some ultimate truth from an Angel on the subject of nadis:

In order to connect with the Highest Power in the Universe, it is wise to turn to the human body for answers. Using the heart as the center, connecting the flow of energy can require the removal of blocks that have formed around the chakras of the body. This removal is anchored in achieving success in the areas of good health, spiritual cleansing and evolving into the truest form of human life.

The strength of your life force depends on the effort and willingness to surrender old thought forms and paradigms that have held you bound to a certain lifestyle or belief. Removal of blocks or resistance creates openings to experience passion at a deeper level, which fuels primal energy.

The power of love is felt at greater levels once the constraints regarding the belief of others have been dissolved. Your core vibrations in the human body are all the truth indicators that one needs to discern the properties of a Divine Life of purpose.

You can inject light to open the nadis by connecting with the spiritual aspect of these core vibrations and with help from your guides. Partnerships with the energy of love, nature and the Highest Power open the nadis through breath, movement, intention and some understanding around the truths held within the heart. Full awareness and enlightenment are not limited to the domain of Saints and Angels; on the contrary, they are available to you in this very moment.

This is a very interesting word to me because it is associated with both a definition and a gesture. Placing your palms together with fingers pointed upwards in front of the chest in combination with a head bow is the gesture associated with this word and can also be performed wordlessly while holding the same meaning.

This word has slightly different descriptions in various geographical areas and from different scholars, which makes it mysterious in some ways. I remember hearing the word for the first time and thinking what a beautiful sound the syllables made, especially when following a prayer in the flow of Divine communications.

*In everyday life, **namasté** can be considered a religious salutation. However, **namasté** is a Sanskrit term which can also be understood to mean "I respect that divinity within you that is also within me."*

The act of namasté unfolds on three levels: the mental, physical and verbal. "I honor the place in you where spirit lives, the spirit in me meets the same spirit in you." Namasté recognizes the duality that has existed in the world and suggests it's an effort on our part to bring these two forces together, ultimately leading to a higher unity and a non-dual state of oneness that pays honor to the sacredness of all.

Let's check in with the angels on the word *namasté*:

The sounds made by words like this evoke a unity through tonal unison. Like Om, there is a connection with Divine Source when evoking energy from the sound. When voices speak this in unison, with actions or through intentional energy, a balance of peace can exist.

If you are seeking the meaning of true ascension of consciousness through intentional living, words like this will find their way into your heart, voice and being. Teaching love means teaching others the meaning behind such energy.

Words and gestures can bridge gaps between people and unify cultures in unique and meaningful ways. Think of how you can change the world with raised consciousness, with simple greetings and departures that acknowledge the Divine Light in everyone. This could represent an exercise in teaching and raising vibrations through energetic connectiveness.

Through this practice of acknowledging the love and light in yourself and others, you will help bring understanding, the light of truth and the shift in belief that is being presented to everyone on the planet as you expand into the unique thread that connects all living matter. Awaken to the wisdom in the reflection of life through namasté.

This word is seen quite a bit in the *Whispers* and appears to be an integral part of the divine aspects of the world we live in. However, the picture that comes to mind when I say *nature* is one of beautiful landscapes and animals scurrying about!

Nature, in the broadest sense, is equivalent to the natural world, physical universe, material world or material universe. "Nature" refers to the phenomena of the physical world, and also to life in general. The term typically does not include manufactured objects and human interaction unless qualified; e.g., "human nature" or "the whole of nature". For the most part, Nature is also distinguished from the supernatural. Nature ranges in scale from the subatomic to the galactic.

There—it just happened again. I can't say that I ever before expanded my thinking of nature to include the stars and the universe. My expressions of nature were limited to the earthly plane and mainly to the outdoors (tee-hee). I am laughing at myself for a lifetime of 'little thinking.' Of course, nature is all around us all of the time, including our daily lives that we spend indoors.

I know that when I am awed by nature, in many ways I become connected with God or Source energy. Now I see that I have attached miracle status to several things that are just purely natural. I can now say with a chuckle, "Oh well, that's human nature!" And now I will ask for something that should be regarded as a natural part of everyone's existence, an angel whisper:

Nature is the supreme example of how you are all one with each other. Nature has a way of bringing together all elements of the life experience. There is knowledge and mystery to be found in nature. You don't have to go any farther than your own breath to find it.

In the beginning, there was only nature in its most extreme and wild form. Man has attempted to control, tame and predict all of nature. If you look at what man has made during his time on Earth, you could make an argument that it is all part of the natural expression of mankind and therefore one with the environment.

Even wars could be viewed as human nature. Yet this is one example of how man has manipulated the environment to include war as a part of everyday life on planet Earth. With the evolution of the human consciousness, true change could eliminate war as a part of human nature.

Divine Source and the angelic realm are consistent with all of nature. When you look into the eyes of an animal or pick up a stone to connect with the essence, you are feeling the energy of nature and the core of Prana. This is the life force that has made the human experience not only possible, but rewarding on the soul level. Look deep inside the heart and you will witness true nature at work!

*According to Wikipedia, a **vacuum** is a volume of space that is essentially empty of matter, such that its gaseous pressure is much less than the atmospheric pressure. The word comes from the Latin term for "empty." A **perfect vacuum** would be one with no particles in it at all, which is impossible to achieve in practice.*

When a low-pressure system moves out of the area, it is usually because a dome of high pressure is pushing in. The same type of condition occurs to form hurricanes and tornadoes, which gives some example of the way nature fills a void.

In the same way that nature fills our physical environment, it must fill the vacuum of our personal energy whenever there is a void. Energy goes where energy flows, and creating a vacuum without the focus provided by intentions or some form of purposeful awareness could inadvertently draw on some unwanted energy or pressure.

In today's world, there are many opportunities to pick up some bad energy. Creating an energetic vacuum as a product of physical healing, spiritual growth, manifestations, or for any purpose might require an intention or focus that includes the replacement of expended energy. The angels must have great expertise to share in regard to the way nature fills a vacuum:

When you are experiencing the depth of an emotional feeling, you have created a vacuum through a shift in energy. Drawing to you the lessons that life has to offer is simply filling the void or the dark aspects of the soul. The Sun shines down in the outer world, but the inner world is dark and needs your light to illuminate the path.

Nature provides that inner light through experiences that fill the void of darkness. Energetically speaking, the more you allow your light to shine, the less 'empty space' there is to fill. You might feel alone as you search the darkness for signs of light on Earth, but this is merely providing a foundation of personally acquired knowledge from which you will gain the wisdom of an experienced soul.

If you descend into the darkness each time you are with a person or facing a particular situation, the vacuum is being created and dark matter can start filling the void. If a person or situation is lifting you in an upward flow of energy, you are filling the void with the naturally occurring vibrations of luminous energy.

The atmosphere of the Earth is analogous with the human journey, in that high pressure will usher in stability and sunlight, while low pressure brings an unstable and sometimes stormy environment. To keep the vibrations high and filled with light, get in touch with your energy and make choices designed to hold a high-vibrational balance in all areas of life. Your balanced energy helps the world find peace.

New Age has become a label with a bad connotation, like so many others in our language, such as *liberal, environmentalists, Lightworkers* or even *contractors* (tee hee). I have friends who interpret the English language by the tone in which it is spoken, and in some ways I think everyone does this in any language, whether consciously or not.

The truth is that we are entering a New Age and as we shift into the energy of the Age of Aquarius, we are repeating an earth cycle that is 26,000 years old. There is nothing new about it, other than it is new to us in this lifetime.

As you may know, I usually include a definition in my Angel Whispers, but as I researched the term, I found ridiculous and condemning descriptions and meanings. Everything from those containing atheistic beliefs to non-Christian traditions, combined with a text 'tone' to have you believe that crystals, Tarot cards and astrology are the newest forms of spiritual extremism. It was a real eye-opener and an affirmation of my resistance to being labeled as such. So no definition this time, except from the angels (lol)! So with that, let's see what the angelic guides have to say about the New Age:

There is nothing new about the language of man and the interpretation of language, except the times. Certain meanings around the use of such terms are often taken and used in order to gain power over people. If someone can trigger a block or resistance simply by using or misusing a word, it can easily become a tool to gain control over the masses.

In addition, this can draw people to the movement with promises of joining a group of like minds to reject establishments and hierarchy. As religious and social structures collapse under the weight of stagnant energy, economic irresponsibility and outdated teachings, people will search for alternatives. The teachings brought to mankind were meant to be expanded by taking a foundation and building on it. It should come as no surprise that these find resistance from those wanting to maintain power.

There are illusions in every aspect of human development, so that people can learn and grow. If you accept this, using basic teachings as your foundations and expanding from there, you will release old paradigms with a conscious flow in the future. The reason that some visions feel negative is part of the process of discernment around these illusions. In that light, you are stepping into a new age of enlightenment, spirituality, living in conscious harmony and learning new levels of trust within your self.

If you create a space in your mind and heart that affirms within every person there is an avatar, you can find success in your New Age discernment, feel the Universal energy that connects all of life and evolve into a higher consciousness. Within this heart space, you can feel the essence of the New Age without attachments to the beliefs of others and with unrestrained love and joy for the opportunity that is before you now.

Dr. Marcel Vogel was a spiritual scientist and one of the most prolific minds of our times. With several patents to his credit, he surprised many people with the profound results of his laboratory experiments. He proved in the lab what he showed in his talks and workshops, that we are what we think. By measuring the electro-magnetic field of the human body, Marcel taught us how one single bad thought toward another individual lowered the energetic field of the person that the thought is directed towards, while a loving and kind thought raised this field or aura.

We could easily use our common sense to recognize the results of these experiments, but he could put it in scientific terms and show the reality of the results of negative thoughts. I started changing my thought process and found we are so conditioned by our society that this was no simple task.

I recently received this quote from DallasNews.com in an article about the current election: "A lot of people ask one question: If Obama became president, would he live?" said Mr. Simon. "That's the scary part. Will someone take a crack shot at him?"
This is a great example of negative thinking sent out to the masses. Mr. Simon was hurling daggers at Obama with this horrible thought based in fears.

After spending some time with a friend this last week, I observed that she was the most pleasant negative thinker I had ever seen. She said everything in such a nice way that usually ended in a joke or laughter. She was the most positive negative thinker I have ever witnessed! In the end, her take on things in almost every area was negative.

Now that I have worked at and changed my thinking, I have realized that even if an event is negative, my positive thought about it is so much better for my mind, body and spirit. As Americans, we usually respond to tragedies in great style, so having the negative thought doesn't really serve anyone. In a way, it instills a total lack of faith. This is where I will use my positive thinking to get a whisper on negative thinking (tee hee).

It is human nature to have negative thoughts, and to some this is a defense mechanism. It is their way to maneuver through life with a way to shelter themselves from disappointment, despair and depression by not only lowering all expectations, but also to change them by expecting the worst outcome.

In the evolution process, mankind must overcome this way of life in order to open up to the joy of living. When you eliminate a negative thought by replacing it with an optimistic view, you have shown gratitude to God, Source and your soul.

The process of having a negative thought can easily be changed by your total awareness. This can create an opportunity to allow yourself the pleasure of thinking and feeling the most positive outcome in any situation.

The purpose in thinking positively is to gift yourself with a happy resonance regarding your future. Therefore you will create a path filled with the vibrations of love, light, faith in mankind and numerous reasons to find the joy of life given to you at birth.

As I engage in the process of studying words, the path to discovery seems littered with remnants of our history. These remnants appear as shiny gems casting beams of light into the darkness and are a reference to the great quotes and word meanings that inspire the 'angel whispers.'

Simply put, an **obligation** *is a requirement to take some course of action, whether legal or moral.* **1.** *The act of binding oneself by a social, legal, or moral tie.* **2.** *A course of action imposed by society, law, or conscience by which one is bound or restricted.* **3.** *The constraining power of a promise, contract, law, or sense of duty.*

Here are a few quotes that best express the meaning of obligation, followed by some quotes from the angels in the form of a whisper:

Our major obligation is not to mistake slogans for solutions. – Edward R. Murrow, American news broadcaster

In other words, a democratic government is the only one in which those who vote for a tax can escape the obligation to pay it. – Alexis De Tocqueville, French social philosopher

"Doing your own thing" is a generous act. Being gifted creates obligations, which means you owe the world your best effort at the work you love. You too are a natural resource. – Barbara Sher, speaker, coach and author

Not only is there a right to be happy, there is a duty to be happy. So much sadness exists in the world that we are all under obligation to contribute as much joy as lies within our powers. – John S. Bonnell, pastor and author

If the energy of an action that has been labeled an obligation stems from toxic emotions, re-evaluation and further discernment may serve you. When an obligation brings up resistance, this could be a sign that your body is messaging a need to take another look at the action step that is before you. Cords of attachments based in negative emotions can support actions that are out of alignment with your true intentions.

It is easy for a false sense of commitment to rule your priorities and thus override your energy in a way that could be self-destructive, but there is always knowledge provided in these actions that carries some insight around the truth of your being. Distractions can be a delay tactic used by your ego and the matrix to fool you into thinking that your obligation is an essential part of your Divine Life-Purpose.

Therefore it is important to discern any obligations based in false illusions around your sense of duty in order to ensure the positive direction of energy. You made but one commitment to the world when you evolved onto the physical plane, and that is an obligation to move in the direction that brings you closer to love for the Highest Power in the Universe, loving life and loving yourself.

When your mind, body and spirit move in harmony with this alignment, you have just successfully made the world a better place to live! Balance what you think with what you feel, to fully express an obligation to love.

When this popped out of my mouth the other day, I immediately thought I had coined a new term (tee hee)! You have heard the phrase 'optical illusion', which is defined as an *optical phenomenon that results in a false or deceptive visual impression.* I think we create obstacles and blocks with our thinking in much the same way that a visual experience can be deceptive.

The Universe is filled with opportunities to trick ourselves into believing something that is fabricated and false, which leaves us stuck, unable to move forward, or giving up entirely on our dreams. Many times I give voice to ideas and beliefs that were built on a premise or assumption, and therefore hold the space for my personal obstacle illusions.

Just telling ourselves we can do something and holding a vision for it may not be enough to overcome obstacles that were nicely formed and promptly buried away like paperclips beneath a mountain of paperwork (lol). Let's see if we can clear the desk and uncover the secret to removing obstacle illusions with the help from an angel that whispers:

It is easy to discount your feelings and allow thoughts that invalidate your ability to manifest a joyful and peace-filled existence. The logical mind can easily latch onto information that, while it may be true for one person, for you it could be that the opposite applies. By attaching to an outcome, you have formed an illusion that may block your flow of energy.

Awareness is the conscious mind's building a bridge in order to cross the layers that blanket an illusion. Listening to the voice that speaks from beyond the physical senses could serve as a way to illuminate the path that best serves. This could take courage and a willingness to leave your comfort zone in the search for ways to unlock the chains that bind you to an illusion.

Getting trapped by your own thoughts is common to mankind, yet you are being given an opportunity to step outside the framework of a social consciousness that is anchored in the past. The greatest opportunities for change has never presented itself with the least number of true obstacles..

During this holiday season, you would be best served to find completions to the projects you have committed to. Simplify your life in ways that bring joy and freedom to the soul. Take responsibility for your actions and face your life in the light of truth as a pathway to the highest level of resolution. Find spiritual food in the script you are writing for the next phase of your life. These steps will serve in the removal of obstacle illusions, which allows the greatest vibration of love to be felt at the deepest levels of your soul.

Opposition could be defined as resistance or the action of opposing something that you disapprove of or disagree with. Competition is the act of competing, as for profit or a prize. But according to Eliphas Levi, "Equilibrium results only from opposition of forces; the active has no existence without the passive, light without darkness produces no form, and affirmation can only triumph over negation. Love again gains ascension of strength from hate. Power is composed of two opposing forces, which unite in love and disjoin in discord; love associates contraries while hate makes similars to be rivals and enemies; hatred succeeds to love when by saturation the void has become filled."

I read this surprising passage on Sunday after an interesting conversation with friends the previous night. We were having dinner at a local trailer eatery in South Austin called "The Odd Duck" when the idea for this whisper came up, specifically within the context of intimate relationships. Life partners teach us lessons when they oppose our views, so why does that feel more like competition at times?

Maybe the angels can help us with a whisper of loving understanding around finding the balance in opposition, by connecting us with the camaraderie of competition:

When examining responses within relationships, it is easy to question what lies below the surface of a reaction. The ego can take energy and create a response that does not align with either party, which is then termed a misunderstanding. Since your experience transfers energy into emotions to facilitate a release, the general feeling might be that opposition is unloving. Feelings of rejection and abandonment along with issues around trust and safety can lead to feeling misunderstood, which in turn, generates a repeating behavioral response from a defensive position when opposed. Opposition meets resistance and communication breaks down.

Competition can feed the spirit in the reward of commitment and discipline before any goal is ever realized. The individuals working together toward that goal can bring opposition that draws the optimum performance. In that respect, the rival has fueled your abilities by providing a focused target and, therefore, is truly a partner in your success. This feeling rarely comes from disapproval or discontent, but rather from empowerment and accomplishment.

A peacekeeper who operates in the energy of opposition, like an angel, is a true being of light. If opposition is met with respect and honor, you are more likely to illuminate the lesson that bridges all gaps to achieve balance. When you create the heart opening that comes from the elevated perspective known as the Christ Consciousness, you allow the flow of energy to be balanced with the heart and mind. Listen equally to both and you will be nurturing your own spirit.

In order to respond with the energy of love, you must first learn how to receive with that same energy.

I couldn't decide on just one of these words due to my deep personal feelings toward both and the apparent relationship between the two. Instead of the half-full or half-empty analogy, you could say my glass is simply halfway at the moment (tee hee). I consider myself to be a fairly optimistic person, yet periods of my life have found me on the other side of that proverbial fence.

Optimism is an inclination to put the most favorable construction upon actions and events or to anticipate the best possible outcome. Optimists generally believe that people and events are inherently good, so that most situations work out in the end for the best. Pessimism, from the Latin pessimus (worst), is a state of mind which negatively colors the perception of life, especially with regard to future events. "A pessimist is one who makes difficulties of his opportunities, and an optimist is one who makes opportunities of his difficulties." (Harry Truman)

When I reflect on my pessimistic years, I see that my faith was at low point, which would indicate a relationship between a person's faith and their general outlook on life. I also will admit that I built illusions around being pessimistic, with mantras like "If I am always prepared for the worst, I will never be disappointed." I turned what I perceived as a coping skill into a way of life (ouch)! I feel the need to optimistically turn to the angelic guides for a whisper on the subject:

No matter how you look at it, you are describing the process of attaching to outcome in order to determine your feelings in the moment. Past hurts can allow the energy around optimism or pessimism to manifest in the form of boundaries. It can also appear that these boundaries protect the heart, but that is an illusion. Filling the heart with discouraging outlooks closes and blocks feelings and can lead to a permanent state of closure.

In terms of faith, do you want to place your faith in the possibility of negative events or positive feelings? The eternal optimist takes the form of an angel on Earth in order to deliver and distribute faith-based energies across the globe. These people emulate angelic energy as a way to connect themselves and others with the Christ Consciousness, which represents the conscious overview of mankind. The belief that everything is in Divine order is the highest form of faith, which leads to optimistic outlooks on life.

The body, mind and spirit have the power to make choices, so it is ultimately your free will that will decide your outlook on life. Truth and realistic views are important features of the purpose-filled life. Within that illumination of all truth that surrounds you, the cup is always half-full. The mental recognition of truth comes from the deepest core of your spirit, which in turn translates emotions, feelings and vibrations. Do you wish to vibrate with the negative or the positive side of life? The choice is yours.

This is a word that is after my own heart! For almost all of time, man has farmed and raised foods that were organic. It wasn't until the 20th century and the invention of synthetics that our food source turned into something else. I like to focus on healthy living and I am organic too (tee hee), so it must be better for me to focus on organic. But I like all things organic and not just food. For example, the more music sounds organic, the better.

It is interesting to me when people make derogatory statements about organic foods, and I must admit that the labeling and certification of products deemed organic have brought up trust issues. I was shopping in a local organic market that offered organic and non-organic Brazil nuts, but I had just read where the entire world's supply of Brazil nuts are found in the rain forests and not certified farms.

Today I am witnessing a generation that is bringing their gifts to the table with a style and ease that couldn't be better described than pure and organic. In today's world of rules and regulations that certify and quality things to be sold as organic, I am proud to be engaged in services and activities that offer some level of a natural experience. And now we will break away to listen for an organic connection with an angel who whispers:

The focus on nature and the environment has placed organic products at the forefront of the minds of many. By placing focus on the benefit of keeping things organic, mankind begins a long-overdue process of healing the Earth and its inhabitants.

One of the beauties of nature is that everything is available to meet the needs of many, but discernment is essential. There is a group of souls that volunteered to help the planet by forming a bridge that connects modern man to the ancient wisdom, so part of the experience offered today is a return to those ancient thoughts, ideas and actions.

When you think of the word organic, it is synonymous with the nature of children. The curiosity, innocence, love and faith inherently found in children are part of the natural make-up of mankind. When you see these qualities of children, you are witnessing the last conscious stream of divine love that soul experienced prior to the journey into the body. Now that's organic!

Man moved away from some aspects of nature in the last century and it is time to return to the courage, comfort and confidence that come naturally. The body, mind and spirit all have voices that are constantly speaking to you about your inherent organic nature. Listen to those voices that are calling like a subtle wind moving through the magic forest of your consciousness.

OK, this is a word that I made up. Maybe I can trick the angels into some deep meaning and have fun with hearing a whisper on this moment of silliness (lol). Words are still being born every day as our languages morph with our own conscious response to evolution, followed by a verbalization of connecting sounds.

I appeared on Alison Baughman's Visible by Numbers radio show on Monday night within minutes of returning home from a weekend workshop in Tulsa. As I listened to her introduction, I was filled with a warm energy of reflection. I opened to receive her kind words with a simultaneous realization of how far I have come on my path in a relatively short time.

I was still buzzing from a wonderful weekend with a beautiful group of people in Tulsa as I drew in the breath of receiving and exhaled gratitude to the angels and the Highest Power. The result was this new word emerging from my mouth as I described the feeling of hearing Alison's words to Beckie, my wife of 32 years this Thanksgiving.

*Overflowing means to fill a space to capacity and spread beyond its limits while glowing means to shine with, or as if with an intense heat. Embers radiating in the darkness or to show exuberance and elation can also describe the word **glowing**.*

I hope all of you had a great Thanksgiving as I now give gratitude to you and the angels with some fun and a smile from me to you. Thank you all for receiving my "Angel Whispers" and sending your comments. May your days be overglowing throughout the holidays and beyond! Now for a whisper on my new word:

The creation of combining sounds is as old as mankind. The first sounds from the human body attached meaning to tones and feelings behind the expressions of communication. As man evolves, the need for language will diminish into complete expression of thought and energy.

Making up words is a reminder to us angels that you are being creative, playful and accepting of new ideas and thoughts that will ultimately lead you down the path of completely divine expressions. Every word that you use is within that same energy, since someone created each word that you use today. The connection between the sound, the thought and the manner of speaking gave someone a resonance with each word created.

Creating words and sounds can be individualized and therefore you should not exclude yourself from the domain of teachers and scholars. Every sound is unique to the moment and the individual as a personal expression from the human body, which is a sound instrument. Speaking each word as a songwriter sings their song will bring greater meaning and heartfelt expression to others as your gift to them.

Overglowing vibrates with the love that it was intended to bring. Abundance, joy, love, passion, gratitude and light combined with warmth exude from the breath released with speaking this word. Your gratitude was felt and received when you spoke this word with laughter and playfulness in your heart. For this reason, we are now expressing that this word is in true alignment with your soul with a greater understanding of who you are.

This last week I had an accident while out on my morning bicycle ride. As some of you have already guessed, this is where I get my Angel Whispers. Riding and exercising around Lady Bird Lake (formerly Town Lake) is my spiritual food, my meditation and my overall wellness program. Apparently I hit a bottle that propelled me into the street, and when I overcompensated, I was thrown off the bike and into the curb.

The result was a broken clavicle and two broken ribs in my back, along with some serious road rash. I somehow managed to break several bones that have no prescribed 'fix' other than pain pills, rest and immobility. I have to say that on a scale of ten, my pain levels reached at least an eleven and stayed there for several days.

As I slowly recovered, I couldn't help but think of the times that I asked my clients, "Has your pain served you in some way?" While most people surprisingly say *Yes* to that question, I often wondered about their answers. I have heard things like, "It made me take a break" and "I had time to reflect" or "My life changed for the better after the accident." I think I have already begun to answer that question for myself.

Pain: 1) a feeling of being hurt; suffering (the death of the one we love causes pain). In my practice, I deal with lots of different kinds of pain, and now I have greatly expanded my knowledge of physical pain (LOL). Did I tell you that laughing hurts? My pain has already taught me valuable lessons on receiving help from others. I really had no choice but to receive, as I had very little to give back. I must say the outpouring of support was overwhelming at times and filled me in a way that I have never experienced before.

My inner voice and angelic guides told me not to go out on that slick rainy morning. I didn't listen, even though I have an honorable excuse. Several have asked "Where were your angels? Don't you talk to them?" Had a car been coming in that lane or had I failed to wear my helmet, that outcome could have been drastically different. Angels can't protect us from the dangers of life or prevent us from feeling pain, but they can help us with how we deal with it. I will now ask for an interruption of pain in the moment of a whisper:

Pain is, on the scale of human emotions, at the opposite end of joy. It is an unavoidable part of life that includes the free will of others. The pain that you experience can be a test of faith and a change in perspective. The lesson that you learn from pain can help you make choices that will serve you in the future. Part of the life experience includes easing the pain of others as a way to serve in the balance of suffering.

Sometimes pain can be unbearable and creates a necessity to cross over. Your society has little to offer in the ways to best deal with this problem. Therefore we have sent teachers to provide lessons in this area. You know these teachers. As you witness pain and suffering in others, you will grow in appreciation of joy, love and contentment. The opening of the heart is often marked by the compassion felt for others. It is not up to Divine Source to limit the experiences of man, only to expand the horizons of the eternal light that shines in the energy of the life force.

Paradigm Shift

First we must understand *paradigm* to really grasp the meaning of one that is shifting. I think the reason this subject came up is due to the movement of energy that is occurring across the globe right now. There is a natural order of the Universal Laws that dictates that we as humans engage in a constant challenge to not only push beyond the limitations we impose on ourselves, but to take it a step further and change the definition of those barriers as we evolve.

Merriam-Webster Online defines paradigm as a philosophical or theoretical framework of any kind. The structure that serves as an individual model for social behavior and development is something that I am attempting to help shift within many of my clients (and me too!). Perhaps the greatest barrier to a paradigm shift is the reality of paradigm paralysis: The inability to see beyond the current models of thinking. This could best describe some emotional states that people find themselves facing while living within a repressive and judgmental framework that obscures their future or view of themselves.

If you think about this from a broad perspective, you can easily start to understand that we can't possibly know the essence of what the ideal structure is or we would all be happily living within it (tee hee). The need for mankind to constantly push on our paradigm can drive the thirst for knowledge about the mysteries of life and death. I have to admit that I have shifted many paradigms on my journey into the world of listening for a whisper from an angel:

Knowledge is something that is presented to you every day and at all levels. This is part of the basic ingredients that make up the human experience. This knowledge comes from several sources and there is always one that resonates within your reach. Even a butterfly can transcend a moment with a transmission of knowledge about your life on Earth.

Understanding is the acceptance of this knowledge. Spiritual knowledge goes to the deepest level of the soul and brings the surrender of paradigms that no longer serve a purpose. This shift can free the heart in a way that lacks description in the written word. Diligence in paying careful attention to the paradigms that are currently in place around you is rewarded with spontaneous energetic movement with every shift that occurs.

Great moments in the history of mankind have recorded paradigm shifts with an imprint on your essence or Soul. From Jesus of Nazareth to the fallen Veterans of the Iraq war, a paradigm shift has exchanged the energy as a transmutation of the ultimate sacrifice. This creates a new opportunity in the evolution experience.

If you want to shift your paradigm, first surrender the self-imposed structure that you have been living with. Give the old thought patterns to the angels and they will help you release that part of you. Feel the energy of freedom from that paradigm and know that energy as your connection with Divine Source. In that loving moment of freedom, your paradigm has shifted and you are free to experience the greater love that exists in your new level of consciousness. In all paradigm shifts there is a new perspective.

I was talking to a friend and spiritual leader the other day when she said something that moved my creative juices, in the form of deep thoughts. She was talking about passion as it relates to the scale of living emotions. She told me that passion was just below love on that chart.

As I thought about that, I realized 'of course it is,' your passion is also your love, and what you love is also your passion, in most cases. I have many passions, including my wife, music, faith and cycling. As a matter of fact, my epiphany was that I have several passions in my life, and I am therefore passionate about life.

After that recent crash on my bicycle, many have asked if I will ride that bike again. That question is usually in regards to facing my fears by riding my bike and following that same route that I took on my fateful journey. I have answered yes to the   question several times, but my answer is more about facing my passions and not my fears.

My passion can get me in trouble over the things that I do. I am sure that Beckie would prefer that I give up my passion to ride in exchange for a passion less worrisome for her. I also extend myself in other areas when my passion calls for action. I might deliver a package that no one has asked for, if you know what I mean.

Passion: 1) very strong feeling (hate and fear are passions); 2.violent anger, rage; 3) archaic: suffering. These definitions surprised me in that they seemed closer to the opposite end of the scale from love, which is hate. The suffering part sure fits in with my passionate bike ride (tee hee). Maybe the Passion of Christ comes into play here, thus linking the word to the suffering of Jesus.

Another passion of mine is my angel whispers and the feedback created by them. I can say without a doubt that this passion lies slightly below love on my scale of life. I will passionately await a whisper on this beautiful word: [Oh, that's good!]

The passion of mankind has created the evolution of a species that affects the world and the Universe. From Source, there is a feeling that is delivered to ignite the passion within. If you are not passionate about what you do, what you do will lack passion.

It is true that passion can fuel such things as anger, fears and hate. But what lies beneath the surface of these emotions is love that searches for answers. Once these have been successfully received, the passion converts all of life to love.

Passion is also purple on the color spectrum, so it is close to the Divine essence that attracts all beings. There is a peace that can be found in passion, and this speaks to the power of wants and desires that eventually lead to satisfaction and contentment.

In the passion residing in the essence of a man, there is an eternal love that fans the flames of the fire. The opening of the heart invites the fire of passion that lights the path to the higher self. Divine inspiration plants the seeds of passion through timeless love.

I think my Mom might say "passed life," but seriously, a recent report indicated that 27% of Americans believe they lived a past life, and that number is up from 23% just a few years ago. I was very skeptical with my belief until I had my own experiences in this area that helped me better understand the issue.

Past-life regression is a psychological or spiritual phenomenon associated with the New Age movement and a belief in reincarnation. It can be conducted through hypnosis, guided or facilitated meditations, or other trance-inducing activities. It takes a variety of forms, though is always the process of a person being regressed to learn particularly about their traumas and karmic events associated with issues and patterns in their current life.

For example, if someone was betrayed in a past life they may have an unusual need to feel trust. Or if someone lost their life because they spoke up about their beliefs, they may be less likely to verbalize faith in this lifetime. These past-life issues are subconsciously driven and can greatly affect this lifetime in the form of negative behaviors or unwanted emotions. On the more positive side, people who experienced great wealth in a past life can draw on the knowledge to maneuver through this lifetime without a fear of lack or worry about money.

This is all about karmic issues beyond this lifetime and the effects, both positive and negative, and how they influence who we are, why we are here, the way we choose our challenges and a plethora of reasons behind an emotional response, including one that may define our life purpose. Regardless, this gives me a reason to be thankful we are not given memory of these events, and to engage in the deep-thinking process that includes a need to ask for a whisper of additional insight:

Past-life experiences shape the evolution of man. These challenges presented in various lifetimes need to be conquered for man to go to the next level of ascension and learning. You don't have to relive these issues, but it does serve you to face them on some level.

There are advanced beings in your midst that can lead you to discovery and insight regarding your essence and the various effects of energetic conveyance of information. Your body, mind and spirit can feel resonance with this information that serves as a way to overcome and release the emotional attachment to these stories of the soul.

Inside of everyone lies a need to understand and become fully aware of your soul journey. As you learn the lessons of this lifetime, you can release the need to know, feel or experience the self beyond this lifetime and beyond this moment.

In each person's story, there is a truth that goes beyond the physical limitations. It is this search for truth that propels humans into lifetime after lifetime. When you can hold and accept the truth about who you are, you are holding the light and love that is the gift from God and Divine Source. Belief in the unknown is your defining measure of faith.

Thanks for the idea and inspiration for this whisper, Bari. I thought that I would write about patience sometime in the next several weeks, but I couldn't wait! In our fast-paced world that we live in, patience is a precious commodity.

Patience 1. Willingness to put up with waiting, pain, trouble, etc.; calm endurance without complaining or losing self-control. 2. Long, hard work; steady effort.

How old is my desktop dictionary? I have two and this one was published in 1965 and it shows. I love old books but I'm not sure how long I can endure this one without complaining.

Seriously, I have been told several times that I have a lot of patience. I think mine comes mainly from working on old houses all those years. It takes patience with the somewhat slower pace that is required to repair old structures. Over the years, I worked with people who were trying to cross over from new construction to restoration work, allowing me to get a firsthand look at someone losing their patience.

Losing your patience really magnifies the old adage, "You don't know what you've got till it's gone." I have to say on those occasions where I lost my patience, I felt overwhelmed by the number of details usually outside my control. The more cluttered my thinking gets, the harder it is to make decisions and this really affects my patience.

I've also noticed that the times where I have misplaced my patience are the times that generate the need to read a self-help book. In other words, anger management is the process of engaging patience. You might say that anger is the opposite of patience, and with anger come those 'cords of attachment.' When you attach a cord of anger, chances are you lost your patience. Now I will patiently await the next whisper:

Patience is a virtue. Those who are surrounding themselves with love in the moment have an abundance of patience. Do you see the relationship? Dissatisfaction with your situation, circumstance or station in life often leads you down the path of impatience.

Music of the heart is a prescription for maximizing your patience level. A song or melody has a tempo that can not be rushed as you are moving and flowing with the music. Each individual has their own 'heart song' that evokes the patience to maneuver through the life process.

Patience begins with an understanding and knowledge of the core issues of your life. Take the time to make an assessment of who you are by holding yourself up to a true light. When you truly know who you are, then you will find peace and calmness.

In the child-self, there lies a truth about who you are, who you want to be and where you are going. When you go into a quiet sacred space such as nature provides, you will re-discover the clarity of purpose and the patience of a child.

Many people across the globe are praying for peace, with a zestful yearning to witness this feeling or state of being with cultures around the world. But what would that look like and what form could that take? The war machines are just that, driven by money, power, individual beliefs and a long history of forcing their will on others.

Personal peace to me is the quieting of the mind, body and spirit. Reaching for a stillness that warms the heart even in the midst of a chaotic and fast-paced environment is something that more and more people are striving for. The increased momentum of stimulating the senses through the experiences our society has to offer no longer brings the thrill or newness original to that energy.

*Derived from the Anglo-Norman pas, c.1140, and meaning "freedom from civil disorder," the personalized meaning of peace is reflected in a non-violent lifestyle which also describes a relationship between any people characterized by respect, justice and goodwill. This latter understanding of **peace** can also pertain to an individual's sense of himself or herself, as to be "at **peace**" with one's own mind. The early English term is also used in the sense of "quiet," reflecting a calm, serene, and meditative approach to the family or group relationships that avoids quarreling and seeks tranquility or an absence of disturbance or agitation.* With that explanation and understanding, I will ask for some peace of mind to reach for a whisper from an angel on peace:

Peace is a word that describes a feeling, therefore the true essence of this word is something that must be felt and experienced rather than simply implied. Discussions in groups are beneficial to creating peace between nations, but it is the people that must make a stand for peace in the name of loving thy neighbor.

Peace is available to everyone, yet there has to be willingness and an intention to achieve inner peace. It is your choice, and choosing peace is saying yes to the Higher Self with acknowledgments toward your personal Soul journey.

A collective majority of people willing to stand up for peace is all that is needed as the power struggles shift from world leaders to the choice and hands of the people. In your meditations, hold the world in your hands as you breathe in the energy of the Divine while breathing out the prayers for peace. In this way, you are giving your powers to manifest peace to the world through individual intentions.

It is important for each individual to hold a space in their hearts for hope to dwell in harmony with the vibrations of love and peace. This is the partnership between man and Divine Source energy that develops world peace through an inner sanctum of communion with spirit. Asking for peace is symbolic of your release of control that represents an invitation for Spirit's involvement in the continuum of movement toward that which serves the highest good for mankind, a peaceful planet.

*According to sapdesignguild.org, **perception** is the process by which organisms interpret and organize sensation to produce a meaningful experience of the world. Sensation usually refers to the immediate, relatively unprocessed result of stimulation of sensory receptors in the eyes, ears, nose, tongue, or skin. **Perception**, on the other hand, better describes one's ultimate experience of the world and typically involves further processing of sensory input. In practice, sensation and perception are virtually impossible to separate, because they are part of one continuous process.*

If sensation and perception are barely distinguishable, that could explain a few things (tee hee). My perception can be altered in a moment where my emotions take over. Hurt my feelings and you change my perspective? This is when it comes in handy to have a brain that can tell you when the heart is over-reacting.

If we perceive based on our sensations, having our emotions in balance would create the healthiest perception. Judgments might emerge from an emotion that tricks us into a belief or makes up our mind. I don't want my position in life supported by falsehoods from the senses, so how do I discern the truth and the illusion? Time for a whisper on perception:

If you remove the drama, the pain, the judgments of others and any illusions, your perception has a better chance to be anchored in the energy of truth and love. There are so many factors like external energy, social pressures, parental models and raw emotions that feed the sensory system, it can be challenging to know that which supports your position. Awakening to the truth of your existence and seeking balance in every relationship will not only serve the senses, but will serve to ground you in the higher vibrations.

Your perception is altered by the choices you make regarding relationships, so you must look at each foundation and your motivations. If you are in a relationship that is virtually void of love and filled with a sense of duty, the likelihood for false perceptions increase. If you are fully committed to love in a relationship, the overall sensory experience can support a healthy perception.

You are guided to focus on your commitments in order to answer the questions of motivation, intention and beliefs, so that you may align with every dimension of your being, Chances are, if nothing is being served in a relationship and there is no defined purpose, your perception could suffer illusions or tricks offered by the Universe.

Your position holds the vibrations that establish behavior patterns, so the experience of joy is what you are ultimately seeking in order to bring perception into full focus.

What a great word suggested by my very own mother after she sent me an email that had a poignant description from the perspective of a child. I couldn't help but think that this child's perspective held a lot of truth in the area of how we view our lives.

Perspective in theory of cognition is the choice of a context or a reference from which to sense, categorize, measure or quantify experience, cohesively forming a coherent belief, typically for comparing with another. One may further recognize a number of subtly distinctive meanings, close to those of paradigm, point of view or reality tunnel. To choose a perspective is to choose a value system and, unavoidably, an associated belief system. When we look at a *business perspective*, we are looking at a monetary-based values system and beliefs. When we look at a *human perspective*, it is a more social value system and its associated beliefs.

So from that definition, I wonder if many of us don't choose our belief first and then accept whatever value system is attached. I like the sound of the reality tunnel and it sounds like something I would pay money to experience (tee hee). The truth is that I have tried to place myself in that tunnel and it can be a tough place to go because it can challenge my beliefs and expose areas that need releasing, changing or accepting.

This weekly column that I write is almost completely my perspective with a whisper of definition added to challenge my own truth about things. This is something that I have had deep discussions with others about. Basically, our perspective is the truth that we hold about ourselves, the world around us and the people we know. But is it '*the truth*'? Maybe we can get more clarity from a different point of view in just a whisper:

When you look at the sun, there is no doubt about the truth. When you look at the 'son', there can be doubt that is formed by your perspective. The point is when you see the light inside everyone and everything; you are a witness to the truth.

Every single accounting of man in all forms of communication represent perspective, therefore it is the resonance of the mind, body and spirit that forms your truth. The more something is limited in your understanding by the parameters that you set, the easier it is for more people to agree on the perspective. The best examples of this are found in Nature and natural phenomenon.

If you want to change your perspective, you need to release certain belief limitation. This can be done by opening your heart and mind to more possibilities in order to allow an expansion of thought about who you are and the way you see others.

If you are seeking the truth about who you are and where you are going, the Divine path will be illuminated and littered with signs of love, honor, joy, respect and gratitude. Look for these signs in the vibrations that message your Higher Self and says without a doubt, 'This is true.'

Play is a term employed in ethology and psychology to describe a range of voluntary, intrinsically motivated activities normally associated with pleasure and enjoyment. Play is commonly associated with children, but positive psychology has stressed that play is imperative for all higher-functioning animals, even adult humans.

I am a highly functioning animal, an adult male that loves to play (tee hee)! It's way too easy to be so grown up that we forget to play. But whenever I see people playing and having fun, the mood becomes infectious. For me, play might mean throwing a frisbee, playing a game, or even using words in a playful manner.

Isn't it delightful to witness animals at play, like a kitten or a cub challenging their mother or sibling to a game of extreme hugging? There must be a basic instinct or desire to be playful, maybe a form of intimacy, that takes ordinary moments and transcends them into a higher frequency of love. Wow, did I say that (grins)? It feels like the whisper is coming through after a shout-out to Jenny for recommending a whisper of play.

Humans love the energy of playing, and for good reason. Play is like entering an agreement of the soul that says you are now committing your time to freedom. That commitment activates the child energy and creates the actions that feel similar to flying. This is the feeling of freedom, freedom to express yourself in a way that messages the body through a kinesthetic connection to the emotion of love.

Play energy feels good because it activates the child within. If you are struggling with creating play time, that could be an indication that the inner child isn't being heard or felt. Focusing energy to make sure you play can yield great rewards, so spending time devoted to what makes your heart sing with freedom is a guided activity.

Play can be intimate with love energy flowing like a river of freedom that bathes the soul. Energy goes where energy flows, and so a playful heart creates freedom in your world, freedom from thinking about the bills, the job, the family or anything that is an issue in your life. This break allows you to return to those aspects of life with creative solutions.

Give yourself permission to play and set freedom of the soul in motion with any movement that validates the reason you left the spirit world to come to Earth. In a playful heart, you will find the greatest measure of life anchored in the foundation of love.

Politics has become a taboo subject in some of my circles and is something I think twice about before bringing up in public, much less the family gathering. The thing that disturbs me is the way conflict and divisiveness have become the hallmark of modern-day campaigns. I find myself doing what most Americans are expressing they do, which is voting against the person whom they like the least.

The millions of dollars spent for these elected officials to obtain an office of service that includes comparatively small pay lends itself to a higher potential for corruption at all levels. And for this reason alone, my trust levels have been slowly dropping as the entertainment value has been increasing!

It is interesting for me to note that most people have a tendency to shy away from the subject of politics. This may be due to the belief that no matter how hard a candidate tries, issues of integrity seem to follow them right into public office. Let's see if the angels can shed some light on the politics of our world today:

The fabric of society is spun around the chosen leaders of the people. As the political landscape changes, so does the moral barometer of the Earth. Placing people in charge to represent you in matters of finances, services, spirituality and protection is a serious responsibility that ultimately affects everyone.

If you decide to turn from the process, you are making the choice to let others become the architects and archetypes of your environment. If you are not willing to face this, then who will do it for you? The mirror can challenge you to see the truth, and yet reflection is essential to the process of evolution.

As long as power drives politics and that power is attached to money and big business, the poor and needy will not have a voice except in empty speeches and promises. The true power is in people, and the people must unite at some level to achieve a balance in politics. Modern politics falls into the category of a paradigm that well outlasted the vision, which translates to change becoming divinely unavoidable.

The arrival of the age of information heralds the end of times for lack of transparency in politics. It only takes a willingness to take a comprehensive view, pay attention to your choices and clearly define the needs of others in a framework of rational thinking. In this light, your personal power to effect change in the world lies in your willingness to speak the truth, remain positive, and refuse to carry a load that is not yours. Your ability to love yourself and the world in which you live will always support you.

Your life process is a long series of conscious decisions about the world that you inherited from your ancestors. All you need to know is that you deserve the life you were born to live and so do all children. This moment in time was built on the courage of others who have handed you the system that will pass through your hands.

Thanks for all the notes and messages that carry your thoughts on 'Angel Whispers.' Your feedback gives me pleasure and power (tee hee)! A reader asked several thought-provoking questions about the word 'power' and its meaning, so I am taking it to the Source for answers.

My knowledge and experience tells me that the power center of the body is in the mid-section of the torso or the Solar Plexus. When a person suffers abuse at the hands of another, they are taking power from that individual with an exertion of free will. That type of event can initiate the need for healing energy to reactivate personal authority, or clear the Solar Plexus energy center. The energy of love and forgiveness can restore that personal power.

In physics, the definition of **power** *is the time rate at which work is done or energy is transferred.* **Power** *can also be defined as possession of controlling influence or possession of the qualities (especially mental qualities) required to do something or get something done.*

Jimi Hendrix once said: **"When the power of love overcomes the love of power, the world will know peace."** Ultimately, I see a person's power as a gift and, like everyone else, I sometimes struggle with accepting that power or gift. We are all powerful beings and it is that acknowledgment that allows us to get things done with style and grace. With that grace, I will listen for a whisper from an angel on *power*:

Mankind was given the power to create within the magic and mysteries of the planet Earth. Acknowledgment of personal power, when used in the highest good, brings freedom to the soul and Divine Purpose to life. It is easy to shrink in the shadow of your personal power under the influence of ego judgments and illusions, so your truest acknowledgment is essential to feel freedom from self-defeating actions.

Those who have awakened to their power and continue to grow within that energy are on the path to unlimited success in the areas of love, relationships and spiritual development. In this energy, all paths lead toward peace. Those who seek to gain power over another individual are seeking knowledge from within darkness, so interaction with others provides the opportunities to learn about the light.

The unexpressed emotions of souls that are stuck in their lower energies need release at some level. Once your soul has agreed to accept these energies, balance can be restored through the practice of mercy and forgiveness. This single act of love provides teachings for everyone involved, including all witnesses.

If you want to focus on your power, you will find the greatest measure in your capacity to love, your ability to forgive and your perspective on life and death. You will find power within faith and your connection to Spirit, and from that perspective all power will reside in the energy of love. The purest energy of power is found in the willingness to surrender to the truth of life on Earth, where the power of acceptance becomes the energy of peace.

As I am writing this, I am wondering if our spirit sends prayers while we are sleeping. That unconscious state might be the best time to send messages of gratitude, requests for help, or any communication that is needed. Maybe the Higher Self knows best what to do and continues that prayer long after we go to sleep.

I have received messages about the way prayer works. We are using a different part of the brain to send vibrations that are 'read' as our messages. This part of our mind is in a direct path from the heart to the crown chakra. Therefore what is occurring is a vibrational form that is unique in its structure to any other vibrational partnerships in the human body. The overall effect from engaging in the prayer activity is creating a resonant pattern that raises the vibrations of the body, mind and spirit.

__Prayer__ is the act of attempting to communicate, commonly with a sequence of words, with a deity or spirit for the purpose of worshipping, requesting guidance, requesting assistance, confessing sins, as an act of reparation or to express one's thoughts and emotions. The words of the prayer may take the form of intercession, a hymn, incantation or a spontaneous utterance in the person's praying words. Secularly, the term can also be used as an alternative to "hope."

It is interesting that the dictionary expressed the alternate meaning as hope. I think praying does give you a feeling in the form of giving your problems to a Higher Power. The more I write about this, the more I want to push away from the desk and engage in the activity of prayer as I listen for a whisper:

Prayer vibrations are translated like no other communications in the realm of Angels. In place of words, there is only a frequency that fills with the vibration of your message. The feeling behind the thought is touched to know what serves the soul. This may differ from your desires, yet Angels must remain in service to your essence.

When you pray and release your problems to God, you are sending the vibration of faith. Prayer for others shows your level of true compassion. When you give thanks, there is a feeling of the love that surrounds gratitude. When you message your wants, Angels feel your dreams and desires while holding a vision that is just for you.

When you show anger to God, the Angels know you have passion. When you sacrifice to Divine Source in service to others, you have just surrendered your heart in order to know the true harmony that exists in the realm of Angels. When you pray for help, you message vibrations of great strength beyond the realm of the lower self.

When you are happy in your prayers, the Angels are playful and joyously dancing in the light that surrounds you. When you give a gift in the name of God, you have just revealed the Godself. When you pray with thoughts and offers of understanding, you message that you have reached a Higher Consciousness. When you send vibrations of love, you are standing in the eternal pillar of loving light and experiencing the core of your being.

Admitting the areas that represent challenges for me is part of my undertaking with writing the 'Angel Whispers,' as I have come to experience. Predictions sure raised some of those issues with me in the past. My angelic guides are very cautious with predictions and so I have been accused of 'holding back' information by those who think I know something I'm not sharing (tee hee).

On the occasions when the Divine Source releases predictions, I have questioned in my mind why some people get that information while others do not. Part of my issue stems from witnessing clients who have held on to a future prediction with white knuckles for twenty, even thirty years. This comes across as a form of damage and creates my own sensitivity to the idea of predicting the future. That may even be the discernment from my guides attaching to my energy in a way that allows my words of predictions to escape to only those who will not hang on to them (insert epiphany here).

The angels often give great practical and meaningful ways to deal with the future along with the occasional prediction. So I must say that the feeling of receiving feedback that confirms the predicted event really happened is an indescribable emotional response. According to the angels we write our own script every day. With free will adding an element that can change the future, predictions are a slippery slope.

Quantum Physics is making predictions based on probability, while the Farmer's Almanac makes forecasts based on scientific data. Predictions by psychics are more of a claim that a particular event will happen in more certain terms than a forecast. On that note, I will make a rare prediction in the form of an angel whisper:

Predictions are visual and intellectual stimulants with great purpose and meaning. The preparedness that evolves from the vision of the future is a necessary element to the survival of man on the planet. The vibrations in the moment are directly linked to the future and your free will.

One burst of energy from the power center of the human body can alter the course of history. This has been witnessed repeatedly with great accounts of events that go beyond the natural state. This shows a relationship between manifestation and the super-natural phenomenon that is constantly occurring in the Universe.

The year 2009 will go down in history as a time of great change. Many souls have evolved to bear witness and be a major partner in the events of this coming year. When a large number of people share a common thread in their life-purpose, the unity of Spirit becomes an even greater force.

If you want a theme or mantra to go along with predictions for 2009, it would be preparedness. The triumphs and challenges for the New Year will come fast, and those who are not ready at some level will struggle. There will be a global shift in consciousness felt around the world as many will experience increased awareness in every facet of life, with heavy focus in the vibrations of peace. Communities will form quickly with fluid harmony in response to the global shift, as systems collapse under the negative influences of war, greed and the abuse of power.

Paying forward by serving causes to help the Mother Earth and environmental causes will bring many great rewards. 2009 will hear the cries of distress from the Ocean with events like the Storm of Tears.

The free will of some men will reach beyond the strength of military forces and bring focus to the social standards with spiritual connections. Concerted effort, compassion, understanding and love will form a bridge between cultural differences.

The Rainbow children will come in mass and bring the energy of the exalted beings across the globe. This will magnify hope as these children touch the souls of many. Divine love will pour from their eyes as they exude unconditional acceptance free from judgment and filled with light.

Leave your comfort zones to experience change at the deepest level and to embrace the human nature connected with the unknown. Being fully present in the world outside your control will bring peace to the body, mind and spirit.

There are so many people seeking or engaging in prophecy today, including me. I personally use extreme caution in this area, and it has been my experience that the angels do the same (tee hee). Each individual response to such information can be wide and varied as some take it with a grain of salt while others may cling to an idea or prediction.

Prophecy usually indicates knowledge of the future which is said to be obtained from a divine source, or a prediction uttered under divine inspiration. An example of prophecy would be this Cree Indian prophecy: Only after the last tree has been cut down, only after the last river has been poisoned, only after the last fish has been caught, only then will you find that money cannot be eaten.

In a recent conversation, a friend was telling me that they had been told by a psychic about an impending a car wreck that might result in the loss of their life. After three painful months of getting into the car and driving every day with this information, my friend was in that dreadful accident and nearly lost their life. Was this some sort of self-fulfilling prophecy resulting from focus on the possibility or probability?

As our world becomes more aware and each person's psychic sense is awakened, I am sure we will hear more prophecy. Between politicians and some news agencies, we hear prophecy reported as fact almost every day, and I for one question the integrity of some deliveries of future information. How about some prophecy inside of a whisper:

There are vibrations related to events experienced by each individual which represent all aspects of life and include the past, present and future. The interpretations of these vibrations are comparable to walking a tightrope in the sense that you must walk the straight line to get to the other side.

Most information expressed as prophecy holds a space for learning in some way. Trust, faith and common sense can lead a person into action steps that are serving even when following a complete illusion. Regardless of future information, mankind is ultimately being led to have complete faith that everything is in Divine order.

Your response to what you think or what you feel could happen, should be carefully discerned, and your interpretation can be affirmed through repetitive signs from Spirit. Your own internal 'guru' has the ability to tap into the intuitive fount of wisdom that is innate to every living creature, and this sets the platform from which to deliver information by reaching beyond the body senses.

In nature, you might observe the way that animals make instinctive decisions about their future, and humans should be no different. Your natural ability to maneuver through life does not depend on the word of others, yet everyone has a helper. It is keeping balance in a world of information that enables you to hold a space in your life for prophecy.

I have been asked about this subject a lot lately, which has sparked deep inner reflection and many requests for discernment from a Divine source. My problem with this word is the way it relates to the fear energy and all the various ways others use that energy to lead us to believe that we need protection.

Protection *means the act of protecting, or the state of being protected; preservation from loss, injury, or annoyance; defense; shelter; as, the weak need protection.* "On life's journey faith is nourishment, virtuous deeds are a shelter, wisdom is the light by day and right mindfulness is the protection by night. If a man lives a pure life, nothing can destroy him." ~Buddha. This quotation and definition perfectly display the dichotomy that surrounds the meaning of this word.

Let us count the ways that our culture has formed the co-dependency that has evolved around the need for protection. Almost every aspect of life on Earth has an insurance rider attached. Government has now assumed the position of world protectorate, which in international law means an autonomous territory that is protected diplomatically or militarily against third parties by a stronger state or entity.

And it wouldn't be right to leave personal protection and all that represents, such as protecting the heart, out of this word study. I will try to find a safe place to engage in lifting the veil for a whisper on protection:

When you leave the energy of illusions behind, the word protection does take on new meanings. Fear breaks down faith, which can create a closed door to your emotions and the way you express them. People and circumstances can fuel a need to build a wall around your heart out of a perceived desired for protection. Over time, this can separate the entire body, mind and spirit from the full presence of life.

The way that you protect yourself from the dangers of life needs careful discernment in order to ensure these ways are serving to you and others. Social ideas around protection have alienated many people with tendencies toward isolation as a vehicle to remove vulnerabilities, which in turn, affect community.

The truth is that taking rational steps and using common sense are all that is needed in the area of protection. The illuminated being rests in the peace of knowing that everything is in Divine order when facing the duality of life. Energy depends on the polar opposites creating a movement. The open heart and mind see the truth around protection and discern needs associated with that energy.

Have the courage to remove barriers that serve as false protection. Embrace faith to experience everything that life has to offer. See through the eyes of compassion to open the door to your heart and the hearts of others. Live in the safety of knowing that your ideas around protection are anchored in the true light of the Highest Power as you nestle into the comforting and nurturing arms of the angels.

For those who need a primer, entanglement is that strange quantum phenomenon that links two particles across distances such that any measurements carried out on one particle immediately change the properties of the other--even if they are separated by the entire universe. Einstein called it "spooky action at a distance." And indeed it is weird, according to this description by Clay Dillon.

With energies connected by an unseen bond, questions emerge around how the whole system of particles is influenced by movements of single supporting elements. Like a flock of birds or a school of fish using the influence of an intuitive individual leader and combining information, like the wishes of a democratic majority, in order to determine the direction, speed and timing of group movement events.

The way humans are 'wired' may be influenced by so many unknown sources that it seems to me that personal choices must contain elements of social and global consciousness, human compassion at a soul level, and a deeply passionate need for community. We are connected to elements on so many different levels. Science is catching up to spirituality, and redefining the idea that we are not alone (tee hee)! Let's feel the influence of energies connecting to spirit and evoke a whisper on quantum entanglement.

The very essence of any species' survival contains a dependency on the natural environment to provide essential supportive elements. The air you breathe contains particles that create a partnership between environment and humans that goes beyond the normal state of consciousness, and therefore can only be 'known' within the deepest layers of existence and survival.

Ancient knowledge and divine energy synthesize entangled energies into wisdom evoked through a shared experience. The heart is at the center of movement that predicts change, utilizing the energy of love as a catalyst for upward movement. In accordance with the laws of nature, a majority of the parts must agree to the effort of the entire system.

For the unconscious mind to find peace with the conscious existence, making a connection with the unseen forces of nature is essential. Knowing that your entire being is a collaborative effort of several sources reassures the soul by bringing an energy of love that is courageous, a love that is willing, and a love that is brilliant.

The only limitation comes from the perspective that defines your place in the world. It's more than creating your reality; it's living your reality and awakening to the things that find their way to your heart openings to reach the soul. Entangled energy creates symbiosis, which in turn clearly defines not only your place in the Universe, but the supporting energy that surrounds you.

This is a great addition to my library of whispers, mainly because I have nothing under 'Q' (lol). T*he Everett many-worlds interpretation, formulated in 1957, holds that all the possibilities described by quantum theory simultaneously occur in a "multiverse" composed of mostly independent parallel universes.* The work of scientists like Marcel Vogel, and movies like *What the Bleep Do We Know!?*, *Down the Rabbit Hole* and *The Secret* beg the question. "What is Quantum Physics?"

Quantum physics is a branch of science that deals with discrete, indivisible units of energy, individually called quantum, or, plural, quanta, as described by the Quantum Theory. There are five main ideas represented in Quantum Theory: 1) Energy is not continuous, but comes in small but discrete units; 2) The elementary particles behave like both particles and waves; 3) The movement of these particles is inherently random; 4) It is physically impossible to know both the position and the momentum of a particle at the same time. The more precisely one is known, the less precise the measurement of the other is; 5) The atomic world is nothing like the world we live in.

"God does not play dice with the universe" is one quote by Albert Einstein, himself one of the founders of quantum theory, who disliked this loss of determinism in measurement. He held that there should be a local hidden variable theory underlying quantum mechanics and consequently the present theory was incomplete. Experiments have been performed confirming the accuracy of quantum mechanics, thus demonstrating that the physical world cannot be described by local realistic theories.

Now that we have that established, my head is spinning in all directions as I try to grasp the collision of science and the mysteries of the Universe. I love it when scientists find evidence that supports metaphysics, as the two were separated by definition around the year 1300AD. It's time for the angelic view on Quantum Physics:

The search for knowledge is in the DNA of every human being. The energy or passion around the thirst for knowing what makes up the physical and non-physical world can be suppressed or released, depending on the choice of each individual.

Scientists are using theories and experiments to try to understand the questions around the existence of mankind with relationships between multiple planes of existence. Within this framework of study live the fundamental basics of energy, spirituality, intellectual power and the meaning of life. Once these basics are explained, others will find answers inside their hearts to questions of the mind, body and spirit.

As scientists find proof for key aspects of life on Earth, the Mother will unveil the deepest connection possible with many supporting features that enhance the various forms of life and multiple dimensions. Knowledge in this area eliminates fears and creates open acceptance in the energy where science meets spirituality.

When the duality of life in the physical finds a center on common ground, all planes of existence meet within the heart. For centuries the intentional misuse of information has helped to create barriers in order to further greed, wars and abuse of power. Equally as powerful are the thoughts of modern men and women that will dispel archaic thinking with the illumination of truth. Love for life and the planet Earth will grow stronger as a result of Quantum Physics.

A newsletter reader wrote, *"Dearest Russell, I have been struggling with situations such as torture, abuse and murder - especially of children. Do you think the angels ever whisper about those things? I'd love to hear what they say about that, if they ever do."*

The question is a good one. Harsh events, especially those that negatively affect children, are difficult to accept. Those who believe in a loving and merciful God may find challenge in understanding why a higher power would let such things happen.

In these whispers, I attempt to gain greater understanding through awareness and then share that insight with you. I have had experiences around young children who have passed, and with those connections, surprising revelations often bring comfort, and unusual information is often found below the surface.

Let's go for a swim beneath the surface to seek comfort and understanding on a quest for peaceful acceptance in the form of a whispering angel:

First, you must understand that there are times when free will is saying no to what the soul has already said yes to. It is easy to build illusions around the suffering that becomes apparent on the surface, but this should not be held as the only truth. The expressing of a harsh energy can require the active participation of another who becomes a partner in the experience. Just as you see people coming together in loving expressions, people can come together with dark-force energy in a binding moment in the journey of a soul.

In your deepest desire to understand the meaning of life, a single thread can lead you into a mystery that is surrounded by darkness. In the light is absolute truth, but in the darkness is energy with force that holds questions that are sometimes without acceptable answers. Rest assured that great purpose can be found in the transmutation of repressed energy.

You might be getting confused or disheartened with regards to justice, which is not in the hands of mankind. Justice is in the domain of the Divine, where all human experiences are resolved at the soul level. So don't let ideas of injustice attach you to an illusion of suffering. Have faith that the children and people you see in harsh situations are moving into the light of love.

For in the greatest sacrifice, you will find an ascended soul dancing across a rainbow.

People are searching this planet like never before in an attempt to discover the meaning of life. This unified effort to uncover information has led to groundbreaking discoveries about ourselves and the planet we share. We can't play dumb anymore (tee hee)!

The result of every individual's raising the bar is a daily witnessing of breaking down old structures to facilitate incredible transformations as an evolving species. The current forward momentum has us leaving old paradigms at lightning speed, and most are feeling the pull to break free from the old framework.

One reader wrote: *I'd like my magnet to shift, so that I am whole without anyone else's love. Maybe it's that I don't believe God's love is enough for me? Maybe I think I 'need' a man's love? Which is why I think security and trust are the issues?? I know that I can't get out of this place with my current tools, so I'm looking for new tools, new insights, new vibrations to help me up.*

Let's see what the angels can whisper that helps us raise the bar.

It's easy to get confused in such a fast-moving landscape where an inherent resistance to change affects almost everyone. Mankind is like a weary warrior that is tired of fighting and resisting, to the point that a readiness has been reached and the bar of success is being raised. Discovering the truths about your life offers a freedom that filters in slowly around the energy of the position. Raising the bar means holding yourself accountable in your conscious choices.

Today, the world is filled with gurus, masters, and teachers who are showing others the illuminated path of truth. There is also a hunger to find a space filled with love on this side of the veil. Through the eyes of spirit, we see the way that people are expanding their awareness in order to raise the bar, or the vibrations, to levels that have not been reached. This would be similar to explorers discovering a new land.

Such journeys into undiscovered territory are not without great risk. Yet there are many with the courage and determination to forge ahead with movement supported by the momentum created by ancestors who came before you. One destined moment after another offers you choice after choice to break old behavior patterns by claiming responsibility for your life, surrendering to love, having the faith that allows you to see the good in the world, and making commitments to fulfill your intentions by living the life you came here to experience.

The reward cannot be expressed, as it is fully realized within the experience.

It is truly a great time to be alive and witness the transformational energies that are bubbling up in our society. It's so exciting and at the same time challenging. As many people move toward taking complete responsibility for their actions, others are still holding on to the victim mentality and a complete lack of ownership.

In these challenging times, as you find yourself taking on more responsibility, the issue of recognition comes to the forefront. You can hardly give yourself recognition for your good deeds in any way that seems soulfully affirming without the energy of ego, so it really falls on others to help with discernment and recognition.

I am often amazed at the things that people recognize in me that I honestly failed to acknowledge about myself. As I was writing this whisper, I opened an email from a friend and 'angel whisper' reader. It was interesting to find a quote in this message regarding the subject I was drawn to write about this week.

"She told me she felt I was courageous. When she said this to me, I had the most beautiful experience of knowing that the courage she spoke of was something that lives through me and gives itself to me, rather than my doing something to create it. I told her this and we went to a very deep place of recognition that exists beyond the mind. We were in the moment, together, communicating from that place. I realized that the conversation we were having was opening my heart, and that I was being 'heard' so completely that I was able to let go of my constant conception of how I hold myself."

In this beautiful light, I will ask the angels for a whisper on recognition with meaning that can exist beyond the mind while finding a thread of light in the soul of every person:

As you recognize things about yourself, you hold a space for the light for others. As you acknowledge your achievements without ego judgments, you are energetically giving others permission to experience success and find joy in life through connection in the Highest Power.

To give is to bathe in the light of Creation. To receive with grace, dignity and without resistance is a form of ascending into the Higher Self. To find balance in the two energies is the sign of a true Master. Therefore the recognition of people who are serving a higher cause falls outside the individual and rests in the hands of the loving souls whose mission is to bring balance to the world.

Across a wide spectrum, the energies of the world have been out of balance and the extremes that all of you have witnessed is the transmutation of the past, designed to bring a flow of energy into the Age of Aquarius. This energy has never been witnessed by mankind as a whole, but has foundations in the ancestry of each individual.

Receiving in the heart and soul is the truest form of balance in energy. The Age of Caring and Sharing will begin with the balancing of energies of giving, receiving recognition beyond the mind, standing in the light of Creation and loving with all the senses. To stay true to the time, you simply have to acknowledge your own capacity to love while you receive love from others. Teach only love and fully open your heart to receiving recognition.

Thanks, my sister, for recommending this word as an Angel Whisper. The word *reconcile* has meanings that relate to the restoration of friendship or harmony, to settle or resolve. I found one definition that said *to cause to submit or accept something that is unpleasant*, and of course there is a relationship with this word and your bank account.

The latter definition sparked some interest from me as it alludes to ideas around reconciliation as being difficult and spells ego to me. Surely, now that I am thinking about it, when we reconcile with another person we are accepting something within ourselves. This easily leads us on a path of challenging our ego, regardless of the details.

Maybe *to reconcile* means to swallow your pride, eat crow, give in, concede loss or experience some other form of reversal of personal policy (tee hee). I am sure that most of you have experienced some form of this energy when you reconcile with someone or something. That makes me wonder why our egos step up to the plate when we engage in this activity. It shouldn't be so hard to change our minds, especially when there is a valid argument, like imbalance in our checkbook, as an example (lol). In that case, there is only one truth, like it or not.

That leads me to think that when we engage in reconciliation, we are really deciding our truth in some form. OK, I am following a thread to my spirit, because reconciliation just turned into forgiveness from within. Let's tune in and reconcile this account with some help from the Angels:

Reconcile comes on the heels of New Age for a divine reason. Everyone on the planet is going through some form of this activity in order to release old thought patterns and false judgments. For mankind to evolve into the Higher Self, this will take on many forms, from accepting the belief of other individual to creating deeper bonds with your energetic essence.

Resolving differences with others and from within is a benchmark for the times and a necessary part of walking on your path. As people are pushed outside their comfort zones, they must reconcile matters of the heart such as loving your relationships, careers and life itself. You have several opportunities for this, but in some ways time is a factor.

There is no reason for you to be left behind in the areas of raised consciousness unless that is the choice you are making. Free will and the ego can raise blocks such as fears, distrust and lack of clarity, but if that's the case then it is clearly the right time for you to reconcile your differences, engage in forgiveness and find a mirror that reflects truth.

Exalted beings that are walking the earth have reconciled differences in the body, mind and spirit in order to experience total freedom from attachments to the material world. If you turn off the 'brain filter' and allow the heart to openly access judgments, you will become free to experience joy and happiness that reach the soul through the breath of Divine Spirit. The gift of life places the choice of peace and love in the hands of every individual with access through the heart center.

Reincarnation, literally "to be made flesh again," is the belief that the soul, after death of the body, comes back to earth in another body. According to one belief, a new body is developed during each life in the physical world, but the soul remains constant throughout the successive lives. The Hindu or Buddhist doctrine supports that a person may be reborn successively into one of five classes of living beings (god, human, animal, hungry ghost or denizen of Hell) depending on the person's own actions.

According to most polls, 20-25% of Americans believe in reincarnation, which is not part of Christian teachings, and I have witnessed some humans throwing this term around rather loosely (lol). Seriously, there appear to be those who regard this lifetime with the cavalier attitude: "Oh, well, maybe I will come back and do it again.......as a dog".(tee hee) Others would like to think that this is their last lifetime, if they get it right; whatever "right" is.

The reincarnation story of an eleven-year-old that is posted on my blog sealed the deal for me! Now I wonder about the different aspects, like how many years between lives, what determines the fate and gender, and of course why. Is it heaven's way of recycling? Questions are now pouring out of this soul, which is the true indicator that it is time for a whisper from an angel on the mystery of reincarnation.

Whatever resistance you feel around this subject might be a reflection of the big picture when it comes to your belief. As limitless beings who are creating their own reality, humans reincarnate as a way to escape the limitations of a single lifetime and the absolutes regarding spirituality.

As the soul travels through the astral plane, all memory is erased and the physical incarnation starts anew. The event is part of an agreement between the Divine Universe and the soul, with focus on resolving spiritual needs. The astral plane contains a life-giving force built within a crystalline structure that allows the repeated penetration of the physical plane. In this holy environment, the energy of love fuels the growth of a seed that becomes part of the Tree of Life.

The reincarnation process allows for a type of remembering similar to a dream of faraway places and times. Some recall a vivid past, while others experience standing in the footprint of another lifetime. Each step you take in every lifetime becomes an indelible imprint on the soul, a part of a pilgrimage, a journey which carries the experience being held as sacred.

The truth you hold within illuminates a mystical journey that begins with the innocence of a child and returns to the waiting arms of a loving energy known as God.

~Herbert Otto~

I was recently involved in a relationship balancing using a technique called Psyche K. An event had triggered unhealthy emotions to come between me and a friend that needed resolution. Isn't that usually the way a relationship becomes unbalanced? The method was unusual but completely effective. I came away from the experience telling the practitioner that every relationship in the world needed her balancing act!

It seems that most difficult-to-resolve conflicts originate from an event where personal boundaries are crossed. This can happen more easily when all the fun is already gone from your time together. One thing that hit me during this resolution process was that relationships can be balanced by adding joy. You have all experienced a friend who becomes so needy that every moment you are together becomes more and more draining of your energy. Maybe in the beginning you had nothing but fun with this person, but now the laughs are gone and so is your eagerness to be in each other's company.

There are so many divorces due to crossing boundaries. In just one event, the lines can be crossed and a distancing factor is formed between two people. The truth is that many marriages end without closure, resolution or peace. The result is an out-of-balance relationship that now affects the children, families and friends. Even if no words are spoken, the children become the innocent bystanders entwined in the relationship issues of the past, forcing them into thinking they have to choose between parents on many levels.

In almost all cases forgiveness can resolve the problems, which raises the question '*Can you forgive someone who hasn't asked you*'? I have realized that the only thing preventing me from taking this step in the past was my own ego. It was silly to make my health and well-being dependent on someone's asking me for an emotional response. Some of the best healings that I have witnessed have occurred when one person surrenders the ego in exchange for love. For further keys to balancing a relationship, I will ask for a whisper:

A relationship is an equal bearing of responsibility. Balance occurs in the flow of friendship energy when an equal exchange of thoughts, ideas, principles and beliefs occurs freely without conditions or repression. Hold the knowing that with each day, the balance can shift.

In all cases, love will balance relationships. When you commit to suspend all judgments in order to find true peace, you are making a conscious choice to follow the pathway of the enlightened soul. Without judgment, there is joy. Without joy, there is judgment. Without love, there is bitterness. Without bitterness, there is love.

When your perspective has defined your truth and there is no resonation, it is an indication that your views may have been influenced by the ego or judgments of others. Within every human lies the ability to vibrate with the truth. Within every truth is a relationship.

The walk of life is taken one step at a time. Before you place one foot in front of the other, make sure your last step is planted firmly on the ground. This way you will avoid falling! The human experience is all about learning to walk.

With the dawning of the New Year, resolutions and the time for making them are upon us. *Resolution*: 1) the act or process of resolving: the act of analyzing a complex notion into simpler ones. 2) the act of answering: solving.

One of the most common New Year's resolutions is to get in shape. Ultimately, this means getting into the gym for a lot of us and then we are on our way to resolving a health issue, for example. With the end of 2007, I really had to think about making resolutions for 2008 and just what that means to me.

Beckie and I decided that we didn't need to resolve any issues as much as we wanted to set some goals for the coming year. In the process, I noticed that when we set goals they should not be limited to a single year. In fact, in 1996 we made a lengthy list of goals that lasted over a ten-year span. We did manage to hit most of those items on the list for that decade.

From that experience, we saw the importance of setting reachable goals and writing them down, as well as discussing what we want, both as individuals and as a couple. One of the goals on that 10-years list was to own a mountain cabin that was free of debt. That goal came to fruition in 2006 and came about from the sale of property in '96.

So for this New Year, Beckie and I are setting our intentions in much the same way we did in '96. I don't find myself with many issues to resolve, but I do have some lofty goals to set. So please join me in setting intentions for 2008. One of those intentions for me is to continue with what I call *Angel Whispers*:

You need to have strong resolve for the future in a way that penetrates the moment. In this way, you are messaging your body, mind and spirit of your intentions to live your future in a way that resonates with your being.

A strong resolve can also speak to your free will and help you accomplish a task at hand. The resolution to improve your life can speak to issues that need change. Change can be difficult for many, so the release of old patterns and habits are a key part of your intentions.

To simply love each other more this year is a resolution that is often unheard. Making a resolution for more abundance, a better job, a new relationship or an improvement with an existing partner, can be simply mean setting a goal to love yourself and others at a deeper level.

A resolution to set firm goals that can resolve many issues at once is what you are looking for. With these commitments and intended goals, you can find clarity in your life with the role that Divine love plays. Find the joy that surrounds you, and happiness will follow you for the rest of your life.

How do you reward yourself? If you are like me, it is usually with food or consumption of some kind, like a big fat chocolate shake and a juicy hamburger (lol). Obviously, some of us find love in the comfort of food and we may tap into that love as we taste our sweet rewards. But is doing something that is considered unhealthy really a reward, or do we all need to go to Hawaii?

*By definition **reward** means something given or received in recompense for worthy behavior or in retribution for evil acts. A satisfying return, result, or profit could also describe a reward. In Psychology, the return for performance of a desired behavior or another form of positive reinforcement is considered a reward.* Earl Nightingale once said, *"Our **rewards** will always be in exact proportion to our service."*

Retribution for evil is a reward? That definition raises more questions than answers, which must speak to the contrast inherent with our language. Since most people I meet are challenged in the area of receiving, you might speculate that rewards from others and even those offered by the Universe can go unrecognized. Maybe the angels will reward us with a deeper understanding of *reward* in the form of a whisper:

Rewards are delivered from the Universe as an acknowledgment and as a response to your energetic participation with an outcome. Without rewards, it is easy to retreat into a shell of illusion and the darkness of lower energies. You can be challenged in opening to the rewards that are offered if you dwell in the lower energies that separate you from faith and hope.

If you place the responsibility of validation in the hands of others, or if you limit yourself from the process of validation, it is easy to become out of balance. So failing to recognize the rewards of life creates disharmony and ultimately results in lowered self-esteem. A gift from spirit can be subtle and easily discounted or overlooked, which can serve in the sense that the need for truth and love to become more present is being illuminated for you.

In the deepest mystery of life, there is a wonderful structure that requires some level of comprehension and awakening to the fact that your commitment to service makes you an invaluable asset. This awakening can help you better understand your place in the world as your defining moments become unveiled in a single instant of reward. Allow yourself to feel and accept your just rewards with a willingness to stand on the podium to receive your 'Gold Medal' as a symbol that you went the extra mile in a devotion and commitment to the process known as life on Earth. Within the energy of love, rewards are without obstacles or limits!

Romance is a word that is not limited to the area of personal relationships, but it is often defined as a love affair between two people. I believe there can be romance in any type of relationship, even those outside the traditional views.

When romance is present, life can offer a greater level of happiness in many ways. Seeing the world through rose-colored glasses is a saying that alludes to seeing the romance found in our daily living. People who are falling in love with their partner, job or any aspect of life, seem to be easily satisfied with anything and everything (tee hee).

The angels often deliver messages about the need to clear away past hurts and harsh experiences in order to find the romance in life. If Beckie and I had stayed true to our commitment to single life, we might have never opened to the romance that was offered upon our meeting. That would have made the last 33 years quite different (lol), so acting on romantic inclinations must be important too.

It must be time to act on a romantic inclination in the form of a whisper from an angel on the meaning of romance:

Romance is a high-vibrational feeling containing elements of the past, present and future connecting with ideals, dreams, desires, wishes and beliefs. Your rich history has a romantic base that gives your body a feeling of guidance for the present and the future. Balancing the energy of romance is reflected by individual combinations of soulful needs and heart readiness.

Being drawn romantically toward someone or something that doesn't quite fit is merely the creation of lessons through experience. Romantic inclinations can be fed by the ego, so be aware of desires that help create attachments to outcome and expectations. Allowing romance into your life invites a world that is witnessed by the heart, so there must be focus on where the mind takes you in your thoughts of love.

Romance has driven men and women to commit incredible acts of courage and sacrifice. Fall romantically in love with yourself and the world will helplessly follow, because romance is the way children experience love. Let the inner child feel the romance in the outer world to experience the most profound romantic energy, and remember, romantic experiences are rarely planned, so child-like spontaneity can offer rich rewards.

Love is the seat of romance, so stop and rest in the energy of your desires and be the messenger who personally delivers your song of the heart to the Universe.

Have you ever felt trapped or without options in one of your commitments? Sometimes the investment we have made, whether it is time, money or other forms of energy, can bring illusions around that intention or desire.

Rubicon *is defined as a limit that, when passed or exceeded, permits no return and typically results in irrevocable commitment.* Friedrich Max Muller once said, *"Language is the Rubicon that divides man from beast."* Maybe that is why I do these whispers, to make that distinction (lol).

At one point in my adult life, I was struggling with a decision around a commitment. It was causing a lot of stress and disharmony in my life, then a wise friend took me aside and asked why I was putting myself through the misery. The main reason was that I was vested in the project that was by all appearances failing to yield any positive energy. After discussing it with my friend, I pulled out of the project and discovered my heart was singing, my soul felt free and the other people involved were equally relieved.

Circumstances, situations and experiences can alter the direction we are heading, and all that it takes is an acknowledgment and ongoing discernment of the divine life purpose we are living. It is time to make an investment of thought and action in order to better understand Rubicon. And now for a whisper:

There are levels of commitments to all aspects of life. There is commitment to your health that includes your spiritual, emotional and physical bodies. There are commitments to your family and friends that involve spiritual growth and life purpose, and there are financial commitments anchored in loyalty and responsibility.

Within all types of energy, there are levels and limits to the human psyche. The Rubicon can appear in various forms, such as limiting beliefs, illusions and false judgments as a way to remind you of you're true alignment with your core existence. Instead of reflecting with judgment on your decision, give yourself the freedom to reassess any situation and approach new information with an openness and willingness that is free of blame. If your commitments are filled with discomfort, your body is sending you a message to take another look. Feeling trapped is usually a sign that illusions have been built in regard to your commitments.

Feeling cornered can also indicate a lack of faith, as if to tell the Universe that it is ungenerous. A caged heart might encourage you to place conditions or find focus on waiting for a single set of circumstances to form that will enable you to love your life. Release any behaviors or thoughts that hold you to any conceived absolutes, for there are none on the path that you walk. The limitations you form around decisions are just that, something you are putting in place. Hold a space for truth that gives you the freedom to make changes based on the current landscape of the heart and soul. In doing so, your family, friends, and lovers will honor those choices above all others as you anchor your love in the illuminated light of faith, truth and the energy of change.

Thanks to Terry for asking about this subject as a response to last week's whisper on Inner Voice. Crystallinks.com states that "Sacred geometry may be understood as a worldview of pattern recognition, a complex system of religious symbols and structures involving space, time and form. According to this view, the basic patterns of existence are perceived as sacred. By connecting with these, a believer contemplates the Great Mysteries and the Great Design. By studying the nature of these patterns, forms and relationships and their connections, a believer may gain insight into the mysteries – the laws and lore of the Universe."

About Sacred Geometry and how it relate to music, Crystallinks goes on to say that "Pythagoreans, who found that a string stopped halfway along its length produced an octave, while a ratio of 3/2 produced a fifth interval and 4/3 produced a fourth, believed that this gave music powers of healing, as it could "harmonize" the out-of-balance body, and this belief has been revived in modern times."

I have to agree with the Pythagoreans because my experience with healing, balance and sound is often accompanied by images of Sacred Geometry. The most profound instances of energy shifting in the body seem to incorporate geometric pathways filled with light. I also believe that angels communicate using Sacred Geometry as a language medium. I will bring these natural designs to my mind's eye as we ask about Sacred Geometry in the form of an angel that whispers:

Angels occupy a space that is vastly different from anything that humans can imagine. The space of sound and breath, music and Sacred Geometry, vibrations and Divine energy all provide an environment for movement and communication.

Nature gives the best examples of geometric designs that are considered sacred as they represent repetitive messages, which are considered Divine. The perfect structure of a spider's web, the hexagon pattern that repeats in a bee's honeycomb and the inner formations found within shelled sea creatures are all natural elements formed within an intricate framework connecting life in the Universe.

Each geometric shape is the result of a combination of energies in motion that are balanced by time and birthed in a still moment. In healing energy, the movement of light within a structure of geometry creates an alignment that brings balance to all systems involved. As a multi-dimensional being, your energy follows a pathway within a soothing rhythm that speaks to the very essence of who you are. This essence defines the sacred nature of the spiritual body, or what some refer to as the soul.

The intelligence held by the spiritual body communicates through a language of the heart, a song in nature, a beat of the primal drum or a vibration that holds a type of spiritual ecstasy. The love that surrounds you is sometimes offered in a spiral energy where Sacred Geometry is accessed for the purpose of communication, alignment, balance and an undeniable connection with the Highest Power.

I received an email from a reader who asked for a whisper on sacred gifts and wrote the following: *I never liked using the term "gifts." It's not that I don't consider them gifts or am not grateful for them. It's just that the term gets bantered around so much that people become referred to as being "gifted" which may suggest that they are better than someone else or in some way a step above them. The truth is that every human being has gifts, and no one's gifts are any better or worse, any higher or lower, on any scale than anyone else's. So I just feel a little uncomfortable with the term "gifts" because it may (but not necessarily should or does) imply something more.*

The term "spiritual gifts" is closer to a truer meaning, but also is misused at times to suggest an elitist mentality. One who boasts of being spiritually gifted is, by default, suggesting that others are less gifted.

I'm sure that others have found terms for what they do that fit their individual circumstances. The term that feels right for me is "sacred gifts." This serves as a reminder that these spiritual things are sacred and that it is the sacredness of life that is most important. Placing the word "sacred" before the word "gift" suggests that accepting the gift does not make one gifted. It fills one with humility and a desire to honor the sacredness of that which has been bestowed on him or her.

I couldn't have said it better myself, as I know we all have gifts that should not be compared. At the dinner table, the first sacred gift that came to mind was just being there at that moment. That gift was generated by circumstances, the schedule of others and an openness to receive what mystery lies ahead. I will ask for a gift from the angels in the form of a whisper:

Everyone is given sacred knowledge, connections and abilities that are geared specifically for them. It is the diversity of individuality that makes up the entirety of the life experience. This can serve as a barometer that measures the willingness to receive.

Without judgment, there is only love for these gifts. The rejection of these natural talents is related to the spiritual beliefs that each person holds or fails to hold. The Highest Power gave you free will to discern for yourself an acceptance of empowerment.

There is a lot of focus on the scientific proof that supports the validity of sacred gifts. The real focus should be directed at the vibrations of the emotions that emanate from each Soul's acceptance of all aspects that govern the Self. There is a relationship between the Soul's purpose and the gifts that are offered.

These sacred gifts are apparent in the individual's reflections and perspective. Your truth is held in your perspective. For more insight, simply go to the nearest mirror and gaze into the eyes of truth. If you think [or believe] your gifts are dormant, it is time to remove the layers and blocks that surround your passion and begin to live life to the fullest measure.

Sacrifice is another word suggested by a reader and an excellent choice to follow on the heels of manifestation. **Sacrifice:** *1) to give of yourself even if you don't want to. 2) retreat from your dreams. 3) loss of something really important.* I just made up those silly definitions since I am without access to my dictionaries and the Internet. Could there be some truth between the lines that express how I may view sacrifice in a negative light?

In my retrospective on this word, I had a realization that I had placed loads of energy in the area of sacrifice when it came to my children. That may have served me with some sort of shield of honor, but looking back I can't say that I was seeing the truth in all situations. At the time I'm sure I was convincingly following my heart!

My bottom line to the daily epiphany is that I am constantly engaged in the decision-making process that leads to change or sacrifice. Whether it is choosing to work rather than go play, fill my time with one person over another or giving up an activity to donate time to a cause, somewhere in there is a choice or many choices.

Sacrifice is used a lot in religious teachings and there must be a connection to our spirituality. It could be conceived that to live a spiritually devoted life means plenty of sacrifice of personal freedoms. But what if that leads to spiritual freedom? It's time to sacrifice a moment to hear the whisper:

Don't become the victim of a sacrifice, even if it is made by someone that you love. Inside every action in the Universe there is an opposing energetic force. The force that follows sacrifice is love, love for yourself, love for God or the Highest Power, love for others, and love for life itself. Sacrifice is found in the same vibrations as passion.

In nature, the ultimate sacrifice is a common element to the life process. This sacrifice is accepted as a part of the total experience. Your perception of another's sacrifice can determine the predisposed feeling of outcome for that person. In this way, the judgment of others who view a sacrificial aspect can only reflect an external perspective. Most will affirm that their personal sacrifice was a bridge to ascension.

If you are contemplating a sacrifice, it could help to assess who is being served. The energies of the Lower Self can support self-serving images of sacrifice through the creation of an illusion. The Universal flow of energy always supports the creative mind. The result can be a fabricated vision that connects your path to paradigms that support sacrifice as the only means to achieve your goals.

Perhaps you should apply the word sacrifice to things like your unhappiness, dissatisfaction or any perceived misery in your life. Sacrifice is surrender. The release of all resistance can be your true sacrifice to Source Energy. The giving heart is the purest form of sacrifice while only the ego would attach resentment or discontent without accounting for the true nature of energetic exchange. Look at your situation through the eyes of an angel to illuminate the truth in your sacrifice, and what do you see, love or illusion?

I love a word with many meanings! *A **sanctuary** is the consecrated area of a church or temple around its tabernacle or altar. An **animal sanctuary** is a place where animals live and are protected. **Sanctuary** was also a right to be safe from arrest in the sanctuary of a church or temple, recognized by English law from the fourth to the seventeenth century.*

The area around the altar came to be called the "sanctuary," and that terminology does not apply to Christian churches alone: King Solomon's temple, built in about 950 BC, had a sanctuary ("Holy of Holies") where the Ark of the Covenant was kept, and the term applies to the corresponding part of any house of worship. In most modern synagogues, the main room for prayer is known as the sanctuary, to contrast it with smaller rooms dedicated to various other services and functions.

When I think of my sanctuary, I think of our mountain getaway that we call Casa Angelis (House of Angels). It is funny how I can hear a song or sound, maybe even a single tone that takes me there in my mind. Once I am there, it seems that I have escaped the urban landscape of sounds that normally surround me by going via this journey of thought into my personal sanctuary.

I would venture to say that everyone needs their own personal sanctuary, whether it is an altar, church, a place to live or a sacred space of the body, mind and soul. How do you find that feeling or place? I think it is something that could be considered part of our life search, to look for something that gives us a feeling of peace, love or comfort and then hold onto it for dear life. Beckie and I call that the 'warm fuzzies.' I will try to capture the essence of sanctuary as I retreat into a whisper:

Sanctuary is the human equivalent of standing in a circle of angelic light. These feelings of protection, safety, faith, and connection are found in the essence and easily exposed when boundaries are removed.

As you soothe the Spirit in the physical world, you open doorways into the mysteries of life. Finding some piece of knowledge about the unknown forces that drive the Human Spirit can bring a feeling of completeness and harmony to your existence, even in the midst of chaos.

Prayer and meditation unlock the gates of the Sanctuary where you will experience oneness. The Higher Self provides a heart space that is always a sanctuary, where an opening can present you with a different perspective of your life and the world around you.

The sanctuary of the Soul is in the freedom of the heart. When you embrace life with acceptance of the Self, the heart is free to openly forgive and experience joy. The sanctuary is the space that allows the ceremonious expression of love to enhance your inner strength through relationships, integrity, spiritual cleansing and connection to the Divine.

Thanks, Richard, for the suggestion to evoke a whisper on the controversial creature called Sasquatch. What a fun word to say or whisper (tee hee), especially since Beckie and I are currently in the Rocky Mountains, whose majestic landscape is providing the perfect backdrop for such a playful discovery and request from a reader.

According to some sources, the **Sasquatch**, also known as Bigfoot, is purportedly *an ape-like creature that inhabits forests, mainly in the Pacific Northwest region of North America.* This creature is usually described as a large, hairy, bipedal humanoid. The term "Sasquatch" is an anglicized derivative of the word "Sésquac," which means "wild man."

A majority of scientists discount the existence of Bigfoot and consider it to be a combination of folklore, misidentification, and hoax, rather than a legitimate animal, in part because some estimate large numbers necessary to maintain a breeding population. A minority of accredited researchers have expressed interest and possible belief in the creature, with the opinion that evidence collected of alleged Bigfoot encounters warrants further evaluation and testing. Let's see what the mystical beings of light have to whisper about the unknown creatures of the forest:

The power held by man to create during an incarnation of the physical may draw on a vast number of energies from the pool of experiences on both sides of the veil. Dreams, memories, visions, and feelings can come forward in order to create countless awakenings. One magic-filled moment of connection with something completely foreign offers upward movement of energy toward endless possibilities.

The Sasquatch is a magical creature that exists in the same way that unicorns and fairies do. People have described seeing all of these creatures in various settings, and one should not invalidate these encounters described by others, as their experience is as real as any. There is an aspect to the grounded nature of a 'Bigfoot encounter' that feeds the soul with a magical spoonful of inspiration. It is that type of reward which serves to light a Divine spark deep within the spirit.

The soul or essence of a human being incarnates into the physical to experience the limitations of life in the body. Valuable lessons are drawn close and presented as opposition or a contrast that appears in your current dimension. Your energy arrived in the body holding the vibrations of the senses that are beyond the physical. These senses include the magical, mythical, mysterious energies that fill a vacuum with inspiration in order to know, without question, that anything is possible.

For inspiration is just another word for God.

One reader wrote: "Scars have so many meanings -- physical, mental, emotional. So how about adding *scars* to the list of future topics? I was reminded of a woman who came into my tattoo shop about 12 years ago to see if I could put a henna tattoo on her double mastectomy scars. She hadn't let her husband see her in 7 years, and she was finally ready but wanted to look good for him. I used the raised scars to create a vine with flowers. We also talked a LOT about what was true about her thoughts, versus the story she'd made up, and she cried a lot. She loved the design, said she felt beautiful for the first time. Apparently her husband liked it too, as she came back to get it as a tattoo."

Most of us have some type of wound that may serve as a reminder of the path we are each on. Some people hide their physical scars and the energetic ones as well. Somewhere in the great scheme of things, there must be a reason that most of us are dealing with some sort of scar acquired while living this incarnation. It is in that energy of love that I will seek to receive a whisper on the subject of scars:

The physical appearance of a wound is what draws the eyes, and therefore draws the focus in a material world. Scars serve as a reminder of the choices made related to survival, whether those choices were made with conscious awareness of the potential wounding or not. For example, scars from an auto accident might bring up a person's decision to drive that day. But even when a person has overcome great challenges, the scar often represents an outcome instead of the journey.

The idea to beautify the scar is brilliant and divine, as it supports the effort to transmute the energy. The scars hold energy until the full effects of the trauma are released, allowing for neutral thoughts to exist. The same holds true for the more subtle forms of scarring that an emotional or spiritual wound may hold. The energetic wound can be held in much the same way as a physical scar, so engaging in ways to beautify those effects could produce dramatic healing energy and allow a balance to occur.

Your perspective holds the Cosmic Heart energy given to all creatures of the Earth. Will you choose to hold the negative perspective of the scar, or will you transmute the energy in order to clearly see the beautiful light from within that overcame hardships experienced in the continuum of life?

A client recently gifted me with some Jade stones that she called 'seeds' because she admitted the urge to plant them on the new walkway that leads to the front door of my home. I thought it was such a good idea that I planted the green gems in the decomposed granite along the sweeping curve from the street to the house.

A few days later, I noticed the birds had some sort of curiosity with the shiny stones. Yesterday, I discovered that the grackles had taken more than half the stones seeds I had planted and placed them together in a grouping close to the birdbath. They obviously had a much different idea of where the seeds should be planted (tee hee)!

By definition, seeds can be anything that resembles a seed, or a small crystal used to start the crystalline process. But what were those birds thinking? I am sure there was some sort of process going on, and I decided not to disturb the re-seeding and simply be a witness from the front bay window.

It's time to plant the seeds of a whisper and witness the impressions that follow the thoughts of seeds:

Seeds represent creation and offer energy around the process of new beginnings. Filling a seed with life-force energy begins an incarnation process filled with nurturing aspects. When you plant a seed, you bring focus to what is important in life through energy that gives hope, dreams, desires and love.

When the season brings about change, the shifting landscape evokes the thoughts of planting seeds. This creates upward and positive movement of energy. The desire to plant a new beginning brings visions of the future that serve the imagination as a force of nature begins a magical transformative process.

Nature is the greatest teacher by example and demonstrates the many ways that life goes on. In the darkest moments of loss, seeds provide a light that reaches the heart with a message and an energy that comforts the soul. Life does move beyond loss and time does heal all wounds, but the essence of your being wants to know that in a way that seeds provide.

Planting seeds can become a ritual that expands beyond the physical to fill the spiritual body with a light connected to the Highest Power. Your thoughts become seeds and so do your actions, so plant them wisely. Setting an intention is like planting a seed, and your focus on that intention is the nurturing source that yields the best results. With faith and love, your seeds will take root and bring growth that is beyond your imagination!

Our self-image of who we are in this world is very important and could be defined as a crucial aspect in regards to discerning and realizing our life path. This is one judgment or perception that is totally in our hands and could sometimes spell trouble. Seeing the truth around who we are can present many challenges and stir the heart with the emotional critique spoon.

Love from our parents and the way that was expressed can be a major factor in shaping our self-image. Therefore, the parental figure provides a reflective surface upon which to view the way we look at ourselves. Breaking a self-image held from childhood can present blocks and resistance for the adult with issues in the area of self-esteem.

Anytime another person abuses their power with you, they take some of your power and that affects your self-image. That is why abuse victims really struggle in this area, and when I say abuse, I include mental, physical, and emotional. Each person has a role in these types of life events, so it becomes a personal and private responsibility to discern the truth in order to gain the proper perspective. Maybe the angels can help with the perception of truth around the subject of self-image:

In order to see the truth and project that energy to others, it is wise to engage in an overall process of releasing illusions and half-truths. Forgiveness directed in the mirror is one of the key ingredients in this process that allows you to remove energy that affects perception.

Since the ego forms and delivers thoughts and ideas that may attack your self-image, it becomes equally important in the process to reclaim your power as a way to reinstate your integrity. By making amends, opening the heart, accepting the true self and placing yourself in the Divine flow of your life path, you can shift your self-image to one of pure love and unconditional belief in who you are.

Since you are the only one with a judgment in this area, your spirit vibrates with your perception. Happiness, joy, love, compassion and inner truth depend on the choices you make in the area of self-image, with the driving energy emanating from this concrete base of your belief system.

If you hold an image of your self that is condemning, how can others go against that alignment? This leads to self-destructive patterns and a focus on the untruth of your existence. In order to overcome this energy, you simply need to focus on faith and your strengths as a way to reject ego judgments.

You are created in the image of love, and this image holds the truth and the simplicity around who you are and why you are here. Align your soul with this image to heal past hurts, to accept the sweetness and bittersweetness of life, to experience love to the fullest and to express to others the light that is found within you.

The last few whispers on *empowerment* and *simple* have led me directly into this week's study in a way that answers many of my endless streams of questions (tee hee). Our bodies are complex organisms with multi-faceted energy and chemistry. So how do we keep life simple in a complex body system?

Self-love seems to hold the key to almost every question of life. When you discover how to truly love yourself, you unlock the doorway to showing others how it is done. This gives permission and information to the people around you in a way that helps them find the love within you. Have you ever tried to show love to someone who is down on themselves? That kind of outlook does not lend itself to a flow of loving energy. On the other hand, when you meet someone who is filled with love for themselves and whose love is not based in ego or narcissism, it becomes easy to fall into that vibrant energy.

Here is a quote I like by W.H. Auden: "*The image of myself which I try to create in my own mind in order that I may love myself is very different from the image which I try to create in the minds of others in order that they may love me.*" This brings up a good point regarding the differences in our views and actions around loving our self and the way others love us. Let's get a view from above in the form of a whisper from an angel:

The competitive spirit places limiting beliefs around the truth of love in the form of thoughts, abuse and control that is often justified in religion and family structures. Competing for love brings the energy of control as the focus for 'winning' love.

The God-self lives within every human being and is accessed through self-love. Without this connection, the individual may face many great challenges as the path of learning begins by looking in the mirror. Once you see love in a reflection of your true essence, you are then free to embrace the Christ Consciousness.

Self-love requires disciplined yet nurturing actions that are in alignment with the true nature of the energy of love, in order to avoid affects that distance one from the self. If you are waiting for the perfect conditions in order to address self-love, you are supporting an illusion. When you love yourself, you are expressing a love for life, a willingness to experience the positive lessons of love, forgiveness at the highest level and acceptance that vibrates with the soul.

If you were to see an image of self-love, it might look like a black hole in the center of the body. Upon closer inspection you would see stars, heavenly bodies and an entire solar system revolving around your essence. This would represent the duality of love that, on the surface, might appear to be without substance, but with discernment could unfold into the deepest mystery and meaning of life.

Seva refers to volunteer work or selfless service; work offered to God. Amma, also known as 'the hugging saint,' has set the model in this area. The means by which she lives her life are minimal, and last year alone her organization took in more than 68 million dollars in donations. Amma has given aid around the globe by offering immediate help to people devastated by natural tragedies, often doing much more than governments and entire countries. She also helps the poor by building houses, schools and bridges.

Amma's example of unconditional love, having personally hugged more than 30 million people, has inspired me in countless ways. My tithe comes in the form of giving back to my community in the work that I do. I must admit that while I am nowhere near sainthood (tee hee), the feeling of giving with conscious purpose has fulfilled an area of my soul that was in desperate need.

When it comes to validation and approval, we should look inward and feel those emotions rather than looking to others. There is nothing more empowering than the response from the body, mind and spirit that comes from the energy of giving. Let's get a whisper from an angel on the selfless service known as Seva:

Rewards in life are derived from sources that are sometimes hidden from obvious view. The subtle energies that surround the human body can be accessed through stillness of the mind and the ability to 'hear' the inner voice. When that inner voice is heard and action steps are formed as a result, that voice begins to sing the song of life.

Through acts of selfless service, the God within is brought to the surface and helps the individual feel the ultimate depths of their life purpose, conscious living and unconditional love. These acts are simultaneously paying forward creative manifestations and/or resolving past hurts and harsh experiences. In other words, acts of random kindness are both giving and receiving from the essence of the spirit.

The body, mind and spirit are soothed with Seva, and layers of guilt, anger, manipulation and all forms of toxic emotions can be released in an instant with grace, ease and simplicity. The result is higher self-esteem, raised consciousness and clarity which, in return, empower and support the daily decisions that further illuminate the path of the eternal soul.

In love there is only Seva, and in Seva there is the god within, shining the light of truth, joy, happiness and the unlimited pursuit of freedom. Follow your voice to the Seva of choice, and you will be a teacher of love.

This is a word that, at times, seems in conflict with spiritual growth, and it is that contrast that is nudging me into wonder around integrating the two. There has to be some connection between human sexual nature and each person's unique spiritual essence that could offer a transcending moment or two.

Have you ever looked up *sexuality* in the dictionary? It was quite the experience witnessing the lack of definition, and then there was the knowing that my Google searches would spring forth many new interesting ads (tee hee). Take *that* Google analytics! I am feeling so empowered by seeking answers to sexuality, which is defined as *"the sum of the person's sexual behaviors and tendencies."* Wooohooo, that sums it up!

I am also sure that religious teachings can make understanding sexuality about as unclear as the definition. Does our sexuality raise or lower our vibrations? Can we integrate spiritual growth with sexuality in a manner that holds high integrity? These are just a few of the questions that come with asking an angel for a better definition of the word *sexuality*:

Sexuality is one aspect of the human adventure that evokes energy so intense, a primal awakening occurs. This awakening parallels the human response that flows from one's consciousness that has a similar euphoric feeling as spirituality or spiritual growth. A person's sexuality can be the intersection of opposing forces which, in a heightened state, can become the balanced integration of spirituality and sexuality.

It is common for mankind to use teachings that support the repression of energy and categorize it as spiritual growth. But the repression of pleasure usually leads to an energetic response in the opposite direction. Therefore, you should integrate your sexuality with your spirituality in a way that aligns with your consciousness. In this way, you stay in integrity and merge the energies as balanced.

With judgments come shame and a feeling that something is wrong or out of order in some way. To feel true freedom of spirit, try to release judgments and beliefs that repress your sexuality, which in turn represses your energy field. In this freedom and spacious environment that you can create, it is important to align with your core beliefs in order to prevent self-inflicted damage to the spirit.

In the Cosmic union of sexuality between two hearts, there are wings that carry your love around the Universe, only to return with the amplified momentum known as God's grace.

In a response to the whisper on abuse, one reader writes: "I have been thinking a lot about this subject even though I haven't called it abuse exactly – shame – the need to punish ourselves because of *tradition*...then rise above it all in some kind of martyrish fashion – yuck."

The dictionary defines shame as *a painful emotion caused by consciousness of guilt, shortcoming, or impropriety.* In my work, I often witness various expressions of shame and I believe there is a connection to abuse. But is shame a product of abuse, or do some actions of abuse emerge from the energy of shame? I will say that shame feels like one of the deepest of the lower energies.

It is a mystery to me when an abuse victim expresses guilt or shame for a situation that they had very little control over. The implications are that humans often take on the responsibility for the actions of others, which is further evidence that we are all connected. When someone wounds themselves, they wound us too. Whew! I am spinning out of control (tee hee) and feeling the need for a soothing whisper:

It is the depth of an experience that ultimately determines the level of reach into the soul. In the energy of shame, there lies a great opportunity to create upward spiraling spiritual movement. There is also an opportunity for the opposite to occur. Out of the energy of unforgiveness lies the potential for the greatest chance to find love. It is not about duality as much as unison and integration of energies that lead to balance instead of extremes.

It is easy to shoulder the perspective and opinions that other people might project on you. But there is also a light within you that can illuminate the truth. Projecting darkness into your being can be neutralized with light and love energy, if you are willing to release the toxic effects of an experience that brought up shame.

Each person in your life will make a choice on how to treat you, and you will choose how to respond to that experience. Divine energy can cleanse the heart and soul if you open to the greater love that is before you now, with movement away from the judgments and opinions of others. Your true connection to the Highest Power ensures your ability to overcome shame.

By allowing the energy of love to travel into the farthest reaches of your Cosmic or High Heart, you evoke emotional cleansing supported by your faith and belief in a power that is beyond karma, beyond the human psyche and beyond the lower energies that mire you in the human drama.

Enjoy the ride, knowing there will be bumps in the road, while simultaneously feeling the rewards that will come to you and gently nudge you over to the smoother side of the road less traveled!

To ***sign off*** *is to complete or end a performance, project, or other matter; to terminate; to withdraw. In the 9th century and for several hundred years thereafter, a person could change his religious affiliation simply by "signing off"; i.e., by signing a legal paper that ended his membership in one religious organization and, if he so desired, enrolled him in another.*

In the construction world, we usually sign off on the papers held by the bank, the owner, the insurance companies and the sub-contractor as a formal way of completing or ending a project. This summer has been filled with completions for Beckie and me. That is why we have been so darn busy (lol)! Some long-standing commitments are coming to a close during a 'one' year, which is usually denoted as a beginning year.

Completions often signal new beginnings, and maybe I won't know the true experience until the endings actually occur. Just last week I could have ended the format on the 'angel whisper' by going straight to the source and ending my silly commentary. No more Russell talking, just whispers! (tee hee). Well, before I sign off, let's see what an angel might whisper on the subject:

Completions occur when the circle is unbroken. The energy that began in a forward movement reaches the end by completing the circle of light that was once only a thought. The form taken during the process of creation is a circle that holds the energy forever as part of your soul journey. The result is the reward that becomes a gift of that energy.

If you are unable to complete your energy circles or projects, that is an indication of an energy leak. Energy leaks from the circle and it remains broken, providing more opportunity for energy to escape. That is an indicator that focus is needed, and you need methods that direct your energy toward that which is necessary, while being directed away from that which is not necessary. Some energy may leak into areas that do not serve, creating a distraction or illusion that leads you away from the direction of your initial focus of energy.

Goals, intentions, clarity of thoughts and prayers can bring the completions of your commitments to fruition, providing you a light of truth in which to stand and to align yourself with. Completions often mean success and can bring peace to the heart and soul, even if the experience was a negative. Your process can be one that gives you knowledge that carries you, holds you and nurtures you, through that knowledge becoming fully integrated into wisdom.

You can discover pathways toward finding the major completion to your life's effort, bestowing the biggest reward of all. That reward is the completion of the circle of energy that moved your light into the body, motivated your discoveries in the physical world, brought lessons of love and filled the soul with all it needs. The ultimate signing off occurs in divine timing and places your soul in the stream of love known as ascension.

Sometimes we just need some sort of sign to know we are on the right path, and I have learned to ask for these little gems. I am sure that everyone has had some sort of experience that translated into an important message. In my world, signs are an integral aspect of receiving guidance.

Daydreams, images, repetitive thoughts and ideas, or words spoken by a friend can be so synchronistic with your journey there is little room for doubt. Maybe you are thinking about taking a workshop in L.A. when a friend pops in and says, "You know, California is beautiful this time of year," providing that magic moment when spirit gives you the affirming answer through a physical connection.

Coins, jewelry, shiny objects, electrical devices, feathers and winged creatures are known to deliver the signs that you are looking for. When I was writing a chapter in my new book about signs and connecting with nature, I pushed away from the computer and went for a walk in the Lincoln National Forest of New Mexico. As I was walking, I felt something in my vest pocket and discovered that it was my phone. I removed it and found a small black feather tucked between the folds off my flip phone!

Once I asked the angels for a sign and within twenty minutes I had received three very clear signs, so I would advise everyone to pay attention to your surroundings after requesting a sign, because the angels are fast (tee hee)! Now let's see if we can solicit a sign from an angel in the form of a whisper:

We can't always appear in the physical and deliver a message of love, nor would you want us to, so signs play an important role in angelic communication. Within the stream of love that surrounds you and your angelic guides, the common thread often lies in the ability to transfer information through signs.

Other people act as Earth Angels and intuitively receive messages for the ones around them, because there is no resistance from receiving within a detached energy. Birds deliver messages as part their extreme ability to align with Natural and Spirit. Shiny objects capture attention and therefore energy flows more easily around the light-giving essence that surrounds such things.

Humans can easily believe in a sign because of a separation of energies that bring a witness closer to the truth and the vibrations that align with each soul. When you ask us for guidance, we move toward the single element that speaks the loudest and delivers the answer with the most speed. It is important for each person to feel their prayers are heard, and signs can anchor you in the deepest levels of your belief while each individual maintains a grounded attitude. Simply ask for your signs and then be willing to receive signals.

Think of it like driving a car on the highway of life: The more confused and lost you are, the more you search for the billboard or sign that says it is time to exit here!

My angelic guides deliver several common messages such as 'eat healthy,' 'increase energy flow through movement,' 'get plenty of rest' and, above all else, 'keep it simple.' When life feels complicated, that could be your signal for the need to simplify.

My wife, Beckie, does organizational and de-clutter work with her clients, and there is a relationship between clutter and non-simple living that could follow a thread to an emotional need. She helps people in ways aimed at simplifying their lives with an assessment of their living and physical workspace. But how do we keep it simple?

I must admit the big belly-laugh that I received while searching the meaning of the word *simple*. **Simple**: *single, not complex, not unfolded or entangled, not compounded, not blended with something else, not complicated; 2) plain; 3) not other than; 4) not given to artifice; 5-23)* many more definitions with the word 'not'*; 24) childlike trust or dewy-eyed innocence* (lol). I was beginning to think that the dictionary was going to infinity with everything simple did not mean, until No. 24 hit upon a simple meaning.

It is my intention to keep angel whispers simple and easy to understand, yet this word clearly demonstrates that our language has so many complexities, no wonder we struggle to communicate in relationships, family matters and certain aspects of life that require language. Finding a simple space to have moments of simplicity to communicate simple basic needs can be challenging. Nonetheless, it's time to find that space to communicate a simple whisper:

Keeping life simple can be the highest form of faith-based living, as you limit distractions or anything that can keep your focus from your divine life-purpose. In the modern world, there are many opportunities to make things complicated without much effort. Unfortunately, negative feelings have been associated with the word simple, such as 'being bored' and 'without substance,' which can lead to a perceived need for constant stimulation. This need can manifest into a lifestyle that becomes disconnected from Divine and Inner guidance.

Simple is also easy, and living with ease can bring peace and comfort to life in a way that leads to expansion and focus on the body, mind and spirit. Within this space, you can find presence, understanding and truth that illuminate the true meaning of life.
In order to live life to the fullest, find a love for the simple things such as enjoying a sunset, taking time to listen to the song of a bird or stopping to smell the roses.

Faith provides the foundation on which to build a simple life with the energy of happiness, acceptance, joy, love and gratitude. If you are working on your vision of the future, keep it positive and simple. This will lead you to take action steps that resonate with your true essence. If you are not ready or willing to see things in this light, complication may be serving a need to learn more lessons in life, or serving an illusion that is fed by the ego.

One common message from the angels that applies to everyone is 'If it's not simple, then it's not right.' I can say that I have a lot experience in this area of thought. For years I reinforced my belief system that I led a complicated life with near-impossible-to-conquer slants on my circumstance. The more we affirm to ourselves that things are complicated, the more we attract this kind of thinking that life isn't simple.

Simplicity *is the property, condition, or quality of being simple. It often denotes beauty, purity or clarity. Simplicity can mean freedom from hardship, effort or confusion. According to Occam's razor, all other things being equal, the simplest theories are the most likely to be true, and, according to Thomas Aquinas, God is infinitely simple. In cognition theory, simplicity is the property of a domain which requires very little information to be exhaustively described.*

Linda Breen Pierce writes that "a more descriptive term for living simply might include 'mindful living,' 'intentional living,' or 'soulful living.' Voluntary simplicity involves unburdening life of needless material things and letting go of anything that interferes with the integrity of life. She goes on to write that one simplicity maven put it like this: We give up a giddy, adrenaline-fueled whirl of changing experience without substance, touch without intimacy, information without meaning and company without community." What could follow that other than a simple whisper?

What is the most simple thing that you can think or feel? In the natural order of life, there is one basic simple premise. Love is the answer. When you shine the light of love onto any situation, you are being present as a witness to the truth. This truth can be as simple as God, the Highest Power and all that is Divine.

Do not confuse simplicity with an idea that equates to living without your needs being met. The abundant world is as simple as nature itself and offers everything you desire. As you move away from simplicity, you open the doors to feelings of having less time, not being connected, lack of clarity and the loss of certain aspects that enhance your life such as balance, centeredness and spirituality.

The greatest spiritual teachers mold lives that are simple, even in the most chaotic environments. The simplicity of life is a conscious choice that each of you will make. Remember that love and simplicity are foundations of the heart, so the Inner Self must separate from the search for peace in the outer World.

If you can find it within yourself to believe that the mysteries of life are part of the simplicity of the Divine plan, you can vibrate waves of peace, love and harmony throughout the Earth. Live simply, embrace the truth, find love for all, feel the light, think and act out of compassion as your personal message of spiritual development and evolution through enlightenment.

The problem that I have with the word and meaning of *sin* is the judgment and perception aspect that is so defining. Everyone has probably heard of the seven deadly sins: lust, gluttony, greed, sloth, wrath, envy and pride. The mention of these words brings up the ideas around religion that lead us to believe that a judgmental overseer and creator is keeping track of all our actions. I like this quote from an unknown source: "Where there is love, there is no sin."

The English word *sin* derives from Old English *synn*. The same root appears in several other Germanic languages and means "to be." Its present participle is "being." Latin also has an old present participle of *esse* in the word *sons*, which came to mean "guilty" in Latin. The root meaning would appear to be "it is true"; that is, "the charge has been proven." The Greek word *hamartia* is often translated as *sin* in the New Testament, and it means "to miss the mark" or "to miss the target."

I must be Greek to resonate with that last definition (tee hee). Anyone can miss the mark when facing the trials and tribulations of life, but who wants the label of sinner? Buddhism does not recognize the idea behind sin because in Buddhism there is a "Cause-Effect Theory" known as Karma or action. It is time for me to take action and receive a whisper from an angel on the word *sin*:

Sin is a word that connects to feelings that are not within the intended meaning of the word itself. Feeling shame, guilt, fear, and turning from faith often replace the feelings of retrospect, spiritual growth and personal responsibility associated with the meaning. Once you go to the judgment aspect, the meaning is lost, only to be replaced by a code or doctrine.

The original teachings are so distanced from Source, the perspective has been altered to create an opportunity to manipulate and control by those that would abuse such a privilege. This has led many to turn from faith and from the true energy that is available to all. Today's society can resonate more with positive focus on living a life of purpose rather than feelings of judgment and negative behaviors.

Every human being is given a moral compass to know the vibrational difference between right and wrong. You need not look any further than your own feelings to know the truth about your existence, without the discernment from others leading you away from the spiritual path of peace.

If you feel unable to keep from the actions that take you from your Divine life-purpose, this could be your signal from your body that you have built illusions around your life as a way to cope with addictive negative behaviors and repeating events. The truth always illuminates the life path, and beyond that are simply the lessons of life. Learn today to live tomorrow in the energy of pure love.

A big thanks to everyone who responded to last week's *Whisper* by hugging a tree. One reader remarked that after hugging every tree in a small stand of oaks, she turned to walk away, only to hear a voice say, "We love you!" I replied to several of the tree-huggers by saying, "When you went outside and hugged that tree, you were hugging me (lol)."

This series of exchanges was fun and unexpected, two energies I really love (tee hee). I've heard it said that where energy goes, energy flows, and these weekly *Whispers* perfectly demonstrate that to me over and over again. This week's focus took to the high road for an elevated perspective and initiated these thoughts around *"It's a small world with a large voice."*

Our Earth does have a large voice and that comes through when we listen. Listening to the tree deliver a message of love was followed by a profound and connected moment with nature. That inspired account led me into thoughts of the healing energy found in nature, the Earth and the Angel who represents the soul of our greatest Mother. I will ask for a connected inspirational moment usually found in the whispering voices of angels:

Most of you have witnessed the full force of nature at least once in your lifetime, and if you listened during one of those events, you surely heard the voice of Gaia. Simultaneously, you are being constantly reminded of the small degree of separation between you and other people who exist in the world today.

The voice of reason can be found in a whisper of vibration that is connecting at the soul level. Finding resonance with a single thought can be your signal that, beneath the conscious radar, the body holds wisdom and the ability to communicate that wisdom with grace and ease. The lower vibrations found in the communications from the Mother Earth come up through the feet and legs first, before reaching the body, so the mind is the last to 'feel' these important messages. Over-analyzing a message from spirit, the body or even the Earth enables the mind to discount what your body has already assimilated.

The heart of the Mother Earth connects to the heart of the human body and becomes a partner in every aspect of life, from suffering to joy. It is important to listen to the voice from within as the true voice of reason, and create action steps that mirror truth, integrity and honor, beginning with your vehicle of transportation, which is your body and the Earth. That voice of nature speaks with a calming and peaceful tone that softly sings a song that expresses love.

This word came up during a 'song harvest,' a term coined by my friend Craig that frames the glorious journey of creating music. The word just came out of my mouth in place of the one I had carefully crafted and written down in my notes. *Solace* replaced the word *silence* in the phrase "finding silence in the soul." I wasn't sure of the exact meaning or the lyrical 'fit.'

The word *solace* is a transitive verb and a noun that means to console or lighten up by making cheerful. To soothe is another meaning and the example in the dictionary used the verb as 'to solace grief.' This was interesting to me as the study of words and the writing of music intersected to form a deeper relationship or 'bond' to my expressed meaning.

The passage in the song was truly more about solace than silence, and completely in the energy of grief. What emerged in the moment was around the way emotions flow and become partners with sound, only to evolve as energy that is without words. This type of communication between body, mind and spirit rarely manifests the way it did this past week. The Mercury Retrograde was in full swing, and that can affect communication in many ways for many people as we pause for reflection and discernment.

It seems like everything I've written about solace has significance regarding the process of writing the *Angel Whispers*, such as silence, solace, consoling, cheerful messages and the feeling of being lighter. Maybe now I can find the meaning that dwells in the depth of the silence in the form of whisper on solace:

Ancient civilizations found many ways to express the feelings associated with solace. Sanskrit writings were channeled messages designed to give the reader solace, courage inspiration and faith in mankind. The meaning, messages and connection with this word have lost strength in modern times with the dismissal of important teachings around spirituality.

Gaining solace can take on many forms and have greatly desired effects, so it is wise to contemplate actions and intentions around solace designed to bring you closer to your heart and soul. Inside solace, you can find silence, acceptance, inner beauty and peace with a connection to your Divine energy source.

As you find balance in your life, include the nurturing aspects of solace that bring harmony to your joy, your grief and everything in between. In this way, you are completing a circle of life that surrounds you and supports you by bathing you in the light of love and connection with Divine Spirit.

The intent to soothe the soul expresses the energy of your willingness to experience the most beautiful aspects of life from a perspective of joy and wonder. Inside the depths of your solace, you will find the highest levels of peace, love and, most importantly, acceptance. In this light, think of solace as the gateway to receptivity and the strands of energy that connect with your heart.

What a beautiful word combination, soul and mate, which can easily translate into companion of the soul. The Angels work with people on a daily basis to help understand the broad scope of meaning this word carries. As Humans, we tend to place limitations inside the confines of the literal meaning of this word and others.

In my thirty-third year of marriage, I am still feeling the love and can easily say that I have found my soulmate. The guides call them help-mates and claim that we have many available throughout our life on planet Earth. Help-mates are constantly connecting with us in this lifetime and, according to the Angels, they find us for a moment or a lifetime.

Twin flames are the next level up from soulmate and I will save that for another whisper. *Soulmate is a term sometimes used to designate someone with whom one has a feeling of deep and natural affinity, love, intimacy, sexuality, spirituality, and compatibility.* Let's ask for a defining moment with the angels on the subject of soulmate:

Soulmate has several implied meanings attached to it. Social and moral structures built by man shine a focused light on the subject that narrows the meaning of soulmate by reducing it into terms that appear black and white. For some, this can contribute to false ideas around love and relationships.

When things start to feel complicated, that is the signal for a moment of solace. Quiet the mind and ask for the simplest meaning to come from the heart, body, mind and soul. As you open to the Higher Self for answers to your love life, resistance is removed, allowing loving energy to enter and dissolve fears around love, misunderstanding in relationships, and illumination of the truth.

The truth is that there are many soulmates and many who have walked through time together. When you chose to emerge onto the physical plane, there was a chain reaction that brought large numbers of loving souls that you vibrate with to incarnate simultaneously. These are the ones that know you at the depth of your resonant frequencies.

To attract your soulmate, or to keep the one you have, learn to love yourself so that others may learn how to love you as well. When you choose to lead the way in self-love, the ones around you can follow. Release the toxins of past relationships, self-destructive patterns and the unwillingness to forgive yourself and others. When you open your heart to self-love, you are shining a beacon of light to your soulmate. Be the lighthouse so that others may find their way around the dangers of life to land in the safety of love.

I have been getting repetitive messages, usually an angelic signal, regarding the current state of our government and political affairs. In addition, I have seen articles about religious leaders entering into the political arena to deliver messages with spiritual content. All of them feeling a calling to express political views from a spiritual perspective.

My repetitive thoughts around this subject include a vision that might completely dismantle the government, changing the way the business of running a country is handled. Using technology to create a streamlined and simple approach to government would be on the forefront of building a new political structure for the future. Policy and legal think-tanks could be used to design laws that support individual and humanitarian positions.

We could move toward a flat tax based on economic factors that would eliminate the need for the IRS altogether. Overhauling the prison system in a way that would allow non-violent offenders the chance to work off their debt to society by building infrastructure, which could help rehabilitate criminals and balance the budget. I believe there is a way to build a government that turns a profit and has little need to tax the people.

In other words we could narrow the focus, and if you elect me as your angel whisperer (tee hee), I will deliver a message on spirituality and politics:

The separation between religion and government was created for reasons that no longer apply. As you have witnessed, the spotlight on the political theater has illuminated an undeniable truth that gives direction and purpose to the actions of your neighbors. There is a need for the injection of spiritual input in all areas of life, including government.

By speaking the truth, you are injecting love and light into a body that governs the people. Your immediate future will define levels of evolution for mankind, and your political process may go through drastic changes as a result. Like the people, government is an evolving process.

The change that people seek in this area will not come without spiritual involvement, and the form that shift takes will center around personal integrity. The current focus on politics is feeding the generation destined to deliver the greatest change, and the nature of that job requires the courage of spiritual warriors. All warrior spirits are having spirit-driven thoughts around various structures due to the Cosmic energy that is directing focus on the framework of success. This energy will serve individuals and the nations of the world because it is the bigger picture.

The Higher Self can deliver the wisdom necessary to maneuver the political path with the highest discernment around your use of energy devoted to this area. Evolution is change and it will take courage and discipline to bring the Earth from chaos into a new peace. Courageous actions are always anchored in the light of truth.

I was kidding around with a friend on Facebook as I jokingly wrote about my new book coming out, titled *The Spiritual Laws of Distraction: A Cautionary Tale for Blind Dating* (tee hee). My little Facebook funny did solicit a response on some level. It made me think of the way humans make laws, but what about the laws from spirit?

Some might argue that laws pertaining to spirit cannot be understood from an intellectual perspective, while others might point toward the Ten Commandments as the foundation of the spiritual laws of mankind. My brain leans to the possibility of finding spiritual laws in the subtle energies of love.

An old Buddhist proverb says, "When the student is ready, the teacher will appear." I believe this may be a type of spiritual law, like the Law of Attraction presented in the movie *The Secret*. It's not that I don't believe these laws are simple, but maybe they can be over-simplified or maybe even understood (smiles). Let's get a whisper on spiritual laws:

The previous whispers on contrast *and* loss *provide examples of the ways that spiritual lessons are taught through an etheric vibration that might be construed as a type of law. Spiritual laws might be better defined as energetic truths. There is no real law, only options that are presented with the choices you make regarding your spirit.*

The free will and the higher self have a deep understanding of spiritual truths. As you witness yourself and others violating human laws, you can start to appreciate the way your own willful acts convey knowledge to the soul that brings the opportunity to synthesize energy into wisdom. When you become clear what is not law, you crystallize whatever you regard as a truth within 'what is.'

Spiritual truths illuminate life on your path to awaken the vibration known as love. If you are unwilling to discover ways to love yourself, you are unwilling to teach others how to love you. The energy that surrounds any issue of self-love evokes spiritual laws that help you identify blocks to create upward movement.

Spiritual laws are anchored within personal truth and integrity. These laws may not be clear or present as they do reside in the subtle layers. What is important to know is that spiritual laws are supportive of your journey and grounded in the energy of all your responses. Completing a life journey is therefore dependent on your willingness to open your heart, release pain, choose happiness, and feel the joy that is available to you in every moment.

Maybe it would serve to view spiritual laws as guidelines or suggestions!

What is that old saying? The squeaky wheel gets the grease or, as my father says, the squeaky wheel gets the attention! It struck me on my morning ride that in some ways, our society has turned toward the energy behind this saying. In almost every aspect of our culture, it seems that the loudest voice gets action or reaction.

Opinion news journalism, "shock the viewer" marketing and outrageous attention-getting entertainment are all phrases that describe ways the media gains the attention of the public. There are several problems with this approach, in my view, as the loudest complainers are now dictating agenda in many facets that affect my lifestyle. It also means that several voices are never heard simply because they are not "squeaky"! A good example is the speed bump that damages everyone's vehicle in order to slow down the two percent of the population that drive recklessly through our neighborhood.

The other problem is that my wheels generally don't squeak unless provoked by anger (tee hee). Admittedly, this is something that I am working on, which is the notion that a loving expression that speaks softly toward an issue goes largely unnoticed.

American humorist Josh Billings (1818-1885) recites in a poem, *The Kicker*: *"I hate to be a kicker [complainer], I always long for peace, but the wheel that does the squeaking is the one that gets the grease"*. However, the idea of the idiom is much older. A manuscript from about 1400 had: "Ever the worst spoke of the cart creaks". Let's listen for a squeaky wheel in the midst of a whisper from an angel.

Your frustration with this aspect of modern society can lead to passive-aggressive behaviors, loss of faith, conflicts and a negative outlook. Understand that the shields of protection enter any conflict where there is a challenge presented. Certain actions solicit a response that is usually filled with some teaching, such as finding ways to communicate with everyone involved with the attempt to solve a problem.

When others stand on the proverbial soapbox, you are given a choice to examine your beliefs and choose your battles. Ultimately those willing to use their gifts and who have stepped into their power are finding ways to effect change within a structure or, better yet, finding ways to completely change the structure to create bigger changes.

The challenge is in altering the contour of thought without the blocks created by forceful methods, and this can be accomplished more easily from the energy of love expressed through a combination of action, thought, compassion and presenting ideas. Once again it is your choice that finds the energy in which your beliefs are expressed.

Leaving behind all judgments around the reception of your perspective and remaining open to guidance can bring peace, understanding and acceptance to both the battle and the outcome. You want to avoid being drawn into actions that undermine your personal integrity or ability to express your truth.

I have never been so arrogant as to believe we are alone in this vast Universe, and in the work that I do, questions surface regularly about this area of study. I came across some articles, just prior to our recent trip, that described an 'alley' of alien activity stretching from Roswell to just south of Albuquerque. We were headed to our mountain cabin, which apparently lies directly in the runway (tee hee).

On one particular evening, Beckie and I were lying on the upper deck on top of our heated air-mattress, enjoying the star-filled heavens, when we observed a very strange thing. I was thinking about travel through space and how it would be ridiculous to think that advanced civilizations would have to travel through the time-consuming dimensions of our reality.

A few minutes into that thought, a beam of light appeared directly above us. The beam was very high up and expanded in size as it dropped into the sky. The way the beam of light appeared, expanded and stopped at a high altitude in the New Mexico sky really piqued my interest. As quickly as it appeared, the beam of light simply disappeared, and when it did, we both saw a vehicle with lights quickly move away from the spot in a northerly direction.

We were in some sort of shock when something else appeared as cloud-like formations to the immediate south of the last observation. It was a completely cloudless night, so this odd sight captured our attention. As this new feature appeared, lights started dancing through haze which turned the cloud green and purple. Then we noticed a triangular outline with lights appear within the cloud before the entire thing moved off in the southerly direction. So tell me, angels, what about star beings?

The Christ Consciousness is an expanded view of the life on Earth. This viewpoint includes the awareness that your actions affect more than just yourself. Life is supported in many ways, and some of those ways are foreign to the thinking of mankind. Your species has developed powerful weapons and ways to create devastating energy, which could easily raise concerns with more advanced civilizations.

To another life form, you could appear as children who are playing with a loaded gun, such as the Atomic and Nuclear energy, which could raise concerns. Your collective power to come together in peace and love, or to create mass destruction, would ripple out into the Universe with force and consequences. This could greatly alter the balance of life beyond the stars.

Truth resides in the heart, and that allows every person to become present with their beliefs and for their free will to decide whether or not each individual will open to a greater possibility of life itself. If you are holding fears around the existence of life forms, that is the experience that you will create. Be careful with your mind, because one of those mysterious life forms includes you.

This could be one of the most disabling types of energy, especially the way it affects our health and well-being. Everyone experiences stress, yet it is largely ignored or discounted, or it's incorporated into our lives in a way that can ultimately mask the source and effects of stress.

Stress is the body's reaction to a change that requires a physical, mental or emotional adjustment or response. Stress can come from any situation or thought that makes you feel frustrated, angry, nervous, or anxious. "Reality is the leading cause of **stress** amongst those in touch with it" is a quote by Lily Tomlin that really speaks to the basic nature of life in general.

There are so many opportunities to feel stress that it should be a priority to spend some time focusing on stress relief. Keeping life simple, making time for joy and play, addressing priorities and well-thought-out action steps with intentions to release stressful situations can all lead to a better quality of life.

Stress seems to compromise all areas of mind, body and spirit in ways that we might not even be aware of. This makes it essential to stay connected and in touch with the physical body, as this is where we can find the most wisdom in dealing with unhealthy choices. Let's see what the angels have to say about stress in the form of a gentle and nourishing whisper:

People often ignore their body and the messages around the effects of stress. Like the tides of the oceans, the human body feels the effects of the natural cycles and rhythms of the planet. High pressure in the atmosphere can remove chances for rain in much the same way that the spirit is repressed from releasing tears during times of extreme pressure. Without this release, the body cannot go deeper into the lower-self energies.

The spirit of mankind is one that easily adapts to all situations in order to ensure the survival of the species. To integrate stress can have a damaging response from the body that makes the cause unclear or not readily apparent, as if coming on suddenly. That is why some focus in quiet moments could help discern stress levels before they become a serious compromise to your wellbeing.

Love, joy, faith, laughter and happiness can minimize the effects of stress, and for this reason many are being led to follow the heart's true desires. Relationships, careers, creativity and life purpose forged without the energy of love can have you facing choices in unexpected ways due to the evolutionary path of mankind. This is the time that mankind has waited for to leave the lower energies and enter a life filled with positive transitions and acceptance in order to fulfill destinies.

Release the pains of the past, follow the thread of love, embrace a planet in flux and discover your heartsong in order to leave stressful living behind and collect the inheritance that is rightfully yours.

This was a subject requested for a whisper that immediately brought up a range of emotions. Most people have been touched by an event where someone took their life, either by accident or by design. Those feelings, combined with what some religions and the law tell us is illegal, can make it hard to resolve the impact from such an event.

The first known use of this word with Latin roots was in 1643 AD. The Sanskrit word sva, which means oneself or one's own, can be traced to the origins of this word and its meaning. The word suicide can take on different meanings, like 'to ruin one's interest,' but is rarely used outside the context of taking one's life.

I discovered that my natural tendency was to block energy around this subject, which is not conducive to an angel whisper (tee hee) That resistance energy was all it took to propel me forward into the contrast in order to gain wisdom, understanding and acceptance, which is always a product of listening to the heart for a whisper from an angel:

The act of committing suicide is a combination of energies merging into one event. The need to feel greater love, the desire to be home with the Creator, the feeling that some part must die, and the inability to move in a forward or upward direction all come together to form the transitional state and mindset needed to create such an outcome. Most often this conditional state is mired with the human drama that gives the feeling of completion to the physical incarnation.

Taking responsibility to end one's life is making a decision to resolve energy on the surface of existence. Beneath the illusion, beneath the story, is an ending or a letting go that begins a process of transmutation. The spontaneous release of energy leaving the body propels the soul into an illuminated space that holds the opportunity to find resolution.

This release acts to remove the desires, emotions and pain connected to the physical body, and in essence, places the entire focus on human energy. From beyond the veil, time ceases to exist for the spirit, now working solely with energetic form.

Spiritual resolution moves easily within dimensions found outside the body. The pressures of life are transformed into an opportunity to be in the light of a higher consciousness. The burdens carried while in the body are lifted, and the free will chooses an upward movement, downward movement or a lateral movement. Anything but the choice toward upward movement of energy is a soul's way of choosing the path toward another incarnation and more lessons of love.

Surrender is such a magnificent word in the way it delivers a broad meaning with a range of emotions, from humble and loving to being controlled and resigned. It seems to take some a large measure of control to allow myself to surrender. Yet when I recently set strong intentions to work through a process without the energy of control, the result was a beautiful surrender that helped to increase my energy in terms of availability.

As a witness to the natural order of life, it seems that the final journey is a complete surrender at the deepest levels. The type of surrender needed at the time of one's passing is the truest form of letting go. Webster defines **surrender** as *resignation, acceptance of despair, giving up, a verbal act of admitting defeat or the agreement to forgo to the power or possession of another.*

There goes the neighborhood with all the control features that bring a negative concept to the word *surrender. "Change is the essence of life. Be willing to **surrender** what you are for what you could become."* That quote by an unknown author better describes the surrender that I have known lately (tee hee).

The part that needs work in this area for me seems to be in the perspective of surrendering that leads us to believe that we must give up, give in or accept an alternative. But when we surrender everything except our heart's truest desire, then maybe we have just cleared the way to manifest those desires into dreams. I will raise my arms in surrender to the energy of an angel and a whisper on the wings of change:

The human experience offers a variety of opportunities designed to support spiritual growth through learning. It requires an open heart and mind to become masters in the areas of your passion and interests. One single inhale can bring in knowledge that allows you to surrender a thought or belief through the subsequent exhale. This speaks to the natural ability to create change within each person.

Complete surrender of illusions and false teachings can result from taking the higher perspective. Mankind's fascination with climbing the great peaks around the world stem from the desire to see from this perspective or to rise above. When your view of the 'big picture' is unobstructed, so are your thoughts and energy, which can then help you direct energy toward a solution or answer to the questions in life. The solution could be as easy or simple as finding acceptance.

As you surrender to the fact that truth as an integral part of Divine light and spirit, you are opening pathways to pure love and peace. Great strength lies in your ability to surrender and move beyond the limitations that are generated from the beliefs of others. In other words, when you surrender the energy of control, you have just taken the initiative to rise above in order to see the highest potential.

In the moment of eternal surrender, your spirit experiences freedom that has been erased from your memory. That is why you practice the art of surrendering.

I was watching a PBS special filmed at the Lady Bird Johnson Wildflower Center and on the highways of Texas. The show focused on wildflowers and plant species that have a symbiotic relationship with each other. Some wildflowers are choked out by natural grasses and other plants, while some types of plants encourage and support growth of another species.

When my ideas around wildflowers shifted to thoughts about the human journey, my brain popped from the expansion (tee hee). In the search for the best possible environment, perhaps we plant roots in areas with conditions that are less than favorable in some way. Maybe we should factor in the subtle features that could support our growth, something beyond good schools and neighborhoods.

One friend put it to me like this as he raised his fist in the air and proclaimed with an angry tone, "Great. Another opportunity for personal growth!" Do we need more opportunities, or just one perfect opportunity? Wikipedia states that *some symbiotic relationships are obligate, meaning that both symbionts entirely depend on each other for survival.*

That statement seems to indicate that mere survival is possible under most natural conditions, but true growth might be best achieved under those circumstances created with certain details that might enhance a specific aspect of life. Before I go off on the search for symbiotic relationships, let's evoke an angel to give a whisper on the subject:

A symbiotic relationship could describe two energies that meet to form one loving stream, like a feather dancing on the wind. The dance represents an alliance formed not within need, but within partnership dedicated to flying. With magnetic pull, energies merge to create a supportive bond and a mutually beneficial agreement or relationship.

Mankind has symbiotic relationships with plants, animals, food, air, other people, the Earth and even the stars. You are connected and in some cases dependent on so many species, elements and conditions that you might find it hard to fathom. In addition, there are the various dimensions and levels of your existence that the evolving and unlimited beings of the Earth are sometimes blissfully unaware of.

Symbiotic relationships support the vital functions of life, such as eating and breathing. But there is also a symbiotic relationship with unseen energy. This energy comes through the crown and spirals downward into the depths of the soul, before starting an upward movement that emerges as song. In this moment, the heart sings the expression of the energy felt by the soul and delivered by the passion of spirit. Inspiration-fed vibrations move through your body, becoming the unified voice of many, and symbiosis is created.

Separate and unattached energies come together to support life in a mystical stream called support. Surround yourself with beauty, join a like-minded community, choose locations that make you feel good, and create symbiotic relationships that mirror and support your values. Now that is love!

There are times when it feels as though unconditional love, no matter how hard you try, just isn't enough. Repeatedly falling short of a loved one's expectations can be discouraging. Then there comes a day when you finally get a chance to voice words from the heart, but that voice isn't met with acceptance.

Focusing on healthy boundaries for the purpose of creating wellness in a relationship can be met with extreme opposition that often leads to a sense of abandonment and isolation, with some form of shaming, manipulation and judgments attached. So where does the focus of energy go when you are feeling pain in a relationship?

What if someone is unwilling to meet you on common ground, leaving you with little choice? Are we supposed to meet their terms in order to simply have a relationship, even if they are unhealthy? And if so, are we supporting that relationship with some form of unbalanced energy? The questions tell me that it is time to set my terms of endearment with an angel who whispers:

This is why it is so important to pay attention to the models that you and others set for children. If they are taught that unhealthy attachments are an integral part of the loving process, that is what they will learn. Love with unhealthy conditions does not support growth at optimum levels and can create more damage than good.

When facing opposition to love, you are given an opportunity to practice unconditional love. Gentle persuasion from a loving heart gives you the best chance for positive movement, especially if you are unwavering in the choices you make. Sometimes the example you trying to establish can best be reflected in the actions you create, but your best choice is to limit your expectations and detach from all judgments. You can find comfort in showing others the truth of who you are, and create peace within the relationship through actions that reflect understanding and acceptance.

I hear you saying, "I am not a Saint ...," but maybe you have some Saintly qualities that could be applied to every situation. I now hear you evoking the definition of insanity, but trying the same thing over and over while expecting different results has the keyword 'expecting' as part of the description.

You can rise above the drama by seeing through the loving eyes of angels. Look for the positive blessings in order to heal from the damage sustained in the past. Above all else, do not allow yourself to fall into a 'tit for tat' response. That will lead you down the path of living life in the lowest vibrations.

I want to give you all big thanks for your support and response to my Angel Whispers. It's because of you that I am inspired to write these. Think of this email like the pumpkin pie to the turkey dinner, combined with some serious talk over a meal.

Recent events involving the passing of a beautiful soul have shaken me to the core, and so I have to carefully consider my gratitude. Sometimes things in life test your belief system, especially when there are no answers to questions that surround a terrible tragedy. This can lead to several emotional responses, but I found myself bargaining. I negotiated over what could have been done to change things.

As I processed through the five stages of grief, which are denial, anger, bargaining, depression and acceptance, I found myself eventually giving thanks for the loved ones that surround me. I have to take a spiritual teaching from this tragic lesson because I know that is what this beautiful soul would want from me.

I'm not saying that the grief process is over; on the contrary, I am saying that part of the process includes my thanks for the life lesson that I have just been taught. It just so happened to be scattered in between my denial and anger. As I discovered from this situation, I felt gratitude for my own family and friends, and even took the time to express my feelings.

Thanks: 1) expression of gratitude and pleasure for something given or done. So what about giving thanks for something that has yet to happen? Some think that this helps manifest your desires, and I have to agree. When you give thanks for something that hasn't happened yet, you are feeling the vibrations. Just like trying on a new suit or dress, sending out the resonance of gratitude for future events can be as rewarding as receiving in real time, while messaging your desires to the Universe:

As I search for answers and process my grief, I surrender myself to Spirit and all things that are unknown, and I give thanks to everyone and everything in all directions of space and time. Thank you friends, family and heavenly guides for this whisper:

Thanks are more than a feeling; it is an expression of hope. As you thank the ones that surround you, a blanket of hope provides a divine moment. If you are open to receive this gift, then you are able to pass it on.

Without thanks, there is no bond of hope. The balance that this brings will serve more than the one. As you walk your path, you should make time for accepting and sharing this gift.

When you become engulfed in divine light, you are filled with gratitude and in a perpetual state of thanks. This is how you are connected with divine source. Giving thanks for something seemingly small is your gateway into the angelic realm.

Gratitude for the moment is the highest honor you can bestow to yourself, the ones around you and the Highest Power. In the divine realm there is a shining star that becomes brighter with prayers of gratitude and remains eternally in the vision of hope.

Thought forms are an interesting subject to me. Some experts believe that some thought forms can become entities that influence each of us into repeating behaviors and patterns that might be negative or even a detriment to our health. Others use stronger language and see thought forms in a broader sense, manifesting into wars and destruction.

Rev. Len Romska from the website mystic.com writes: *A thought form is a structured inter-dimensional energy form intentionally created to carry out a specific task for which it has been programmed. It is created by you with the co-operative efforts of the universe.*

A thought form is different from the random thoughts we have every day which also create, positively or negatively, but are chaotic and without structure. Common thoughts, as I call them, take on a life of their own, seek out areas of like energy to combine with, and become even more powerful if created out of fear, anger, hate, and revenge. This is called a negative thought form and is instilled with destructive negative programming.

This is a pretty good description and I do believe that a type of programming occurs, especially when we form a limiting or negative belief with our thoughts. Dr. Doreen Virtue teaches that our thought forms 'love us,' making it is challenging to disconnect from them as a result. There is another form of energy that loves us enough to connect in the gift of a whisper on the breath of divine love from an angel:

The power that man holds to create is often reflected in the thoughts that emerge from the physical experience. Within the gift of creation, there is an energetic component that requires opposite poles working in harmony to attract an experience upon demand.

Some men, in an attempt to dominate and control others, abuse their powers by instilling fears through an expression of non-truths. When you fully trust someone and they speak outside the truth, negative thought forms can be created. Misinterpreting your own truth can also lead in the same direction with regard to creation of thought forms.

It is important that you purify the mental body in a way that nurtures your mind through a careful discernment of the truth. The integrity of the soul is weakened by negative thought forms and so it is important that you treat your thoughts with the same compassion you give to individuals.

It may be a much more simple process than you might give credit. Simply measure your thoughts by the infusion of love energy and do not commit to thoughts that are absent of the energy of love, whether they are directed at you, at others, or at the world. The Universe co-creates with you, so it is necessary to consider the far-reaching effects of your powerful thoughts.

The final chance to say good-bye to an unwanted thought form com

We set timelines in every facet of life, and those timelines connect us with our past, present and future. When my father predicted the day of his passing, I had to wonder if that timeline was already in place or one that he manifested. It could be that the vibration held the energy of both.

Timelines are defined as a schedule of activities or events; a timetable. Timelines can also refer to a chronology, representation or exhibition of key events within a particular historical period, often consisting of illustrative visual material accompanied by written commentary and arranged chronologically.

In an article titled ***The Art of Jumping Timelines***, Tom Kenyon writes, "Although it may seem paradoxical to some, your timeline—your life—is only one of many simultaneous possibilities. And it is quite possible, indeed it is your birthright, to alter your timeline and the potentials of your life. Your culture, for various reasons, has hypnotized you into believing that you are limited to one timeline."

By opening the mind to the expansive thinking around timelines, there might be an opportunity to better create joy, peace and happiness in your life. So on that wave of divinely expansive energy, let's dive right into a whisper on timelines:

"Created in the image of God" is an expression that gives meaning to the Creator within each person. In the future days of empowerment and enlightenment, all souls will be looking upward toward a timeline of energy known as ascension. In modern times, people are learning that they have a God or Goddess self that can alter the perception of reality. In one sense, it is similar to an infant's learning to crawl.

The survival instinct that is triggered within any adrenalin-filled experience, allows people to experience deep lessons about control and power as they relate to the senses beyond the body. The purest instinct around time will allow movement within a space where the mind has held limitations, especially around the experience of creating the future using timelines. The exploration of space holds knowledge and information around the manipulation of time in the interest of travel. This will teach man how to travel through time and dimensions or planes of existence.

The timeline of the past sets a vibration that influences the direction of the future. This explains why individuals are reluctant to alter their course consciously. Know that this generation will bridge the knowledge from the elders of ancient history and modern science to create a positive vision of the New World. In this transformational space, mankind will synthesize the elements of spirituality, creativity and positive visions into action steps that create the new models for civilization.

Within your reach is a timeline that offers profound peace, divine love, healing energy and the unity of cultures through art and friendship.

The first part of this word is 'trans' and when used as a prefix, carries the meaning "across, over, or beyond." *To move beyond your form* could describe the meaning of this word in very simple terms. Another definition for **transformation** might be *a swift translation of thought into action,* like this angel whisper (tee hee).

"In today's neo-evangelical church, the term 'transformation' is currently in vogue. Various churches and denominations claim to be undergoing 'transformation.' This word no longer refers to the humble sanctification of the individual believer. Rather, it now refers to an orchestrated, systemic and revolutionary overhaul of the global church, including the 'transformation' of cities, societies, cultures, marketplaces, and more," according to Lynn and Sarah Leslie, who also state:

Transformation--the measurable supernatural impact of the presence and power of God on human society, sacred and secular. In the church, this is characterized by increased holiness of life, accelerated conversion growth, reconciliation in relationships, mobilization of gifts and callings, and an increased relevance to and participation in a greater society.

I am not sure I can completely agree with those assessments, but in this word study I found several contradictions among scholars and spiritual leaders. This quote from Marianne Williamson seemed to capture my thoughts on the subject: *Personal **transformation** can and does have global effects. As we go, so goes the world, for the world is us. The revolution that will save the world is ultimately a personal one.* Let's see what the angels can allow in the energy of transformation:

Every minute of life on Earth creates an opportunity for transformation in the energy of thoughts, dreams, ideas, experiences and awareness. To change is to be transformed, and that energy can bring movement with the smallest level of willingness to embrace this basic constant that surrounds your essence.

Paradigms and structures collapse under the weight of transformation in order to ensure growth through conscious awareness. The evolution of mankind is dependent upon keeping an eye on the future while holding the lessons of the past. This brings grounding and centered openness to the concept of living in the moment.

Transformation shows an unwillingness to continue with old patterns and behaviors as you integrate teachings into your life. Fear energy can slow or stop the process of transformation, especially if supported by beliefs and the thoughts of others. This interruption in the growth process can also represent an internal delay tactic or ego trick.

Would a butterfly refuse the gift of flight after a lifetime as a caterpillar? This illuminates the fact that transformation is a part of the natural order of life, and to resist change simply means that you are not ready to fly. The energy of love is always transformational.

I hear this word more often than most in my angel readings. It seems that most of us are in some sort of transition, whether it be career, relationships emotions or a number of other areas. Our earth is in a transition!

When I left my job of thirty years recently, this word took on a whole new meaning. Granted it was my choice to close the doors on my successful home business as well as refuse clients that are my friends and part of my social circle, but I spent a year planning every aspect of my new life(ha ha).

When I made my break, I found that I was emotionally attached to my old life in several ways and on several levels. I also found some friends that were really attached to my old career and that was unexpected. Anger surfaced in the area of career. Guilt, manipulation and a wide range of negative emotions can follow you around the jobsite and usually does in that harsh environment. I held on to some of those more negative events.

As I began repairing my emotional soul, I had to say no to being manipulated. This was important to me because I allowed a family member to abuse and manipulate me for years. This was the original reason that I set out on this journey of transition. It just so happened to affect my career. On this day, I asked Archangel Michael to help me with answers about transition.

"What did you expect? It was all your choice to raise your vibrational level and to address your needs by rejecting guilt, anger, manipulation and fears. You have witnessed within yourself and others, the immediate reaction to your boundaries and their rejection of your beliefs. As those people have stepped aside, others have simply walked into their space. These new friends have your best interest at heart and are vibrating at a level similar to yours.

I am asking you to release all attachment to the forms that you thought your life would take. Let go off attachments to the old thought forms that give you expectations. Just for the moment, forget about looking at everything in the most positive light, take off the rose colored glasses and momentarily erase all the times that you saw the 'Secret'. Now think of your future in the most realistic way that you can. This doesn't mean to think of the worst case scenarios to prepare you for what might happen. This doesn't work any more than filling yourself with the expectations of a bliss-filled existence. You can look at your life in the most realistic way possible by accepting people for who they are and by accepting your situation for what it is. When you take these steps, you will find that not only will the reaction of others be very predictable, the decisions you make will become more apparent.

To create change and move to the next level, we must give up a part of our old life. This is often felt as giving up a freedom, so it is only natural to mourn for those old friends, old ways, even the old city that you loved. You can be guaranteed certain things in life and one of them is change will happen. It's up to you to decide to how you will receive those changes. When you ask God how you can serve, the self-serving types are bound to scatter. Realistic goals, comprehensive studies and down to earth planning will give you a clear picture of your intended purpose.

One more thing, you can't do it all alone so asking for help from the ones you can most trust will help to ease you through transition............ and that includes the humans."

With the current disaster in the Gulf of Mexico, it is hard to be distracted from the environmental concerns that we face. Once again, we all have to find ways to live with such a tragedy in the face of mounting evidence that it was a man-made event. So today, I turn to our friends the trees to help me stay grounded and centered in the truth. Then I turn to the children for another perspective.

I watched the daughter of a friend stand in my driveway, hugging a tree with such passion and determination that I asked her what she was doing. "Loving this tree," she replied in a blissful state. After several minutes of this, I asked in the form of a statement, "That tree needs a lot of love tonight."

"Well, just look at it. It's so tiny to be holding up so much!" she exclaimed as she pointed to the tree top. So I backed off and let her have all the time she wanted hugging that tree. The next day the tree fell over with no wind or storm; it was top-heavy. So today, I am going to ask the angels to help me know whatever any seven-year-old knows about trees (tee hee):

The tree sustains life on Earth as a bridge between the land and sky and creates an exchange of energy that becomes known as breathable air. Without trees, most forms of life on the planet's surface would cease to exist. They are also the ultimate barometer, marking the events of time, the seasons, environmental challenges and foretelling [?]the future.

The partnership that trees have with man was forged in the Divine Providence, and now supported by the Universal laws that govern your world. Symbols and images around the globe use trees to represent life as communicated in the most ancient text know to mankind. The Tree of Life represents the way faith and knowledge are synthesized into action within every natural act of survival by every species on Earth.
Your relationship with trees speaks to the heart of your perspective on life, creation and the energy that surrounds you.

In the center of everything that is held sacred, there is a magnificent tree. Some of mankind's most peaceful gestures were treaties signed under the canopy of a tree. The gates to Heaven are adorned with beautiful tree specimens that evoke the eyes to look upward. The roots of the tree hold steady the spinning Earth, to bring the silence that awakens the senses of mankind.

While on a sabbatical in the mountains of New Mexico, I awaken every day in the magical fairy glen of the Lincoln Forest. So naturally, I drew some cards from Doreen Virtue's "Healing with the Fairies" that said *Awakening to Your True Self* and *Be Honest with Yourself.* How can I, or anyone else for that matter, do one without the other (tee hee)?

What is the true self? I certainly hear this term thrown around a lot in the metaphysical circles. These two words conjure up images and ideas around duality in personality, and a sort of struggle or challenge to be true to one's self. It becomes apparent that reaching for the true self can bring many chances for personal growth.

On the other hand, maybe we are at a point in evolution where advanced thinking takes over as we are transforming into a true light as a species and a culture. I would like to think that my authentic self is represented most of the time (grins). If these are the insights and questions arising in the awakening to my true self, may they now connect to take on the form of a whispering angel:

It is only natural for human beings to rise with energy on the journey of evolution, for evolution carries components of ascension. In today's fast-changing world, upward movement of energy removes the layers from the past to create new beginnings, new ways of thinking, new approaches, and a view on life that can unfold from an elevated perspective.

The evolving process brings the higher self into the realities of the moment and enhances an environment that allows more freedom, presence and authenticity. This shift is noticeable and has created an awareness within the teachings from the spiritual world. The term allows others to be taught new patterns of thought as a way of deepening an experience.

Spiritual teachings help to create focused energy in movement toward a goal or intention. Part of your experience is within the global shifts and the external sources that facilitate such awareness. The excitement of the times and the possibilities should course through your body like a river, bringing release, fresh ideas, cleansing, and renewed energy.

A magical energy surrounds the true self and offers a vibration to create in a boundless reality. Once again, this is why there is such focus in an area that offers such potential in personal growth, energy movement, health management, and spiritual journeying. When you think of the true self, think of love, joy and the magical mysteries of life! Truth is light, and light is love.

Trust

Thanks to Danielle for the suggestion to create a whisper on the word *trust*, a sometimes elusive feeling amongst a vast landscape of opposition (lol). I am merely referring to the challenges with trust, whether it is with your faith, other people or with one's own self. By definition, **trust** means to *have confidence or faith with reliance on the integrity, strength, ability, surety, etc., of a person or thing.* But what if that trust connects with optimism to form illusions?

In my quest for answers, Google held 300 million possibilities (tee hee). But here is what I found at ChangingMinds.org: *Trust is both an emotional and logical act. Emotionally, it is where you expose your vulnerabilities to people by believing they will not take advantage of your openness. Logically, it is where you have assessed the probabilities of gain and loss, calculating expected utility based on hard performance data, and concluded that the person in question will behave in a predictable manner. In practice, trust is a bit of both. I trust you because I have experienced your trustworthiness and because I have faith in human nature. We feel trust. Emotions associated with trust include companionship, friendship, love, agreement, relaxation, comfort.*

If a person who is trustworthy commits an act that displays the opposite, does that mean we should no longer trust that person? And what if that person is looking back at you in the mirror (tee hee)? My brain is hurting, and that is my sign that it is time for a whisper from an angel on *trust*:

In the grand scheme of things, trust is an essential ingredient to the enjoyment of life. Like anything else that appears to be lost, trust can be found in the most unlikely places. If you are lacking trust in general, that could indicate the need to address issues relating to self-worth, lack of faith, the fear of failure or some sort of limiting belief about yourself, your environment, or the world in general.

You are constantly bombarded by a variety of energies that individually may be very subtle, but in unison, these energies can create feelings around the distrust in the world. It is important to separate yourself from actions that manifest distrust. Second-guessing yourself, seeing the world or the human journey as being without hope, living with damaging and negative emotions, or belief in an ideology that does not align with your true essence can support the emotion of distrust.

Building faith, supporting your spiritual growth, self-forgiveness, surrender to a higher power and a willingness to let go of things that do not serve are all ways to build trust. Giving through sharing always builds trust by spreading throughout the world like ripples of water across a pond. If you could elevate your heart to extend trust to someone who might not have earned it, you are teaching that person the value of trust. In order to accomplish this act and then feel the rewards, you might view it as sharing your trust, and in that way you are not giving up a part of yourself as much as you are moving loving energy through the Cosmic heart!

Learn ways to trust yourself first in order to experience trust with others.

*The meaning of the word **truth** extends from honesty, good faith and sincerity in general, to agreement with fact or reality in particular. The term has no single definition about which the majority of philosophers and scholars agree. Various theories of truth continue to be debated. There are differing claims on such questions as what constitutes truth; how to define and identify truth; the roles that revealed and acquired knowledge play; and whether truth is subjective, relative, objective or absolute.*

So if the truth is subjective to the rules of definition, then how do we discern the meaning? Some things are so rooted in our reality that there isn't much of a question of truth, like the color of snow and the price of oil in China. But when someone tries to tell you things like what you are thinking, what you meant to say or defining your belief system, something like the truth takes on a new meaning.

No matter what you meant to say, if someone takes the meaning differently than you intended, then isn't that their truth? If you try to defend yourself then that feels like ego. I strongly dislike being stuck between ego and the truth, but isn't truth worth fighting for? I am finding that I have more questions about the simple truth than I have answers. It must be time to ask for as whisper and hope it rings true:

Live in the light of love, and truth becomes illuminated for everyone to see. Truth is not a concept or a science; it is a belief and a feeling that resonates at the deepest level. The Higher Self operates in the vibrations of love and transcends the deepest meanings of truth into the essence of who you are.

As truth becomes apparent to the mind, the spirit has just created your epiphany through a vibrational response. The Ascended Masters walked the earth inside of truth and therefore words manifest into truth, not in the reverse order. Breathing in the air of truth, you can release all questions about its validity through the surrender of an exhale.

You should respect the truth of others in the light of love. Your acknowledgment of their vibrations is the gift of acceptance and acknowledgment. You don't have to embrace their beliefs by abandoning yours; it's the opposite. When you accept that others are holding their truth, you have opened to receiving everyone is Every One.

Your part in the process of ascension is to accept your truth and the truth of others as being one and the same and without attachments. In the opening of the heart, love makes everything a truth. In gratitude, you are asking to know the truth. In sorrow, you are releasing that which is not true. Teach only love and you are teaching the greatest of all truths as you operate within the realm of Divine energy.

Do you ever feel lonely, abandoned or incomplete, as if a part of you were missing? Does it seem like you have a spirit guide who helps you with balancing Karma or male/female energies? Do you live with someone who seems like your opposite, yet you are inexplicably drawn to them? All of these questions could evoke answers regarding your Twin Flame.

The thought behind this term revolves around our soul's origination that is sometimes compared to a flame. When you separate one flame into two, each individual fire burns with the equal intensity. The flames easily rejoin to make one and this is a metaphor for the seed of the soul.

It is noted by some spiritualists we incarnate with our Twin Flame in our last lifetime on Earth and until that time, our Twin Flame resides on the other side of the veil, helping us with relationships, balancing energy and raising our consciousness.

As we shift and engage in spiritual growth, we are opening our heart to the Twin Flame experience. 'Near flames' or soulmates can help us with this aspect as they teach us about love. Dreams of unicorns or magical creatures can be a connection with our Twin Flame, as this relationship is magical in its mystery. Twin Flames in the same physical body are highly enlightened beings and are often great spiritual teachers or saints. Now for a magical and mystical message from an angel on Twin Flames:

As the world experiences a shift in the areas of raised consciousness and spiritual ascension, Twin Flames will incarnate together more frequently. This is part of the Divine plan of bringing loving energy to the pinnacle of the hearts and minds of everyone who experiences or witnesses true love.

Those who are not ready to look in the mirror and accept themselves with unconditional love will find conflict in the search for their Twin Flame. The search ends at the flame within, for that is where peace, balance and acceptance reside.

The emergence of information around such ideas and terms are social indicators that mark the evolution of man. As the human spirit ascends into the light of pure love, a truth comes forward to bring nurturing energy to each individual. In this light, you can find further resonation with spiritual development and Divine teachings.

Twin Flames draw close in connection with the Higher Self, and for this reason can evoke feelings of spiritual guidance from an outside source. These guides are leading you to discoveries that ultimately have bearings on lessons of love. This half of your eternal flame can hold you in a way that expresses unconditional love to your soul in a frequency that exactly matches yours. This gift is human in nature and therefore helps those that have turned from religion, archetypes and the Highest Power.

Twin Flames unite to complete an individual's capacity to love in the highest vibrations of the body, mind and spirit and to form the ultimate relationship.

Over the last few weeks I have received validations on several different levels. Recent events have changed the way that I view many aspects of life. It is a wonderful feeling to experience such deep changes followed by validations in very unexpected ways.

I think one of the rewards to life is to be validated, starting in our childhood. Since we challenge our parents and siblings with our beliefs, their experiences can make it difficult to accept our knowledge and how we interpret things that on the surface might seem similar.

But as an adult, it is easy to have made up your mind regarding these life lessons. Therefore, a profound change in the way we view such things as death, spirituality, and even the way we present ourselves, can make an immediate validation seem unlikely due to the mental traps associated with being set in our ways.

Validation: *1) In psychology and human communication, validation is the reciprocated communication of respect which communicates that the other's opinions are acknowledged, respected, heard, and (regardless whether or not the listener actually agrees with the content), they are being treated with genuine respect as a legitimate expression of their feelings, rather than marginalized or dismissed.*

I found this definition in the Wikipedia and received a larger opening to my thoughts after reading it. To acknowledge and respect the opinions of others is a validation, whether you share the belief or not. What this says to me is that we should respect and validate the ones around us with some way of telling them that we hear who they are and what they stand for, regardless of anything else. In this respect it's as easy as sitting back on a cold night with a friend or loved one and simply listening. I will now listen intently for a whisper on the subject:

Validation is a cornerstone to faith and therefore supports hope, freedom and spirituality. The importance can hardly be expressed in the written word. One small dose of acceptance can heal nations or save a single life.

Every thought that serves as a new beginning is ultimately validated to move from an abstract expression to an action. This is the structure of change and change is the basis for all of life.

When you take a moment to open a door that has been closed, you are planting a seed of possibility. Whatever grows from that seed will bring birth to something that might otherwise fail to exist.

The best example of this is the belief in God or Source. The validation emanating from the heart and expressed feeling of one human being to another has survived outside the physical world. Now it is a common belief and a uniting factor in the thread of life.

What a luscious word to fill page after page of whispers with today's various meanings, theories and implications. My beliefs around healing emerged from studies in science, philosophy and personal experiences with vibrations that emanate from sound, light, and the human body. We have all heard the term "good vibes," which illustrates the cultural acceptance of vibration in relationships with people, music and almost every aspect of life.

As you know, the human body is made up largely of water, so the effect that vibrations have on water is something to consider. There is currently new technology that is coming to the surface that will provide clean and inexpensive natural energy by using vibrations in our streams and waterways. This could be half the cost of harnessing wind and solar energy!

This is just one area where vibrations are being studied to find ways of helping mankind. Another is the sonogram and ultrasound, both being studied for their healing aspects as well as for being the least intrusive way to diagnose human conditions. You can start to imagine the ways that good vibrations could be used to offset those vibrations that are considered destructive. Sonar vibrations, while considered helpful to mankind, are known to be destructive to aquatic life and might be an example of negative applications.

In the activities that I engage in, it is necessary to align with the vibrations of others for the purpose of gathering information and messages. I will now feel my way into the vibrations of angels for the purpose of experiencing a whisper:

Vibrations are integrated into all life forces, even in the case of things considered inanimate objects. Stones, for example, are the result of years of vibrations that form the size, shape and information programmed by nature. The vibrations of the earth are subtle, yet strongly felt at the lowest levels of energetic movement.

The use of destructive forms of vibrations has grown proportionately with the population of the planet. This produces a counter-balancing effect that is illustrated by the current rise in consciousness among people from all backgrounds. This raised awareness by the masses can no longer be controlled by governments or individuals in power.

The vibrations of peace fill a void left by dictators and rulers of the past that is creating a global shift in the balance of powers. Leaders with vision, integrity and a commitment to service will find themselves aligning with the vibrations that are sweeping the globe. Collectively, you are all headed toward destined fulfillment of the promises made by the ancients.

In essence, as you reach for Source Energy in the higher vibrations of your existence, peace and joy will follow. Repelling the thoughts, ideas and actions that were forged in the darkest times for mankind, you will transmute the energy of the past with waves of light and love that illuminate the future. The past, present and future are all represented in the vibrations of the moment, so that you can know who you have been, who you are now and who you will be tomorrow. Stand in that light and feel the vibrations of truth that remove you from judgment and surrender you to complete acceptance.

Whether someone is truly a victim seems subjective, so that allows room for opinions and judgments. There are teachings that support that everything happens as part of a plan or a contract, which does not support anyone's becoming a victim. If we are all part of a larger Divine plan, then it stands to reason that what some might view as a harsh event could also be seen as an extreme life-lesson. Could I become a victim of my own thinking while driving Beckie crazy (tee hee)!

Victim is defined as a person or animal killed as a sacrifice to a god in a religious rite, or someone or something killed, destroyed, injured, or otherwise harmed by, or suffering from, some act, condition, or circumstance. Peter McWilliams' definition of a victim: a person to whom life happens.

Confusion sets in with that definition of killing, and my determination to do these word studies comes to the surface with thoughts that define my existence. This also shows me how important our language is. In a moment we can go from empowerment to blame, depending on the perspective. Please join me in a moment of stillness that evokes understanding of the word *victim*, through a whisper from an angel:

There will be victims in a society where free will can sometimes remove choice. Even your planet Earth has free will and can shift energies quickly and unexpectedly. If there was a measure of victimhood, it would evolve from the perspective of each individual. That mental assessment can view the victim role as subjective behavior, which brings you back to individual assessments from those who witness and those who experience an event.

The external forces of the world brings challenges that can be hard to meet and harder to resolve. Most people you might consider a victim could argue the contrary. It is the contrast that offers the greatest teachings and the fastest way to resolving an issue. In the spirit world, when someone commits a grievous act against another human, both are considered wounded by the event.

The emphasis placed on suffering as a way to salvation is a religious control that encourages the victim mentality. Forgiveness and acceptance can quickly lessen the victim mentality. The energy of love and faith moves beyond definition, as these qualities are found in the brightest light and within the deepest darkness of human emotion. A shooting star becomes a victim to gravity as it shines a light across the night sky in a move that becomes empowered, bold and daring! A descending instant where light turns into darkness simultaneously embodies authoritative power and victimhood.

What a deep subject to explore! How do we use this ability to communicate with the most effectiveness? It is certainly one of my challenges in all aspects of my life. Even in this writing, I am using my true voice as I express my thoughts. I believe your true voice can be heard in many ways.

Sus, my evoctuer, helped me to claim my true singing voice. What I discovered was that the singing voice is always true; it was I who wasn't open to receiving everything that my heart and soul had to say.

As I was using my singing voice in a band called 600 Voices or DCVOX, I realized that the idea of more voices making a point in unison appealed to my artistic side. I personally love the idea of expression with melody and harmony. What is my voice trying to say here? I love music! And that's my next point. Sometimes we speak many words to say something that takes three. I love you!

This was illuminated in a restaurant last night when the owner came up and asked what beautiful project I was working on now. I struggled to find the words to tell him that I had switched from General Contractor to a psychic and medium doing Angel Therapy®. I thought of the exact words to answer his question in a concise, easy-to-understand manner........after he walked away with that strange look on his face. Isn't it interesting all the great things we can think to say *after* the moment is long gone?

So many people are trying so hard for their voices to be heard today. Have you been in a public place lately? It surprised me recently when I was around a family that yelled every communication, just like their two-year-old. Are we so repressed as a society that we have to raise the voice constantly for others to hear? I choose whisper.

The gift of the voice is a powerful one. Not all beings are blessed with this ability. Although it may sound glorious to communicate without words, the angels often deliver messages about the power of the voice.

When you listen to the many languages that are spoken, you can hear tones that are similar to music. The ancient languages are filled with sounds that flow together like a chant or song. When a language is no longer spoken, a message is lost forever.

The fears associated with speaking the true voice can be deep in the subconscious mind and therefore without reason to the individual. The rational behind the fear can often be found in the history of mankind or with the one that is listening.

Embrace the voice as if it is a new discovery. You can find the mysteries of the Universe in the single tone of the voice, whether it is yours or others, just by taking the time to receive instead of reflect. This is a choice of free will to open your soul to sound. Listen to the voice of a soul when it is merely a whisper, then you avoid hearing the soul as a cry. If the noise around you is drowning the whisper, then seek the silence of nature as a sanctuary where you can receive the true voice.

Gratitude goes out to Martha for today's whisper request and to all of you who sent me photos of the Sasquatch (tee hee). Fun needs to be a part of any angel-related activity, and the last whisper was a good reminder. But then again, I think the subject of defining a vortex can bring some giggles and grins.

Remember in The Wizard of Oz when Dorothy leaves Kansas in that tornado, only to eventually wake up in her own bed? Was it a dream or did she experience a vortex that took her to another dimension? The tornado represents a vortex of air, like a whirlpool uses water. The scientific community might challenge any idea of a vortex that does not include a rapid movement of tangible matter.

Vortex energy has become a big business with tourism exploding in places that advertise areas having such energy like Sedona, Arizona. Vortex energy is thought by some to be ley line intersections (Earth grids lines), electromagnetic energy or geomancy which is a form of dowsing. Mystics see vortices as energetic doorways that connect and open to another dimension.

Whatever your belief, these areas that have been discerned as vortex energies have been used for healing, spiritual experiences, and shifting consciousness. You might not find the yellow brick road if you enter a vortex, but you might experience a shift in energy. Let's shift some energy and see what an angel might whisper on the subject of vortex energy.

The energy vortex is considered a phenomenon surrounded by mystery. There are occurrences in nature that can be seen and explained by science, but so far science has been unable to explain certain types of energies and dimensions. Doctors know that energy travels through the human body, but are unsure of the pathways used to usher that movement.

Being 'in the flow' of life and feeling like everything has aligned can place you in that warm and comfortable zone. This could be a partial description of the feeling that occurs when placed in a vortex created by your own personal energy field. Being out of the flow, or out of the vortex, could lead to disharmony, illness, or simply feeling stuck. Energy shifting can be useful for optimal health and high-vibrational living, which is why vortex energy is used in healing arenas.

The chakras found in the human body represent another type of energy vortex, so when one of these energy centers gets blocked, the body responds with low energy, feelings anchored in low vibrations and a reduction of upward movement. People are drawn toward the vortex in a search for increasing or shifting energy, better connection with spirit, and releasing toxic emotions through a greater movement of energy.

Nature fills a vacuum, and vortex energy is a naturally occurring balancing tool provided to create movement and flow like a river returns to the ocean. Find a vortex in nature and create magic with energy. It's as simple as that!

Vulnerableright

The words that conjure up mixed feelings seem to draw me in; I guess you could say I was vulnerable to that (tee hee). A discussion with a friend led me into thoughts around the true essence of being vulnerable, which means *capable of, or susceptible to, being wounded or hurt. Vulnerable* also means *open to moral attack, criticism and temptation.*

If you are open to all those things through vulnerability, then it would stand to reason that you are open to receiving love, nurturing and basically all emotions. The idea of being vulnerable seems to carry negative connotations around a state of weakness, but in truth, should carry a more positive response as the apparent gateway to receptivity.

A quotation from Anne Morrow Lindbergh that I really like is, "*I do not believe that sheer suffering teaches. If suffering alone taught, all the world would be wise, since everyone suffers. To suffering must be added mourning, understanding, patience, love, openness and the willingness to remain vulnerable.*"

In reflection, some of my most profound experiences resulting in a conscious shift emanated from my own personal moments of vulnerability. In those instances where I became vulnerable, I also became aware and, through that consciousness evolved the positive features of my story. Now for one of my most vulnerable activities, I will engage with angels for a whisper on the subject:

The heart must open fully in order to receive love, so you must remove boundaries in order to assist in manifesting the balanced heart. A warrior can express the loving spirit while wearing armor, yet finds it difficult to receive love while covered with protection. This represents the true nature of boundaries and being vulnerable.

Tremendous courage and the highest example of the human spirit shine in the light of vulnerability. In this state of being, barriers and limitations are removed, making available possibilities that were not apparent in the moments prior. Without limiting factors entering the mind, the spirit is free to explore new opportunities and experiences.

The depth of feelings experienced in a vulnerable state reaches levels within your existence that can uncover lost information and feelings in the energetic search for truth. Within your highest vibration, truth and vulnerability illuminate purpose, integrity, faith and love with extreme clarity.

To fully experience all aspects of life, be willing to allow yourself to be vulnerable and present in moments of strength as well as times of weakness. The energy of receiving love from being vulnerable creates a wave of relief that washes away all barriers standing between you and the playful, compassionate, nurturing light of the Highest Power in the Universe, God and the angels.

Analogy (from Greek "ἀναλογία" – *analogia*, "proportion") is a cognitive process of transferring information or meaning from a particular subject (the analogue or source) to another particular subject (the target).

In a recent session, the angels were brilliant in presenting awareness through the use of an analogy. The comparison was between the human body and a computer. My client had a pact or agreement that was below the conscious radar because it was made as an infant or small child. The agreement was a response to an experience that the angels referred to as a 'homepage' and when others 'pushed her buttons', they were accessing her emotions through 'links'.

Being the creative and spirited human, I asked if we could just delete the homepage and the problem would be resolved (tee hee). The answer was no, we cannot remove the experience from the energy. I thought, "This is a lot like cyberspace; once you put it on Facebook, it is there forever!" The solution was to create a link that would route traffic toward the positive blessings that occurred around the harsh experience and, through awareness, release the need to visit that area again. It sounded so simple.

The interesting part of the story is that after the analogy brought awareness and a way of explaining things, the release of energy occurred with love and understanding on a conscious level without the need for further discussion. On that note, let's see if we can glean more simple suggestions from the whisper of an angel:

Communication is an essential tool when it comes to connecting the senses to the analytical mind. There is an energy that surrounds each person, and that energy is filled with information. The balance of energies occurs when the mind meets the body within the space of the heart. That is when your soul can truly listen as well as be heard.

The analogy is used to reach a greater understanding by presenting information in a way that resonates. The human adventure includes creating models that mirror a light of truth from within each person. In some cases that model is referred to as art, but regardless, the analogy can hold a Divine answer. The words of an analogy spoken to express an emotional status, target the heart area where the highest vibrational response can effect change through a heightened feeling or awareness.

There has to be a way to shift the analytical aspects of the experience in order to feel the emotional response. Analogies create the opening that allows the full emotional benefit to be reached and therefore the need to uphold a pact or agreement is lifted.

Love opens the eyes enough to allow the soul to gracefully gaze upon the truth, which offers you the elevated perspective on life and a Divine connection with the God or Goddess within.

This word comes up a lot in the Angel Whispers and in each of our personal journeys. Willingness could translate to some as sacrifice, release, shifting perspective, spiritual growth and any number of emotional responses. Sometimes it might serve to become a 'Yes Man' (lol) in order to experience the benefits of being willing to try new things or break free from old patterns.

According to Miriam-Webster's, **willingness** is a noun from the 14th century that means *inclined or favorably disposed in mind,* or *ready, w*illing and eager to help. Being willing can be a call to act or respond to accept without resistance. Willingness can be associated with sacrifice through choice. Wentworth Miller once said, *"Confidence is at the root of so many attractive qualities, a sense of humor, a sense of style, a willingness to be who you are no matter what anyone else might think or say, and it's true, I do have a certain fondness for women that have dark hair."*

That quote adds a certain playful romance to the idea of being willing to show others who you really are! Maybe I should seriously think about adding this word to my romantic charm: "Beckie, is there willingness to _____ (blank)?" instead of the usual wink, wink and nod, nod (tee hee). And now for a wink and a nod from the angels in a whisper on willingness:

Growth springs from a willing heart. A heart that is open can receive information on love through experiences and feelings presented with the energy of willingness. Love lessons can lead to challenges around the freedom to open the heart, especially if harsh experiences led to feeling hurt.

Trusting that the heart can open and receive without pain is in the energetic response that springs forth from your willingness, which is a demonstration of holding faith in a shifting paradigm or a changing landscape. Your willingness to expand or take a risk can be as simple as opening the arms in a flowing gesture that tells the world your heart is open to receiving on this day.

The sacrifice associated with willingness has the light of truth, whether it is letting go of a thought pattern, leaving a bad situation or altering a belief system. Sacrifice can lead to improvements in the quality of life, so willingness can release you from any illusions you may be following.

Why would you be anything but willing to completely open your heart and to witness everything that life has to offer? One simple moment of your willingness to forgive can release a heaviness that you have carried which may have offered lessons through contrast. Without that weight and with a willingness to move forward, your awareness offers magic, love becomes more present, and your life fully illuminates the miracles that litter your pathway to ascension.

Be unwilling to commit to the absence of love and then simply receive into your open heart.

Sometimes it is easier to accept ourselves or another person when we use the phrase "I'm just wired that way" or "He has always been wired that way."

But what if we want to change a behavior or a pattern? Does that mean we have to change the way energy travels?

It is probably true to some degree that we all have characteristics and idiosyncrasies (body habits) that are a part of our DNA. Even writing those words feels like an excuse that says some things simply cannot change (tee hee).

I would think that free will could be a factor in determining any kind of shift, especially a cosmic one (grins). Maybe saying you're 'wired a certain way' is simply describing an unwillingness to accept change and personal growth on some level. On the other hand, resistance to change, whether it be for better or worse, could be another way to explain the way we are wired.

Being wired to receive a message from the angels comes in handy when pondering such questions, so let's quiet the mind, clear the heart, and open to a whisper from an angel:

Strong energies align with each individual in order to fulfill a destined commitment. These alignments serve intentions that are anchored in the body of will, making them difficult to change or alter in any way. The serving nature of these energies is as deep as the tissue and bones.

In the future, healers will be able to better use technology to 're-wire' certain aspects that have found completion and are now playing in a repeating loop that serves no real purpose. The pathways of energy will be re-routed to enlighten and illuminate ascension qualities within the individual.

Mankind is on the cutting edge of such breakthroughs in the way that energy moves, with focus on upward-spiraling shifts in patterns. Acceptance of an individual's personality elements is an essential aspect of social integration, but acceptance of unhealthy behaviors is not, and leads to apathy and descending energies.

Beings are currently falling to the Earth, wired as aspirants searching for the truest forms of love. This energy of ascension and love is found within relationships, and that is why the Indigos' focus is highly tuned to this area of life experience. It is also the reason they are chosen as warrior spirits. Passion is the burning ember that creates a Divine Spark that offers the greatest opportunity to be wired for love.

Wisdom is a word that seems to go beyond knowledge and great teachings in order to be found in all living matter. This places wisdom within the reach of every living being. This word seems to bring a combination of energy with dualistic meanings, such as simple yet deep, knowledge without understanding, comprehension beyond belief, and the list goes on.

Seeking spiritual knowledge would seem to give way to wisdom if we incorporate the teachings into our actions. *Life is the only real counselor; wisdom unfiltered through personal experience does not become a part of the moral tissue.* ~ Edith Wharton, Is wisdom retained and carried with the soul as it journeys from one life to the next, or is everything erased as we travel through time and the etheric plane?

Many children exhibit the traits of wisdom as energy moving forward through the loving eyes of innocence. This provides hope and courage that we as a people are emerging from the darkness of the past with wisdom for the future. Let's hear the wisdom of angels in the form of a whisper:

Like love, wisdom is eternal and completely present for your awareness. Part of the process of evolution involves increasing levels of consciousness that spring from knowledge to become one with your essence.

Wisdom can come to you as a knowing or a deep truth emanating from the core of your beliefs. You do not need to know the origin of this material, only the truth in the vibrations that connect with your wisdom.

The human body holds wisdom and can discern the truth without analyzing or using the brain as a filter. Mankind has long been disconnected from this source of truth due to false information and the power to control the thoughts of man. The truth is that your body, mind, and spirit hold all the answers to life as the gateway to wisdom.

Allow the wisdom of the heart to lead you into your highest vibrations. Accept the wisdom of the soul as the God-self that is speaking directly to you. Embrace the Highest Power through connections and consciousness as the human body mirrors the meaning of life. Hold the purest form of love as an example of your faith and wisdom to know the seed that formed your life.

Perceived knowledge can be a trick to distract you from the truth that wisdom comes from the eternal heart.

To me, words represent communication of the mind and heart. I certainly have found with my 'Angel Whispers' that words can have many different meanings when they stand alone or in a group, and then there is the ever-present particular tone of your voice. The tone is sometimes more powerful a statement than any words.

Mankind has developed many languages over time. There are Universal words that everyone understands, like Aloha, which is one of my favorite expressions. It is not only a greeting but a good-bye as well and the word means affection, love, peace, compassion and mercy. Now that's what I call a word!

A word is a unit of language that carries meaning, has a phonetical value and consists of one or more morphemes which are linked more or less tightly together. Words can be combined to create phrases, clauses and sentences. A word consisting of two or more stems joined together is a compound. A word blended with another word forms a portmanteau (two or more words combined to create a new word).

In my Angel Therapy© it is very important to choose words carefully. I am using Claire senses to discern an angelic message, which is an art form in itself. The results of misinterpretation in this area could be very damaging to the individual. I think the same is true for each one of us who try to put feelings into words. Let's see if I can discern some words in the form of a whisper from the angels:

Words are connected to the vibrations of the heart and soul. It is the mind that can change the interpretation or meaning. The analytical process of communication is best served without attachments to the wording.

Think of life without words and you will find a vibration in the evolution of mankind. Without the ability to speak words, your transmission of knowledge becomes the purest medium of delivery. Our angelic messages are often short and to the point with simple meanings. These are easily accepted and absorbed as they represent a lesson in communication itself with the addition of the feeling of belief.

Not everyone can stand behind the words of an individual without finding the resonation and passion. If words stir passion, you are experiencing a soul reaction to a feeling through communication. What you do with that passion should be up for discernment around the issues of love, integrity, truth, justice, and purpose.

The words of the angels are living in the light of Divine love for God, Spirit and the Mother Earth. They take on many different forms including music, sound, vibrations and a knowing from within. If you take a moment to ask and receive the words from the angels, they will be delivered on the wings of Living Light as they ride on the breath of all that is Divine. Stand in this light and your words will take on a whole new meaning.

While preparing for an internet radio show last Friday called "Lifting the Veil" with Anita Ahuja, which featured a panel of psychics doing spring predictions, I 'tuned in' to the topic of 'spring predictions'. Minutes before the show went to air – I was a guest panelist from the comfort of my home – I received an unusual communication to go to my computer, close my eyes, type in a word and Google that word to find the message for the audience.

Through the process of typing with eyes closed, guidance unveiled the word Wunjo. *Vun-yoh* (**Wunjo**) *is the pronunciation for the symbol that represents the Rune of Joy.* As it turns out, Wunjo is a Rune which is one of the symbols of a pre-Latin alphabet that formed the basis for the German language.

I believe the message was that we should seek happiness, understanding, and feelings of emotional satisfaction with eyes open to the truth in order to experience joy. So much of life is rooted in the negative that we must actively work with ourselves and partner with others to find joy, since joy is not usually a solitary emotion.

This Rune teaches that working toward happiness to find balance and harmony illuminates truth, and for happiness to last, it must be founded on truth and honesty. The converse will make success elusive, imagined love false, and strain partnerships through secretive behaviors. The expansive thinking around the Rune makes a great segue to receive a little more on the subject from an angel who whispers:

The way that Spirits delivers meanings and feelings from symbols and language are the examples being presented. What you describe took several elements combining to create an energetic movement into the future with focus that is enhanced using an ancient symbol. Without trust as an element, the loving words that were eventually spread across the country could have easily been discounted.

Not only did you generate an immediate response when you requested a whisper prior to the show, your story created an opening for others to hear the message through your belief in the truth and integrity of what you received. As you witnessed, when time ran out on the radio show and it appeared there would not be an opportunity to deliver the message of joy, the producer extended the show which allowed time for the expression.

Wunjo is a Rune with some of the highest vibrations that connect the history of the planet with today's human experience. Upon your request, you followed Spirit to find the message that would serve the highest good for that listening audience. As the show progressed, the vibrations were raised by the group, and openings into the human body were created to receive the message of joy in the light of Divine truth.

Study the ancient symbols for joy and love in order to open the body, mind and spirit to the journey that many have made in order to bestow such teachings. Teaching love is the highest purpose within the God-self, and to truly be a teacher you must first be a student.

I had a suggestion to let the angels whisper on anything they want! The truth is, that is what usually happens (lol), some type of energy transfers a topic or subject that is in the moment. Well, here goes, Jen. Whisper whatever you want, sweet angels:

Beings of love energy were created from an explosion that scattered particles of light throughout the Universe. In an instant, wisdom, love, compassion and a balanced body of illumination emerged throughout the dark corners of the Universe. From the Highest energy of love came a spiritual partner, as if a loving parent sent a beam filled with hope that could reach out and help all of their children.

The act of incarnating into the body created a movement that removed your energy from the spiritual plane and placed you into the body to experience life in a physical world. Such an act defined the need for spiritual light bodies to accompany each person on their epic human journey. A guiding light was offered in pairs of unique energies that fit the life contract and alignment of each individual.

Darkness offers all the opportunities, and illusions of opportunity, that one will ever need to evoke upward and positive movement. The energy movement created between light and dark is the force that brings balance to each person. Peace follows balance and spreads through a collective consciousness to effect change in the evolution of a species known as humans.

In your lifetime, there is the greatest opportunity for collective energy to bring positive change, caring and sharing, Divine wisdom, and a level of faith unmatched in the history of the planet. The immense change before you might have a lengthy approach, but when it arrives, change will sweep the planet in a wave of momentum.

Every human being has a personal responsibility to bring their biggest love energy to the table. Within each person's capacity to love is personal responsibility, with a focus on integrity that will ultimately lead to the alignment of One. The energetic reach of each person will extend to the next person, creating the chain reaction that will move across the globe like the tides of time. The old cycle will end and a new one will usher in love like never before felt in the human body.

To be an active participant, all you need to do is be your best self, spread love and light, beautify the world and feel the presence of spiritual beings as they cry out, "You're Not Alone!"

On our travels over the Christmas holidays, Beckie and I had a lot of time to talk as we enjoyed the Texas countryside. As these conversations often do, an epiphany was offered.

Thinking back on the '50s and '60s, we saw that it was a simpler way of life, and for good reason. There were only three TV channels to choose from, you always did whatever the doctor said, you didn't get to choose what retirement program your income investment would go into, and so on. No one chose whether to answer the phone – any call was important back then (lol)!

In today's time, even a traffic ticket gives you several choices. You can have it dismissed through a program, you can pay it, you can fight it or hide from it. Every aspect of life in today's world presents several options.

My epiphany was that, starting in the '60s, people woke up and became empowered. This movement started to spread across the globe, and with the aid of technology, we choose how to live in ways that were never available before. People are awakening to the potential in their lives like this planet has never seen, and this may be what the Mayans were marking with the end of their calendar. Happy New Year and may 2012 provide you with abundance, incredible awakening, and several whispers from an angel spirit:

The spirit warriors who have come to Earth are showing the world a power found in the choices that are available to everyone. The potential to serve has never been greater, and the rewards of empowerment have never been at this level. You are truly blessed to be having the physical experience of witnessing the largest transformation in the human journey.

The year 2012 will usher in opportunities that are enormous in magnitude. The Cosmic Heart of the Universe will expand within the consciousness of the human mind, and that will transfer to a collective whole. Those who choose to focus on self-gratification may find the journey to be extremely challenging, but individual ascension will offer safety for all.

In the larger scheme of things, everyone has a choice to make. You can lift yourself from the lower energies that mire the human journey, or you can jump onto the wave of higher consciousness that was prophesied for centuries by the ancient people, who would have traded their lives to be in your shoes. Whatever choices you make in 2012, refuse to commit energy to an absence of love, follow your heart, align yourself with joy, focus on the path to joy, and bring a mental illumination to the process of peace.

In Gratitude

You have my deepest and most sincere gratitude for purchasing **Angel Whispers 2007-2011**, with my hopes that you received something that holds value for you. If you like the Angel Whispers, you can go to www.russellfortsyth.com and sign up to receive one every Sunday in your mailbox.

I would like to take this opportunity to thank the following people for all their efforts:

Jenny Meadows
editor
www.mycopyeditor.com

Alan Ray
artist
www.alanrayfilm.com

Deli Lajoie
webmaster, consultant and sister

I would also like to thank Beckie Forsyth, my wife and partner in this creative process. She lends me the inspiration, support and love that allows me the freedom to create and to be my best self, as well as her beautiful art featured in the table of contents. Without her, I would not be the person that I am today, so that leaves me forever in gratitude to Beckie, my angel on Earth.

This book is dedicated to my other, Glenna Forsyth, who also graces the pages with her wonderful art. Without her unconditional acceptance, my life would not be present to the messages from spirit and the way angels gift everyone with their whispers.

with many blessings,

Russell Forsyth

ISBN-10 1620301849
ISBN-13 9781620301845